BETTING MAIDENS & 2-YEAR-OLDS

ANALYTICAL APPROACH TO FUTURE WINNERS

by
Dan Illman

DRF Press
NEW YORK

Published by
Daily Racing Form Press
100 Broadway, 7th Floor
New York, NY 10005

ISBN: 0-9726401-4-2
Library of Congress Control Number: 2004101009

Cover and jacket designed by Chris Donofry
Text design by Neuwirth and Associates

Printed in the United States of America

All entries, results, charts and related information provided by

EQUIBASE
C O M P A N Y

821 Corporate Drive • Lexington, KY 40503-2794 Toll Free (800) 333-2211 or
(859) 224-2860; Fax (859) 224-2811 • Internet: www.equibase.com

The Thoroughbred Industry's Official Database for Racing Information

To Mom, Dad, Smere, George, Marian, and Nick

Contents

Acknowledgments

MANY THANKS TO Steven Crist, Charles Hayward, Mandy Minger, Brent Diamond, and Dean Keppler for having the faith in me to pursue this project. Also, a big thank-you to Robin Foster for an excellent editing job. Much love and thanks to Staci Durante, Mike Beer, Sarah Feldman, Marc Attenberg, John Eastwood, Geoff Faustman, Jennifer Lusk, Lonnie Goldfeder, Meg Wrenn, and Chris Donofry for their tireless efforts and encouragement throughout the process. A big shout-out goes to my PR boys, Tim O'Leary and Scott Cooper, for getting me some great radio and television gigs.

Thanks also to my fellow handicappers: Mike Watchmaker for giving me an opportunity to do this for a living. Brian Pochman, Paul Malecki, Jim Kachulis, Steve Grabowski, Art Gropper, Kenny Peck, and Scott Ehlers comprise the greatest group of handicappers and workers that I could ever be associated with. Thanks for your support and friendship. Thanks to Chuck Kuehhas, Rich Wroble, Ken Davis, Noel Michaels, Rob Perocier, Ted Holmlund, Daniel Kim, Ken Band, and Steve Marcinak for ideas and encouragement.

Thanks to Duane Burke, Suresh Samwaru, David Cabrera, and all the information-technology guys who were able to decipher my handwriting and come up with some very useful stats. Much gratitude goes to Tom Spellman, Jim Amoroso, Hirma Carter, Eddie Schiffer, Matt O'Connor, and all the quality-assurance boys and girls past and present. You are simply the best.

I'm sure I'm forgetting several people so please forgive me if your name is not on this page. I'd also like to thank all of the horse-racing fans. You truly are the lifeblood of this game, and are an inspiration for me and for everyone at *Daily Racing Form*. And a universe of thanks to Jen Feldman.

Introduction

"Go to law school, kid."

I WAS 17 years old and in love for the very first time. The lady was beautiful, cultured, and extremely popular, and I swooned whenever I gazed upon her. That lady was Saratoga Race Course, and I obviously wasn't the first to be mesmerized by her charms. While my parents wasted their week of summer vacation staring at gardens, lakes, statues, and assorted artwork, I was caught up in the buzz of the greatest race meeting in the world. For a kid accustomed to the drab and colorless Big A, Saratoga was the promised land. Where else would you find $2 punters mingling with patricians of impeccable pedigree? I felt at home.

Every racing day, the great Harvey Pack would host the Paddock Club, a half-hour forum where public handicappers would present their insights on the afternoon's card. Harvey was, and still is, the most beloved and recognizable racing personality in the country, and the Carousel Mini Theatre was "packed" to capacity with fans looking for a chuckle and a winner. After Harvey's usual witty repartee, he introduced the speakers, and one of them immediately caught my attention with his obvious passion for the game. He was well-spoken, confident, and chock-full of information. He wrote for a New York daily newspaper, and seemed to love his job. I had to meet this guy.

After the seminar, I shyly approached the handicapper, and blurted out, "I want to be you one day." Expecting a pearl of wisdom or some advice on how to get started in the game, I was horrified when he flatly stated, "Go to law school, kid." He then walked away.

I guess I took the less-traveled road. I went on to study Gulfstream Park and Calder Race Course while attending Nova Southeastern University in Davie, Florida. I threw myself into learning everything about Thoroughbred racing. I voraciously read every handicapping book I could get my hands on, and studied the *Daily Racing Form* with zeal. I discovered an interest in pedigrees, and tried to spot good horses before the rest of the public caught on. As sports editor of Nova's school paper, *The Knight,* I found little time for men's basketball, or women's softball. The back page was often littered with articles such as "Soup's On: Alphabet Soup Wins Breeders' Cup Classic." I'm not sure if subscriptions to *The Knight* increased during my reign there, but I definitely annoyed the publicity-seeking athletes.

I was fortunate to get an entry-level position with the *Form* a year after graduation, and was promoted to handicapper in 2000. When DRF's national handicapper, Mike Watchmaker, asked if I'd like to be a *Daily Racing Form* handicapper, I replied, "It's what I've wanted to do since I was four years old."

So why the biography? I think it's important for the reader to understand that at heart, I'm still a wide-eyed racing fan. There have been some big scores, and there have been some days when I have left the track scratching my head, but, through it all, I can't wait to open up the *Form* and solve the eternal riddle. Handicappers are part of a special fraternity. We are all searching for that holiest of grails, the correct formula that solves the handicapping equation. While I won't guarantee any such "perfect" system, I do hope to pass on some tips that may help your handicapping process. Every race is a learning experience. Let's learn and profit together.

I would like this book to proceed like a mile-and-a-half turf race. We're going to start out slowly, analyzing the top juvenile debut sires and trainers in the world. We'll find a good tracking position for that long run down the backstretch by discussing bloodlines, auctions, pace, speed, trip handicapping, workouts, and body language. Then we quicken on the far turn, evaluating older maidens, turf maidens, European imports, record-keeping, form cycles, "nicking" patterns, and more. Hopefully, we'll be flying late with an analysis of juvenile allowance and stakes races, with a special emphasis on the Breeders' Cup Juvenile and Juvenile Fillies.

This is the greatest game in the world. I might have made a fairly good lawyer, but if my love for horse racing is a crime, then I am certainly guilty as charged.

GETTING OUR HOOVES WET:
Introducing the Top Juvenile Debut Sires and Trainers

*T*HE TWO MOST important words that handicappers should use in analyzing juvenile maiden races are "how" and "why."

How is this firster going to perform today?

Why is this trainer running in this exact spot?

How is that gap in the work tab going to affect the runner's performance?

Why is the $100,000 yearling being offered for $32,000 in his debut?

Being inquisitive is the key to finding overlays in these kinds of races.

Over the last three years I have compiled an extensive database of debut winners, and have broken them down by sire, trainer, age of the debut winner, distance, track, and race class. For juveniles, I have noted every North American-bred debut winner throughout the world. Older maidens have been taken from the charts of *DRF Simulcast Weekly*.

In early 2004, I took 30 names from the sire and trainer database, and had the excellent information-technology staff at *Daily Racing Form* run some numbers for me. I think you'll find the results very interesting. Certain juvenile maiden races are inscrutable on paper. Sometimes the right way to play these heats is to go with the proven debut sires and trainers. So without further ado, here are some names that you need to know.

BOUNDARY

Pedigree: Danzig—Edge, by Damascus
Race Record and Earnings: 8 starts, 6 wins, 1 second,
   1 third, $217,777
2004 Stud Fee: $10,000
2004 Stud Farm: Claiborne Farm (KY)
2001–2003 Juvenile Debut Statistics: 46 runners, 13 winners (28%)
2001–2003 Return on Investment: $7.09
2003 Juvenile Debut Statistics: 15 runners, 6 winners (40%)
2003 Return on Investment: $8.07

Quite simply, Boundary is the most underrated debut sire in the country. He was unraced as a juvenile, but won his first five starts, including the six-furlong Grade 3 Roseben Handicap at Belmont with a 107 Beyer Speed Figure. Trained by Bill Mott, Boundary was never off the board in eight lifetime starts. He finished his career with a sparkling win over champion sprinter Cherokee Run in the six-furlong Grade 3 A Phenomenon Handicap at Saratoga with a 113 Beyer.

He is by champion sire Danzig, and crosses very well with Raise a Native-line mares by Mr. Prospector, Alydar, Forty Niner, and Seeking the Gold. Boundary also does very well when bred to mares with Damascus, Round Table, and Northern Dancer blood. Perhaps a reason for Boundary's success is that each of his first four dams was a major stakes winner. A top sprinter, and very solid sire,

Boundary's most notable runners include Irish juvenile champion Minardi, and graded stakes winners Conserve and Roxelana. He is a great stallion to consider for handicapping purposes, as his off-spring generally sell at auction for between $35,000 and $75,000, and thus are not considered as flashy as those by the "boutique" sires. Boundary's juvenile firsters won at a 28 percent clip in 2001 with an ROI of $4.25. He "faltered" a bit the following year when he "only" scored with 15 percent of his juvenile firsters, but the ROI exploded to a mind-boggling $9.88. It should also be noted that Boundary had a pair of juvenile debut winners overseas in 2002 that were excluded from the study. Boundary sires hard-hitting, precocious racehorses that do well on turf or dirt.

Juvenile Debut Sire Ranking: A+

DISTORTED HUMOR

Pedigree: Forty Niner—Danzig's Beauty, by Danzig

Race Record and Earnings: 23 starts, 8 wins, 5 seconds, 3 thirds, $769,964

2004 Stud Fee: $50,000

2004 Stud Farm: WinStar Farm (KY)

2002–2003 Juvenile Debut Statistics: 60 runners, 12 winners (20%)

2002–2003 Return on Investment: $4.69

2003 Juvenile Debut Statistics: 29 runners, 7 winners (24%)

2003 Return on Investment: $4.14

Distorted Humor will go down in history as the sire of 2003 Kentucky Derby and Preakness Stakes winner Funny Cide, but he is also one of the top juvenile debut sires, and is one of the most promising young stallions in the world. Like Boundary, Distorted Humor was unraced at 2, but he did win at first asking, at Gulfstream Park, with an 86 Beyer. At 3, he won the six-furlong Screen King Stakes at Saratoga with a 105 Beyer. Distorted Humor got better as he aged: At 4, he won the Salvator Mile Handicap at Monmouth with a 112 Beyer. The following season, trainer Elliott Walden turned him back to seven furlongs, and Distorted Humor found his true calling. He took the Commonwealth Breeders' Cup Stakes at Keeneland with a 116 Beyer Speed Figure, and then came right back to set a track record in the Churchill Downs Handicap. His last major victory came in the 7½-furlong Grade 3 Ack Ack Handicap at Churchill, and he ended his career with a solid third-place finish in the Grade 1 Cigar Mile at Aqueduct.

From his first two crops to race, Distorted Humor not only gave us Funny Cide, but also graded stakes winners Awesome Humor, Go Rockin' Robin, and Humorous Lady. He seems to cross well with mares by Raise a Native-line stallions like Saratoga Six and Majestic Light, and should also do nicely when mated to mares with Northern Dancer blood. Both of Distorted Humor's first two dams were graded stakes winners.

He made an excellent showing with his first-crop juveniles in 2002. They won at a 24 percent clip in their debuts with an ROI of $5.36. A future star, Distorted Humor is definitely a sire to follow when playing juvenile maiden races and he consistently gets above-average results with his debut runners.

Juvenile Debut Sire Ranking: A+

TALE OF THE CAT
Pedigree: Storm Cat—Yarn, by Mr. Prospector
Race Record and Earnings: 9 starts, 5 wins, 1 second, 2 thirds, $360,900
2004 Stud Fee: $75,000
2004 Stud Farm: Ashford Stud (KY)
2002–2003 Juvenile Debut Statistics: 94 runners, 20 winners (21%)
2002–2003 Return on Investment: $2.44
2003 Juvenile Debut Statistics: 57 runners, 10 winners (18%)
2003 Return on Investment: $2.30

The young stallion Tale of the Cat has stamped himself as a dominant force with juvenile debut runners. He had 21 (one in Great Britain) juvenile debut winners in his first two crops, and my gut feeling is that the best is yet to come. As with Boundary and Distorted Humor, Tale of the Cat was unraced as a 2-year-old, but like those two peers he was fantastic on the track from the very beginning. A $375,000 yearling purchase, Tale of the Cat won his first two lifetime starts in route races at Monmouth Park by a combined 15¾ lengths. Trainer John Forbes thought enough of his stable star to try the nine-furlong Grade 1 Haskell Invitational for the colt's third start. He finished a solid fourth behind top 3-year-olds Touch Gold, Anet, and Free House.

Tale of the Cat showed his extraordinary ability in his next start, the seven-furlong King's Bishop at Saratoga. In only his fourth lifetime race, and first at a sprint distance, Tale of the Cat won the Grade 2 event by 5½ lengths, and earned a 113 Beyer Speed Figure for the effort.

He went on to finish third in the seven-furlong Grade 1 Vosburgh at Belmont in his final start at 3. As a 4-year-old, Tale of the Cat won on both turf and dirt, and was Grade 1-placed in the nine-furlong Whitney Handicap at Saratoga, and in the Vosburgh for the second year in a row.

Interestingly, Tale of the Cat is a half-sibling to Irish juvenile champion Minardi (by Boundary). His dam is a full sister to Grade 1 winner Preach, she herself the dam of the successful sire Pulpit. His second dam was a graded stakes winner from the family of the great Round Table.

A versatile sort, Tale of the Cat has done very well with his female runners thus far. Be Gentle, Whoopi Cat, and Feline Story have all won graded stakes races. His son Lion Heart finished second in the 2004 Kentucky Derby. His progeny have sold in the $60,000 to $125,000 range, and it wouldn't be shocking if those numbers grew over the next few years. He should cross well with dams from the

Nasrullah and Raise a Native lines. A sire with a very bright future, Tale of the Cat won with 27 percent of his juvenile debut runners from his first crop, and can be counted on for double-digit juvenile debut winners each season.

Juvenile Debut Sire Ranking: A+

ELUSIVE QUALITY

Pedigree: Gone West—Touch of Greatness, by Hero's Honor
Race Record and Earnings: 20 starts, 9 wins, 3 seconds, 2 thirds, $413,284
2004 Stud Fee: $50,000
2004 Stud Farm: Gainsborough Farm (KY)
2002–2003 Juvenile Debut Statistics: 73 runners, 16 winners (22%)
2002–2003 Return on Investment: $2.53
2003 Juvenile Debut Statistics: 36 runners, 6 winners (17%)
2003 Return on Investment: $1.25

I remember sitting in slack-jawed awe when Elusive Quality smashed the world record for a mile on grass in the Grade 3 Poker Handicap at Belmont in 1998. Here was a powerfully built horse that was very, very fast. I couldn't wait for him to go to stud so I could see his progeny in action. I haven't been disappointed. Thank you, Smarty Jones!

As with the sires mentioned above, Elusive Quality did not race as a juvenile, but made a winning debut at 3. He won first time out for Bill Mott by more than 11 lengths at $8\frac{1}{2}$ furlongs over a sloppy Belmont track, and earned a phenomenal 102 Beyer Speed Figure. The normally conservative Mott entered Elusive Quality in the Grade 2 King's Bishop Stakes for the colt's fourth lifetime start, and he was just nosed for all the money by Honour and Glory. At 4, Elusive Quality set a track record for seven furlongs on dirt at Gulfstream Park. He stopped the clock in 1:20.17, and earned a 122 Beyer Speed Figure. A true horse-for-course at Gulfstream, he ran a 123 Beyer over the South Florida strip in his first start as a 5-year-old.

Elusive Quality wasn't tried on the turf until late in his 5-year-old season, but was a natural on grass. He won the Grade 3 Jaipur going seven furlongs on Belmont's Widener Course in his turf debut, and then followed up with the aforementioned Poker score.

Elusive Quality's dam is an unraced half-sister to a multiple European Group 1 winner. His second dam, Ivory Wand, won the Grade 3 Test Stakes, and his third dam won the Alabama Stakes.

From his first two crops to race, this bright young stallion has already sired French juvenile champion Elusive City, graded stakes winners Chimichurri and Omega Code, and of course, Smarty Jones. He won with 27 percent of the juvenile firsters in his first crop with a $3.76 ROI. He has done very well with Northern Dancer-line mares, most notably ones by Dayjur, but has also had success when inbred to descendants of Raise a Native. Although he only had six juvenile debut winners in this study, it must be noted that he had another one abroad. Elusive Quality's progeny have sold in the $65,000 to $135,000 range, and should continue to trade very well, especially at juvenile auctions.

By Gone West, one of my favorite sires, Elusive Quality should continue to get precocious juveniles. The public is beginning to catch on, however, as his juvenile debut ROI dropped noticeably last year.
Juvenile Debut Sire Ranking: A

APPEALING SKIER

Pedigree: Baldski—Jealous Appeal, by Valid Appeal
Race Record and Earnings: 26 starts, 8 wins, 7 seconds, 3 thirds, $579,610
2004 Stud Fee: $3,500
2004 Stud Farm: Green Willow Farms (MD)
2001–2003 Juvenile Debut Statistics: 57 runners, 13 winners (23%)
2001–2003 Return on Investment: $3.10
2003 Juvenile Debut Statistics: 24 runners, 5 winners (21%)
2003 Return on Investment: $2.32

To me, Appealing Skier is the prototypical regional sire. Although not a "hot" stallion from a commercial point of view, there was no doubting his speed on the racetrack, and he sires plenty of precocious juvenile winners. While he may not pass on the class of the aforementioned stallions, Appealing Skier will give his offspring the speed to be major factors in juvenile maiden races. Horseplayers will often pass over Appealing Skier's firsters when they see his moderate stud fee, so he usually provides plenty of mutuel value.

He won his first three starts at 2 by a combined $15^3/_4$ lengths, and wasn't headed at any call of those races. In start number three, he took the Grade 3 Laurel Futurity at $7^1/_2$ furlongs, and trainer Ben Perkins had no qualms about tossing him into the Breeders' Cup Juvenile for his next outing. He set a sub 46-second half-mile over a muddy strip in the Juvenile before fading badly.

Perkins regrouped with his $100,000 yearling, and they turned the tables on Juvenile winner Unbridled's Song in his first start at 3, the seven-furlong Grade 2 Hutcheson Stakes at Gulfstream. Appealing Skier also took the Grade 2 Withers Stakes over a one-turn mile at Belmont, and set a track record defeating older horses in the six-furlong Grade 2 Kentucky Cup Sprint Stakes at Turfway Park.

Appealing Skier went on to place in five stakes events at 4, including a 115 Beyer effort in the five-furlong Eillo Handicap at Gulfstream. He set another track record in the six-furlong Virginia Is For Lovers Stakes at Colonial Downs, and also won on turf that season.

A half- or full brother to three stakes winners, including the ultraquick Grade 1 winner Trippi, Appealing Skier is an attractive outcross to Northern Dancer- and Mr. Prospector-line mares. His babies usually do not sell very well at auction, but don't be afraid to play them first time out. In his first crop of juveniles, Appealing Skier scored with an astounding seven of 12 debut runners, and produced a phenomenal $9.75 ROI. He was affected by the dreaded sophomore jinx in 2002 as his juvenile firsters only went

1 for 21, but rebounded quite nicely last year, and should be a good fit in the Mid-Atlantic and Northeast regions.
Juvenile Debut Sire Ranking: A-

MUTAKDDIM

Pedigree: Seeking the Gold—Oscillate, by Seattle Slew
Race Record and Earnings: 17 starts, 5 wins, 3 seconds, 2 thirds, $126,174
2004 Stud Fee: $10,000
2004 Stud Farm: Hill 'n' Dale Farm (KY)
2001–2003 Juvenile Debut Statistics: 47 starters, 13 winners (28%)
2001–2003 Return on Investment: $3.57
2003 Juvenile Debut Statistics: 12 runners, 4 winners (33%)
2003 Return on Investment: $3

Mutakddim, a small but sturdy stallion, never raced on dirt and never ran in the United States, yet he is one of the most underrated juvenile debut sires in the world. A result of the potent Seeking the Gold-Seattle Slew "nick," (more on "nicking" in Chapter 16), Mutakddim graduated in his second start at 2 going seven furlongs at Ascot in Great Britain. Trained by John Gosden, the $200,000 yearling never really distinguished himself in Europe. His only stakes win came as a 4-year-old in the John of Gaunt at Haydock, at about seven furlongs.

Looking at his pedigree, one might theorize that Mutakddim might have been a star if given a chance to shine on dirt. He is a half-brother to Grade 1-placed filly Smooth Charmer out of a winning half-sister to champion juvenile Rhythm and excellent debut sire Not For Love. Mutakddim's second dam, Dance Number, was a Grade 1-winning half-sister to noted sires Private Account and Polish Numbers, while third dam Numbered Account was champion juvenile filly in 1971.

Mutakddim's offspring haven't done well at auction, as they generally sell in the $10,000 to $35,000 range. He crosses nicely with mares from the Turn-to line, most notably Southern Halo. Mutakddim has also had success when inbred to mares with Northern Dancer, Mr. Prospector, and Buckpasser blood. He is certainly capable of getting the big horse, as his Lady Tak won the Grade 1 Test at Saratoga in 2003, and he has sired many classy runners in the Southern Hemisphere, shuttling to Argentina for stud duty when the North American breeding season is over.

A direct descendant of the foundation broodmare La Troienne, it is no surprise that Mutakddim has been a success at stud. What is amazing is that horseplayers consistently overlook his debut runners. He has connected with at least 25 percent of his juvenile firsters in each of the last three years, yet his ROI is simply outstanding.

Juvenile Debut Sire Ranking: A-

REGAL REMARK

Pedigree: Vice Regent—Male Strike, by Speak John
Race Record and Earnings: 19 starts, 7 wins, 5 seconds, 2 thirds, $279,879
2004 Stud Fee: $4,000
2004 Stud Farm: Horizon Farm (AB)
2001–2003 Juvenile Debut Statistics: 52 runners, 11 winners (21%)
2001–2003 Return on Investment: $2.96
2003 Juvenile Debut Statistics: 13 runners, 2 winners (15%)
2003 Return on Investment: $3.22

Here's a sleeper sire for the fans in Western Canada. Regal Remark is a solid veteran stallion that consistently provides profits for handicappers shrewd enough to play his juvenile firsters. A $60,000 yearling purchase, Regal Remark prevailed in the six-furlong Bull Page Stakes at Woodbine as a 2-year-old, then pulled off his biggest coup when winning the Grade 3 Tampa Bay Derby the following year.

The son of Vice Regent was a stakes winner all three years he raced, and his pedigree is quite classy. Regal Remark is a half-brother to multiple Grade 1 winner On the Line out of a multiple stakes-winning dam. Fourth dam First Flight won 11 of 24 starts in the 1940's, including the Futurity, Monmouth Oaks, and Fall High-weight Handicap.

Regal Remark's juvenile firsters went 7 for 24 in 2001 with an ROI of $3.12. They showed a flat-bet profit in 2002–2003 as well, and are almost automatic plays at smaller tracks such as Northlands Park, Stampede Park, and Marquis Downs.
Juvenile Debut Sire Ranking: A-

SLEWDLEDO
Pedigree: Seattle Slew—M'lle. Cyanne, by Cyane
Race Record and Earnings: Unraced
2004 Stud Fee: $3,500
2004 Stud Farm: Paulson Thoroughbred Ranch (WA)
2001–2003 Juvenile Debut Statistics: 53 runners, 12 winners (23%)
2001–2003 Return on Investment: $2.95
2003 Juvenile Debut Statistics: 23 runners, 6 winners (26%)
2003 Return on Investment: $3.27

At age 22, Slewdledo topped the Washington sire list by progeny earnings in 2003. He consistently sends out precocious, ready-to-rumble juveniles, and has connected with at least 25 percent of his 2-year-old firsters over the past two full years. He is the first stallion on our list that never made it to the racetrack, but his classy pedigree afforded him the opportunity to become a quality stud, and he has certainly run with the ball.

Slewdledo is a son of the legendary Triple Crown winner Seattle Slew out of multiple stakes winner M'lle. Cyanne. His second dam, M'lle Dianne, won or placed in 15 stakes races in the 1950's.

He has sired multiple statebred champions in Washington, and his juvenile debut runners have had success in Northern California as well. His runners probably fit best at the maiden claiming level, but don't be afraid to back them at the windows.
Juvenile Debut Sire Ranking: A-

STORM CAT

Pedigree: Storm Bird—Terlingua, by Secretariat
Race Record and Earnings: 8 starts, 4 wins, 3 seconds, $570,610
2004 Stud Fee: $500,000
2004 Stud Farm: Overbrook Farm (KY)
2001–2003 Juvenile Debut Statistics: 61 runners, 12 winners (20%)
2001–2003 Return on Investment: $1.47
2003 Juvenile Debut Statistics: 20 runners, 3 winners (15%)
2003 Return on Investment: $1.01

No sire list would be complete without the inclusion of arguably the world's greatest stallion, Storm Cat. Foaled in Pennsylvania, Storm Cat would go on to be a Grade 1-winning juvenile, a two-time leading sire, and a six-time leading juvenile sire by progeny earnings. His stud fee says it all. Breeders go to Storm Cat for precocity, speed, toughness, and plenty of class. Storm Cat won the Grade 1 Young America at 2, and placed in the 1985 Breeders' Cup Juvenile. He never panned out at 3, winning only one of two starts, but has been nothing short of a sensation at stud. His offspring are among the most coveted at auction as they often sell in the $550,000 to $1.5 million range.

A three-quarter brother to multiple graded stakes winner Chapel of Dreams, Storm Cat is out of the fleet multiple Grade 2 winner Terlingua, a half- or full sister to noted sires Encino, Pancho Villa, and Royal Academy. His second and third dams were also stakes winners. Storm Cat crosses very well with Raise a Native through Alydar and Mr. Prospector, and has been very successful when inbred to mares with Bold Ruler and Northern Dancer blood.

Unfortunately for handicappers, there isn't much value in backing most Storm Cat juvenile firsters. He is simply too famous, and his progeny are usually hammered at the windows. Also, it should be noted that much of his best stock is exported to Europe and Japan for racing. Over the last three racing seasons, Storm Cat has sired 11 juvenile debut winners overseas that were not included in this study. His ROI and juvenile debut winning percentage have declined in each of the last three years.

Horseplayers should always fear young Storm Cat firsters, as he is bred to the very best mares, but they don't necessarily offer the greatest wagering opportunity.

Juvenile Debut Sire Ranking: A-

VALID EXPECTATIONS

Pedigree: Valid Appeal—Mepache, by Iron Constitution
Race Record and Earnings: 27 starts, 12 wins, 3 seconds, 6 thirds, $596,092
2004 Stud Fee: $12,500
2004 Stud Farm: Lane's End Texas (TX)
2001–2003 Juvenile Debut Statistics: 110 runners, 23 winners (21%)
2001–2003 Return on Investment: $2.03
2003 Juvenile Debut Statistics: 38 runners, 11 winners (29%)
2003 Return on Investment: $2.30

Valid Expectations was a quick little runner, and has found his niche standing for Will Farish in Texas. The Lone Star State's leading sire in 2003, Valid Expectations usually is bred to swift mares, and this generally results in precocious juvenile runners.

Sold for $68,000 as a yearling, Valid Expectations was successfully pinhooked for $225,000 the following year, and scored his first victory in his second lifetime start at 2 for Steve Asmussen. A multiple juvenile stakes winner, Valid Expectations had his best year at 3, winning the one-mile Grade 3 Derby Trial at Churchill Downs. He also scored in the seven-furlong Grade 3 Sport Page Handicap at Aqueduct with a career-high 112 Beyer. At 4, the dependable Valid Expectations won the six-furlong Thanksgiving Handicap at Fair Grounds in the final start of his career.

Valid Expectations is kin to three other stakes winners, including Grade 3 winner Little Sister. His sire, Valid Appeal, is known for getting very quick juveniles, and Valid Expectations definitely inherited that trait. His dam was a stakes winner from the family of Kentucky Derby winner Foolish Pleasure. Valid Expectations has crossed well with Nasrullah-line mares, and has sired quick runners from mares with In Reality and Damascus blood.

Valid Expectation's auction runners usually sell in the $30,000 to $60,000 range, although it shouldn't surprise if he hits a home run with one of his 2-year-olds in training. He did have juvenile debut winners at Hollywood and Saratoga in 2003, and his Saratoga County won the Grade 3 Gotham in 2004, so perhaps he is ready to shed the "regional sire" label. He is a stallion that handicappers should follow.

Juvenile Debut Sire Ranking: A-

GOLDEN GEAR

Pedigree: Gulch—Fineza, by Lypheor
Race Record and Earnings: 26 starts, 12 wins, 1 second, 4 thirds, $634,009
2004 Stud Fee: $3,000
2004 Stud Farm: Blooming Hills Inc. (CA)
2001–2003 Juvenile Debut Statistics: 49 runners, 10 winners (20%)
2001–2003 Return on Investment: $2.11
2003 Juvenile Debut Statistics: 18 runners, 3 winners (17%)
2003 Return on Investment: $1.70

Golden Gear was a solid sprinter/miler who wasn't very popular during his short stud stint in Kentucky. Now in California, it is expected that Golden Gear will get more opportunities to prove himself as a quality sire. After finishing third in his 2-year-old debut at Arlington, Golden Gear rolled off a pair of victories before finishing a nose shy of eventual Preakness and Belmont winner Tabasco Cat in the seven-furlong Fort Springs Stakes at Keeneland. He won a stakes at Ellis Park at 3, but like several other sires on this list, he improved as he matured. The son of Gulch won the Grade 2 Commonwealth Breeders' Cup at 4 with a 105 Beyer Speed Figure, and finished only a length behind the winner in the Grade 1 Vosburgh that same season. As a 5-year-old, Golden Gear finished first in all three of his starts, and he ended his career with a gritty win in the Grade 3 Equipoise Mile at Arlington with a lifetime-best 107 Beyer.

Golden Gear is a half-brother to multiple Grade 1 winner Keeper Hill. His dam, Fineza, was a stakes-placed half-sister to millionaire Clabber Girl. Second dam Jedina was a stakes-winning half-sister to successful sire Fappiano. Golden Gear's family is loaded with class, and he has proven to be a very useful sire. Canadian juvenile filly champion Ginger Gold and Grade 3 winner Mr. John are two of his best performers.

Handicappers did very well backing Golden Gear's juvenile firsters in 2001. Those horses won at a 23 percent clip, and produced an ROI of $2.35. He should continue to provide plenty of value.

Juvenile Debut Sire Ranking: B+

IS IT TRUE
Pedigree: Raja Baba—Roman Rockette, by Proudest Roman
Race Record and Earnings: 15 starts, 5 wins, 2 seconds,
   1 third, $819,999
2004 Stud Fee: $8,500
2004 Stud Farm: Hartley/De Renzo, Walmac South (FL)

2001–2003 Juvenile Debut Statistics: 56 runners, 11 winners (20%)

2001–2003 Return on Investment: $3.07

2003 Juvenile Debut Statistics: 16 runners, 1 winner (6%)

2003 Return on Investment: $1.26

Is It True broke my heart when he downed Easy Goer in the 1988 Breeders' Cup Juvenile, but he has more than made up for it with his precocious and profitable juvenile debut runners.

After being plucked from the fashionable Keeneland July yearling sale by D. Wayne Lukas in 1987 for $550,000, Is It True won a maiden race at 2 by over 15 lengths at Belmont. He finished second to Easy Goer in the Grade 1 Champagne before pulling off the monumental Breeders' Cup upset. Is It True was a multiple graded stakes winner at 3, and even successfully stretched his speed to nine furlongs in the Grade 2 Jim Dandy.

His first dam was a stakes-winning half-sister to graded winners Singing Susan and I Am the Game. Is It True's best son, Yes It's True, captured the Grade 1 Frank J. De Francis Memorial Dash on his way to millionaire status, and Is It True has crossed well with Northern Dancer-line mares. His yearlings haven't sold well in recent years, and it's possible that he is getting lost in the shuffle with many promising speed stallions in Florida right now. Still, it's hard to ignore that his juvenile firsters went 10 for 40 in 2001 and 2002 with an ROI over $3. He should continue to get good-priced firsters in the years to come.

Juvenile Debut Sire Ranking: B+

NOT FOR LOVE

Pedigree: Mr. Prospector—Dance Number, by Northern Dancer

Race Record and Earnings: 29 starts, 6 wins, 7 seconds, 5 thirds, $178,870

2004 Stud Fee: $20,000

2004 Stud Farm: Northview Stallion Station (MD)

2001–2003 Juvenile Debut Statistics: 60 runners, 16 winners (27%)

2001–2003 Return on Investment: $6.21

2003 Juvenile Debut Statistics: 17 runners, 1 winner (6%)

2003 Return on Investment: $0.94

Not For Love never lived up to his impeccable pedigree on the racetrack, but he has to be considered one of the premier juvenile debut sires in the world. An Ogden Phipps homebred trained by Shug McGaughey, Not For Love only won two of his first 11 starts at ages 2 and 3. He hinted at his potential with a 98 Beyer effort in a N3X allowance at Saratoga at 4, and placed in the Bob Harding Stakes on turf at Monmouth that season. While he achieved a 99 Beyer in an allowance win at Laurel as a 5-year-old, he never prevailed in stakes company.

Not For Love's pedigree is strikingly similar to that of Mutakddim. He is a full brother to champion juvenile Rhythm and Grade 3 winner Get Lucky. His dam was a Grade 1-winning half-sister to Private Account and Polish Numbers, and his second dam was the brilliant Numbered Account. Third dam Intriguing was a multiple stakes-placed half-sister to Poker, the broodmare sire of Kentucky Derby, Preakness, and Dubai World Cup winner Silver Charm.

Another direct descendant of the legendary La Troienne, Not For Love does very well when bred to mares by Smarten, and has also been successful when inbred to Raise a Native and Northern Dancer. Expect his sales numbers to increase in the near future, as he has proven to be more than just a win-early stallion. In recent years, his Duckhorn and Presidentialaffair have won graded stakes for older horses at route distances.

Although he slumped in 2003 with his juvenile firsters, it must be noted that he went 5 for 17 with a $5.91 ROI in 2001, and 10 for 26 with a $9.86 ROI the following year. He passes on speed and should rebound.

Juvenile Debut Sire Ranking: B+

Lest you think I would leave you with an "unlucky 13" list, here are several more sires that should be followed in juvenile debut races:

JUVENILE DEBUT SIRE RANKING: B

A.P. Indy
Classy, underrated sire of juvenile debut runners

Cape Town
23% juvenile debut winners in 2003
$2.50 juvenile debut ROI in 2003

Carson City
25% juvenile debut winners in 2003

Defrere
Three-year juvenile debut ROI of $2.81
23% juvenile debut winners in 2003

Grand Slam
$2.42 juvenile debut ROI in 2003

Kingmambo
$3.11 juvenile debut ROI in 2003

Lil's Lad
$3.88 juvenile debut ROI in 2003 (First crop)

Pioneering
Three-year average juvenile debut ROI of $2.37
26% juvenile debut winners in 2003
$3.97 juvenile debut ROI in 2003

Roar
Three-year average juvenile debut ROI of $3.32
28% juvenile debut winners in 2003
$7.55 juvenile debut ROI in 2003

Salt Lake
Three-year juvenile debut winning percentage of 20%
20% juvenile debut winners in 2003
$2.37 juvenile debut ROI in 2003

Smokester
Three-year juvenile debut ROI of $2.06
$2.54 juvenile debut ROI in 2003
Tactical Cat
21% juvenile debut winning percentage in 2003 (First crop)
Tomorrows Cat
Two-year juvenile debut ROI of $2.98
$3.94 juvenile debut ROI in 2003

JUVENILE DEBUT SIRE RANKING: B-

Gone West
Very classy sire; always dangerous with juvenile debut runners
Honour and Glory
Three-year juvenile debut ROI of $2.27
In Excess
Three-year juvenile debut ROI of $2.64
Silver Ghost
Three-year juvenile debut ROI of $3.21

JUVENILE DEBUT SIRE RANKING: C+

Double Honor
$2.68 juvenile debut ROI in 2003
El Prado
$2.12 juvenile debut ROI in 2003
Forest Wildcat
24% juvenile debut winning percentage in 2003
$2.10 juvenile debut ROI in 2003
Formal Dinner
$2.67 juvenile debut ROI in 2003
Maria's Mon
$3.66 juvenile debut ROI in 2003

Smoke Glacken

$2.74 juvenile debut ROI in 2003

Souvenir Copy

$2.58 juvenile debut ROI in 2003

You and I

20% juvenile debut winning percentage in 2003

JUVENILE DEBUT SIRE RANKING: C

Capote

$2.60 juvenile debut winning ROI in 2002

Devil His Due

21% juvenile debut winning percentage in 2002

$2.36 juvenile debut ROI in 2002

Gold Case

21% juvenile debut winning percentage in 2002

$2.63 juvenile debut ROI in 2002

Langfuhr

$2.74 juvenile debut ROI in 2002

Storm Boot

$2.44 juvenile debut ROI in 2002

Take Me Out

25% juvenile debut winning percentage in 2002

$2.20 juvenile debut ROI in 2002

I usually feel very lonely during the early part of the Thoroughbred season, as there is no juvenile racing for me to follow. While I'll analyze stallions that do better with older or turf maidens later on in the text, it's worth mentioning that the sires listed above do pretty well with their older firsters as well as their juveniles. Don't believe me?

FOURTH RACE

6 FURLONGS. (1.074) MAIDEN SPECIAL WEIGHT . Purse $24,000 MAIDENS, THREE YEAR OLDS. Weight 122 lbs.

Laurel

MARCH 13, 2004

Value of Race: $24,000 Winner $13,680; second $5,040; third $2,640; fourth $1,440; fifth $720; sixth $480. Mutuel Pool $86,701.00 Exacta Pool $78,097.00 Trifecta Pool $55,138.00

Last Raced	Horse	M/Eqt.	A.	Wt	PP	St	1/4	1/2	Str	Fin	Jockey	Odds $1
	Bound for Victory	L f	3	122	7	2	1½	12½	14½	14½	Maysonett F	6.80
22Feb04 7Lrl4	Collier Slew	L b	3	122	3	6	62	41½	22	22½	Kreidel K J	2.90
27Feb04 3Lrl4	Tommy's Palm	L b	3	122	5	7	73	5½	45	31	Hamilton S D	1.70
24Oct03 9Lrl11	Capow	L	3	122	1	8	51½	2½	3½	46¾	Karamanos H A	2.10
27Feb04 4Lrl6	Ole Flat Top		3	115	2	4	32	61	64	51½	Fitzpatrick A7	51.00
27Feb04 3Lrl6	Town Squire	L	3	122	8	1	4½	3hd	51	61¾	Castellano A Jr	9.70
12Feb04 3Lrl7	Viva Riccio	L f	3	122	4	3	8	8	76	714½	Delgado G R	68.30
21Feb04 5CT3	Rockhills Jet Set	L bf	3	117	6	5	21	75	8	8	Goodwin N	35.70

OFF AT 2:41 Start Good . Won driving. Track fast.

TIME :22⁴, :46¹, :58³, 1:11 (:22.92, :46.36, :58.76, 1:11.05)

$2 Mutuel Prices:	7 – BOUND FOR VICTORY..............	15.60	6.00	3.40
	3 – COLLIER SLEW.....................		4.20	3.00
	5 – TOMMY'S PALM....................			2.60

$2 EXACTA 7–3 PAID $80.60 $2 TRIFECTA 7–3–5 PAID $226.80

Dk. b or br. c, (May), by Boundary – Green Heights , by Miswaki . Trainer Tammaro John J III. Bred by Bruce Smart (Ky).

BOUND FOR VICTORY set the pace in the two path and was under energetic urging in the stretch. COLLIER SLEW , very wide, failed to menace the winner and gained the place. TOMMY'S PALM lacked speed and rallied inside horses. CAPOW broke slowly, race in the two path on the turn and weakened. OLE FLAT TOP raced along the rail, chased the pace and weakened. TOWN SQUIRE , wide, gave way. VIVA RICCIO , rank and checked near the five eighths pole, raced wide and was outrun. ROCKHILLS JET SET pressed the pace three wide and faltered.

Owners– 1, Tam David; 2, Souder Donald E; 3, Heft Sylvia E; 4, Martin Jr Mrs J W Y; 5, Sun Burst Stable; 6, Henson Frank; 7, Kling Barry; 8, Powers Floyd O

Trainers– 1, Tammaro John J III; 2, Souder Donald E; 3, Jenkins Rodney; 4, Murphy James W; 5, Ambrogi Leo J; 6, Salzman Timothy; 7, Kling Barry; 8, Mayo Timothy M

$2 Pick Three (4–5–7) Paid $202.40 ; Pick Three Pool $10,363 .

FIFTH RACE

Oaklawn

MARCH 27, 2004

6 FURLONGS. (1.07⁴) MAIDEN CLAIMING . Purse $8,500 (includes $1,200 Other Sources) FOR MAIDENS, THREE, FOUR, AND FIVE YEAR OLDS. Three Year Olds, 117 lbs.; Older, 124 lbs. Claiming Price $15,000.

Value of Race: $10,000 Winner $6,000; second $2,000; third $1,000; fourth $600; fifth $400. Mutuel Pool $198,248.00 Exacta Pool $153,249.00 Trifecta Pool $116,172.00

Last Raced	Horse	M/Eqt. A. Wt	PP	St	¼	½	Str	Fin	Jockey	Cl'g Pr	Odds $1
	Belle Arti	L . 4 124	8	1	3$1\frac{1}{2}$	3$2\frac{1}{2}$	12$\frac{1}{2}$	1⁴	Ortiz F L	15000	10.10
12Mar04 10OP6	Confidential Ave.	L 3 117	7	6	7²	7hd	3$1\frac{1}{2}$	2$1\frac{1}{4}$	McKee J	15000	3.60
7Mar04 5OP6	Tankit Or Leaveit	L 4 124	1	3	1hd	1$\frac{1}{2}$	2²	3$1\frac{1}{2}$	Hightower T W	15000	a- 23.40
	Heathersspacecdet	L 3 118	2	5	8$2\frac{1}{2}$	8$2\frac{1}{2}$	4$\frac{1}{2}$	4$\frac{3}{4}$	Martinez S B	15000	12.40
18Mar04 10OP5	Two Rows of Gold	L b 3 117	10	7	4$\frac{1}{2}$	4$1\frac{1}{2}$	6$2\frac{1}{2}$	5$1\frac{1}{2}$	Doocy T T	15000	4.50
12Mar04 10OP12	Up Henshaw Hill	L b 3 117	4	12	12	10¹	8²	6hd	Murray K M	15000	36.10
19Mar04 10P4	First Away	L f 4 124	12	4	5$1\frac{1}{2}$	5hd	7$\frac{1}{2}$	7nk	Johnson J M	15000	3.80
11Mar04 10P3	Jettin Bear	L b 4 124	3	2	2hd	2hd	5hd	8$1\frac{3}{4}$	Berry M C	15000	4.60
12Mar04 10OP4	He's Tricky	L 3 120	6	10	10hd	11$1\frac{1}{2}$	9$\frac{1}{2}$	9$1\frac{1}{2}$	Norwood J K	15000	10.30
21Mar04 4OP6	Ruston Drive In	L b 3 117	11	8	6$\frac{1}{2}$	6$\frac{1}{2}$	10³	10$2\frac{1}{4}$	Marquez C H Jr	15000	10.80
11Mar04 10P10	Jen's All Aboard	L b 3 117	9	11	9$1\frac{1}{2}$	9$\frac{1}{2}$	11¹	11$\frac{1}{2}$	Kuntzweiler G	15000	47.70
19Feb04 3Hou7	Darned Traitor	L f 3 117	5	9	11⁴	12	12	12	Garcia D	15000	a- 23.40

a–Coupled: Tankit Or Leaveit and Darned Traitor.

OFF AT 3:05 Start Good . Won driving. Track fast.

TIME :22, :46, :59, 1:11⁴ (:22.17, :46.18, :59.00, 1:11.99)

$2 Mutuel Prices:

7 – BELLE ARTI	22.20	11.20	8.40
6 – CONFIDENTIAL AVE.		6.00	4.40
1 – TANKIT OR LEAVEIT(a–entry)			7.60

$2 EXACTA 7–6 PAID $157.00 $2 TRIFECTA 7–6–1 PAID $3,009.00

B. g, (Apr), by Boundary – Swoop City , by Carson City . Trainer Rose Michael. Bred by W Bruce Lunsford (Ky).

BELLE ARTI with the pace from the start, vied three wide into the turn, drove strongly clear. CONFIDENTIAL AVE. saved ground off the pace, continued along the rail through the stretch, finished willingly. TANKIT OR LEAVEIT narrowly set the pace closest to the inside, allowed the runner up the rail, lasted best of the rest. HEATHERSSPACECADET turned in an even effort off the rail. TWO ROWS OF GOLD within striking distance, came up empty for the drive. UP HENSHAW HILL off a bit slow, trailed early, displayed a modest amount of late interest. FIRST AWAY raced outside, no response in the drive. JETTIN BEAR vied up front between foes for a half, faltered in the drive. HE'S TRICKY failed to menace. RUSTON DRIVE IN five wide out of the turn, outrun in the drive. JEN'S ALL ABOARD tired. DARNED TRAITOR trailed most of the way, well beaten.

Owners– 1, Rose Michael and Kathryn; 2, Rand Jeff S; 3, Von Wise Kriston; 4, Pure Gold Stable; 5, Poe Jim Tucker Robert L and Wigginton Jessie; 6, Smith Don R; 7, Lerblance William J Pr; 8, Owens Gary; 9, Hwy 1 Racing Stable LLC; 10, Bird Richard L; 11, Tate Gary; 12, Von Wise Kriston

Trainers– 1, Rose Michael; 2, Brennan Terry J; 3, Von Wise Kriston; 4, Smith Kenny P; 5, Wigginton Jesse N; 6, Smith Don R; 7, Page Thomas K; 8, Lozano Martin; 9, Roberts Stanley W; 10, McKeever Billy C Jr; 11, Walt Nicole L; 12, Von Wise Kriston

SEVENTH RACE

Hawthorne

APRIL 24, 2004

6 FURLONGS. (1.07¹) MAIDEN SPECIAL WEIGHT . Purse $26,000 (plus $9,360 IOA – IL Registered Own Award) For Maiden Fillies and Mares, Three Years Old And Upward. Three Year Olds 114 lbs.; Older 123 lbs.

Value of Race: $26,000 Winner $15,600; second $5,200; third $2,860; fourth $1,560; fifth $780. Mutuel Pool $94,522.00 Exacta Pool $68,429.00 Trifecta Pool $56,872.00 Superfecta Pool $19,280.00

Last Raced	Horse	M/Eqt.	A.	Wt	PP	St	¼	½	Str	Fin	Jockey	Odds $1
	Humorous Tune	L	3	114	3	5	4hd	5²	4²	12½	Molina T	16.80
1Apr04 8TP5	Jessie's Chance	L	3	114	11	2	3¹	3²	2½	23½	Campbell J M	13.00
20Mar04 12GP5	PentelicusDnc-Ecu		3	116	5	8	7hd	6½	7³	3½	Trujillo E	2.80
27Mar04 7Haw6	Miss Expectations	L	3	115	8	4	1hd	2²	1hd	4nk	Sterling L J Jr	13.30
9Apr04 10Haw5	Anita's Charm	L	3	115	6	3	5¹	4¹	5½	5¹¼	Lopez U A	8.10
27Mar04 7Haw3	Aloha Rosa	L	4	116	2	6	8¹½	9½	6hd	6²	Morris L K7	4.00
12Dec03 7TP5	Peekaboo Cat	L	3	114	7	1	2¹	1¹	3¹½	7¹	La Sala J	2.70
27Mar04 7Haw7	Bewitching Blonde	L	3	115	1	11	11	11	10¹⁰	8hd	Chen M B	23.70
16Aug03 7ElP7	Quill Play	L	4	123	4	9	9hd	10⁶	8¹	9½	Meier R	23.70
9Apr04 10Haw9	Clever Comique	L f	3	115	9	10	10⁴	8½	9²	10²³¾	Emigh C A	81.60
4Oct03 8Haw7	Apple Rose	L b	3	116	10	7	6²	7½	11	11	Razo E Jr	11.90

OFF AT 4:00 Start Good . Won driving. Track fast.

TIME :22², :46⁴, 1:00, 1:12⁴ (:22.52, :46.98, 1:00.10, 1:12.85)

$2 Mutuel Prices:				
	3 – HUMOROUS TUNE	35.60	15.80	8.60
	11 – JESSIE'S CHANCE		14.60	6.60
	5 – PENTELICUS DANCE-ECU			3.40

$2 EXACTA 3–11 PAID $492.20 $2 TRIFECTA 3–11–5 PAID $4,489.80
$1 SUPERFECTA 3–11–5–8 PAID $14,460.00

Dk. b or br. f, (May), by Distorted Humor – Hit Tune , by Mr. Leader . Trainer Gore Terrel. Bred by Charles Nuckols Jr & Sons (Ky).

HUMOROUS TUNE saved ground near the middle of the field, came four wide into the stretch, rallied through the lane and won going away. JESSIE'S CHANCE raced close up outside, rallied to the lead between calls in deep stretch then was no match for the winner. PENTELICUS DANCE (ECU) raced near the middle of the field and rallied belatedly. MISS EXPECTATIONS contested the pace just outside but could not last. ANITA'S CHARM raced near the middle of the field and lacked a rally. ALOHA ROSA lacked speed and improved her position. PEEKABOO CAT vied for the lead inside and tired. BEWITCHING BLONDE lacked speed and showed little. QUILL PLAY was always outrun. CLEVER COMIQUE was also outrun. APPLE ROSE raced near the middle of the field and gave way.

Owners– 1, Bartels Nancy and Gore Lizabeth; 2, Tomoka Hills Farm; 3, Bueno Marcelo and Zoldan Isaac; 4, Lloyd W Belpedio G and Cherrywood Racing Stable II; 5, Merlo Joe and Kilpatrick Mark; 6, Summerplace Farm and Ernie T Poulos Racing Stable Inc; 7, Carmy Cat Racing Stable; 8, Inman Barr H; 9, Webb Gene; 10, Nienast Lamont; 11, Bonomo Rose and George

Trainers– 1, Gore Terrel; 2, Scott Joan; 3, Salazar Marco P; 4, Boyce Michele; 5, Lynn Jeffery C; 6, Poulos Dee; 7, Berndt Joel; 8, Livesay Charlie; 9, Bettis Charles L; 10, Scherbenske Percy E; 11, Granitz Anthony J

SEVENTH RACE

Oaklawn

FEBRUARY 1, 2004

6 FURLONGS. (1.07⁴) MAIDEN SPECIAL WEIGHT . Purse $31,000 (includes $2,500 Other Sources) FOR MAIDENS, FILLIES AND MARES THREE, FOUR, AND FIVE YEARS OLD. Three Year Olds, 116 lbs.; Older, 124 lbs.

Value of Race: $31,000 Winner $18,600; second $6,200; third $3,100; fourth $1,860; fifth $1,240. Mutuel Pool $205,794.00 Exacta Pool $174,024.00 Trifecta Pool $154,073.00

Last Raced	Horse	M/Eqt.	A.	Wt	PP	St	1/4	1/2	Str	Fin	Jockey	Odds $1
	Dash of Humor	L	4	124	6	5	2¹	2hd	1¹	1¹¹⁄₂	Berry M C	17.60
	Speedy Sunrise		3	116	9	6	5¹¹⁄₂	3²	3¹¹⁄₂	2¹¹⁄₄	Lopez J	11.30
24Sep03 ⁴AP⁶	Touch of Victory	L	3	116	7	7	8²	6hd	5¹¹⁄₂	3nk	Doocy T T	8.70
	Ashleys Art	L	3	116	2	1	4hd	4hd	4²	4hd	Lejeune S P Jr	13.90
	Flight Wings	L	3	116	11	4	1hd	1¹	2¹	5⁴¹⁄₄	McKee J	0.80
1Nov03 ⁵LaD⁶	Belle Toujours	L	4	124	1	11	11	11	8¹¹⁄₂	6¹⁄₂	Kuntzweiler G	52.80
	Powdered Wig	L	4	119	3	8	10⁵¹⁄₂	10hd	7¹⁄₂	7no	Shepherd J⁵	41.90
14Mar03 ⁸OP⁷	Struttin'	L b	4	124	5	2	6²¹⁄₂	5³¹⁄₂	6³	8⁴³⁄₄	Johnson J M	9.80
	Sapphires N Halos	L	3	116	8	9	7¹	8¹⁄₂	10¹²	9¹¹⁄₂	Pettinger D R	15.20
	Golden Symphony	L	4	124	4	10	9¹⁄₂	7¹¹⁄₂	9hd	10¹⁰³⁄₄	Thompson T J	5.00
10Aug03 ⁴PrM⁶	Firetail	L b	3	116	10	3	3¹	9²	11	11	Shino K A	85.30

OFF AT 3:46 Start Good . Won driving. Track fast.

TIME :22³, :46³, :59⁴, 1:12 (:22.60, :46.69, :59.98, 1:12.02)

$2 Mutuel Prices:

6 – DASH OF HUMOR	37.20	14.00	7.60
9 – SPEEDY SUNRISE		11.40	8.20
7 – TOUCH OF VICTORY			5.20

$2 EXACTA 6–9 PAID $370.00 $2 TRIFECTA 6–9–7 PAID $3,926.20

Ch. f, (Feb), by Distorted Humor – Dot Dot Dash , by Nureyev . Trainer Moquett Ronald E. Bred by Dullea Farms LLC (Ky).

DASH OF HUMOR vied early, fell back off the leader a bit into the turn, asked for run along the rail late turn, regained advantage, edged clear. SPEEDY SUNRISE allowed the pace to go while outside, moved a bit closer late in the turn, lost some ground to the winner into the stretch, managed to close the gap some in the late going. TOUCH OF VICTORY lacked speed, angled out steadily the upper half of the stretch, mild rally. ASHLEYS ART within striking distance, lacked a winning kick. FLIGHT WINGS set or forced the pace for a half off the inside, faltered. BELLE TOUJOURS last away, far back back, belated rally. POWDERED WIG improved position into the stretch, finished evenly. STRUTTIN' lacked a response in the drive. SAPPHIRES N HALOS not a threat. GOLDEN SYMPHONY off a bit slow, lodged a tepid middle move, backed up late. FIRETAIL forwardly placed early, gave way.

Owners– 1, Conway James D; 2, Grum D Janelle; 3, Cranston Mel; 4, Jiles Beavers Deanna L; 5, Fly Racing LLC; 6, Baker Mike and Cindy; 7, Holm Thoroughbred Company; 8, Ebert Anita; 9, Cheyenne Stables LLC and McNeill Don; 10, Spence James C; 11, Olson Paula

Trainers– 1, Moquett Ronald E; 2, Wiggins Hal R; 3, Hobby Steve; 4, Smith Kenny P; 5, Holthus Robert E; 6, Whited David E; 7, Jones J Larry; 8, Hartlage Gary G; 9, Von Hemel Donnie K; 10, Nicks Morris G; 11, Gleason Tim M

Scratched– Soldier's Angel (15Jan04 ¹⁰Hou²)

THIRD RACE

Gulfstream

JANUARY 29, 2004

6 FURLONGS. (1.074) MAIDEN CLAIMING . Purse $24,000 FOR MAIDENS, FILLIES THREE YEARS OLD. Weight, 121 lbs. Claiming Price $62,500, For Each $2,500 To $57,500 1 lb.

Value of Race: $24,000 Winner $14,400; second $4,320; third $2,640; fourth $1,200; fifth $240; sixth $240; seventh $240; eighth $240; ninth $240; tenth $240. Mutuel Pool $184,918.00 Exacta Pool $194,917.00 Trifecta Pool $166,411.00

Last Raced	Horse	M/Eqt.	A.	Wt	PP	St	1/4	1/2	Str	Fin	Jockey	Cl'g Pr	Odds $1
	Intrueflight	L	3	121	9	2	2$\frac{1}{2}$	11$\frac{1}{2}$	1^3	1$^{7\frac{3}{4}}$	Chavez J F	62500	8.00
	Calcite		3	121	3	5	3^1	4^2	3^1	2$\frac{1}{2}$	Coa E M	62500	11.70
28Dec03 10Crc6	Blue Grass Dancer	L	3	119	7	9	7^{hd}	6^{hd}	5^{hd}	3^{nk}	Boulanger G	57500	11.90
4Jan04 8GP4	Micki Michelle	L	3	121	1	1	5^1	3$\frac{1}{2}$	2$\frac{1}{2}$	4^{hd}	Prado E S	62500	0.80
	Starship Elaine	L	3	121	2	8	8^2	5^{hd}	6$^{2\frac{1}{2}}$	5$^{2\frac{1}{2}}$	King E L Jr	62500	36.00
4Jan04 8GP7	Quisty	L f	3	121	5	7	9^1	9^2	7$\frac{1}{2}$	6^7	Peck B D	62500	41.50
19Dec03 4Crc7	Showtime Dancer	f	3	119	8	3	10	10	10	7^{hd}	Toscano P R	57500	96.30
	Lady Tara	L	3	121	4	6	1^{hd}	2$^{1\frac{1}{2}}$	4^1	8^1	Santos J A	62500	3.90
	C D Player	b	3	121	10	10	6^1	8^2	8$^{1\frac{1}{2}}$	9^1	Castro E	62500	18.60
	Fierce Resistance		3	121	6	4	4^1	7^{hd}	9$^{1\frac{1}{2}}$	10	Beckner D V	62500	19.10

OFF AT 2:26 Start Good For All But C D PLAYER. Won ridden out. Track fast.

TIME :22^1, :45^4, :58^3, 1:11^3 (:22.28, :45.88, :58.75, 1:11.79)

$2 Mutuel Prices:

9 – INTRUEFLIGHT	18.00	9.00	6.60
3 – CALCITE		9.60	7.80
7 – BLUE GRASS DANCER			5.60

$1 EXACTA 9–3 PAID $103.80 $1 TRIFECTA 9–3–7 PAID $1,040.00

B. f, (Mar), by Is It True – Inmusicalflight , by Temperence Hill . Trainer Bignault W Paschal. Bred by Dee Jannise (Fla).

INTRUEFLIGHT forced the pace outside LADY TARA, moved to take over from that rival on the turn, then drew off while being ridden out. CALCITE chased the pace along the inside, then closed to gain the place while no match for the winner. BLUE GRASS DANCER reserved off the pace after breaking slowly, split rivals on the turn, angled out for the drive and closed to be up for the show. MICKI MICHELLE tracked the pace off the rail into the stretch and gave way. STARSHIP ELAINE was caught in tight early, saved ground around the turn and had no late response. QUISTY failed to menace. SHOWTIME DANCER was no factor after being outrun early. LADY TARA set the pace under pressure along the inside, then tired in the drive. C D PLAYER broke poorly, raced four wide on the turn and faltered. FIERCE RESISTANCE showed early foot, raced three wide on the turn and faded.

Owners– 1, Dubb Michael; 2, Oxbow Racing LLC; 3, Devault Sue; 4, Bronzine Michelle; 5, Starship Stables; 6, Eaglestone Farm; 7, North Land Farm Inc; 8, Wira Richard and Yvette; 9, Shaw John E; 10, Wilson Robert J

Trainers– 1, Bignault W Paschal; 2, White William P; 3, Gambolati Cam; 4, Asmussen Steven M; 5, DiMauro Stephen L; 6, Nafzger Carl A; 7, Muench David L; 8, Simon Charles; 9, Olivares Luis; 10, Casse Mark

Lady Tara was claimed by Prime Time Stable; trainer, McCarthy Michael J.

While pedigree handicapping is a valuable tool in the analysis of any juvenile maiden race, it is equally important to discover which trainers have their youngsters cranked up and ready to go at first asking. Some trainers take a very patient approach with their runners, while others like to immediately have their pictures taken in the winner's circle. Again, when handicapping trainers, it is necessary to ask questions. How has this trainer done with previous firsters? Does the trainer use any workout patterns that consistently produce "live" runners? Why has the trainer put this firster in this spot? Is the trainer willing to risk a hot firster in a maiden claiming race? And so on, and so on. With this in mind, let's go back to my three-year database, and find out which trainers are most likely to send out precocious juvenile runners.

STEVE ASMUSSEN

2001–2003 Juvenile Debut Statistics: 318 runners, 60 winners (19%)

2001–2003 Return on Investment: $2.51

2003 Juvenile Debut Statistics: 109 runners, 28 winners (26%)

2003 Return on Investment: $2.87

How does he do it? How does one of the most influential trainers in the game show a positive return on investment with his debuting juveniles? Steve Asmussen has started at least 90 2-year-olds in each of the last three seasons, and his winning percentage and ROI have increased incrementally each year. In 2001, Asmussen won with 14 percent of his 90 juveniles for a $2.03 ROI. The following season, he clicked with 16 percent of 117 runners for a $2.58 return. He exploded with 28 separate debut winners in 2003, and it doesn't look like the Asmussen debut train will be slowing down anytime soon.

Asmussen's stable is so far-reaching that he uses a variety of go-to jockeys on his hot firsters. Shane Sellers, Jeremy Beasley, Corey Lanerie, Gerard Melancon, Frank Lovato Jr., Jerry Bailey, Guadalupe Macias Jr., Casey Lambert, Timothy Doocy, Curt Bourque, Steve Bourque, Richard Migliore, Dominic Terry, and Roman Chapa have all ridden successful Asmussen firsters in the study. He dominates the juvenile standings at Keeneland and Lone Star Park, and is very, very dangerous at Churchill Downs, Louisiana Downs, Fair Grounds, Retama Park, Sam Houston Park, and Arlington. He has also slowly made his presence felt at Saratoga and Belmont over the last few seasons.

Asmussen has sent out juvenile firsters for myriad owners as well. His satisfied clients include Heiligbrodt Racing Stable, Grunwald Racing, James Cassels and Bob Zollars, Nelson Bunker Hunt, Ocean Front Property, Gentry Farms, Ackerley Brothers Farms,

Padua Stables, and Cashmark Farms and Janeen Oliver. He also has sent out a slew of winners owned by, or in partnership with, family members Keith and Cash Asmussen.

He likes to work his young horses in company, so astute handicappers might gauge their ability level by regularly glancing at the daily work tab. Of Asmussen's last 57 juvenile debut winners, 26 used Lasix, one wore front bandages, and one wore blinkers. He spots them where they can win, so don't be discouraged if he enters a firster in a maiden claiming heat. He usually has at least one or two hot streaks a year. Between April 4 and May 2, 2003, he sent out six winners. Between May 11 and May 30, 2003, he knocked out another six. Four more came in the period between October 9 and October 23, 2003.

Whether it is April at Keeneland, or December at Sam Houston, Asmussen's firsters must always be taken seriously. He is truly one of the best trainers in the world.
Juvenile Debut Trainer Ranking: A+

TODD PLETCHER
2001–2003 Juvenile Debut Statistics: 182 runners, 40 winners (22%)
2001–2003 Return on Investment: $1.62
2003 Juvenile Debut Statistics: 71 runners, 17 winners (24%)
2003 Return on Investment: $1.74

The New York railbirds used to chant the same old mantra: "Mott and Bailey." "Mott and Bailey." "Mott and Bailey." Times have changed a bit, however, and now the refrain is "Pletcher and Velazquez." There is no doubt in my mind that there are Eclipse Awards in the futures of both trainer Todd Pletcher and jockey John Velazquez. Each will likely credit the other in his acceptance speech. Velazquez rode 28 of Pletcher's 35 juvenile debut winners in this study, and their team should continue to knock them dead on the NYRA circuit. If Velazquez isn't readily available, then Pletcher "settles" for Jerry Bailey, Robby Albarado, Javier Castellano, Richard Migliore, or Edgar Prado.

Pletcher's owners read like a who's who of the American turf. Michael Tabor, Dogwood Stable, Donald and Roberta Zuckerman, Starlight Stables and Paul Saylor, Edgewood Farm, James Scatuorchio, Peachtree Stable, So Madcapt Stable, Alan Kline, Padua Stables, Eugene and Laura Melnyk, Wertheimer and Frere, Bonnie and Sy Baskin, and Anstu Stables are among the many patrons who send their prized young horses to Pletcher.

Like Asmussen, Pletcher loves to work his horses in company, and his good young runners usually stick out on the daily tab. His live runners usually debut with Lasix (31 of 35 in the study). One wore front wraps while another wore blinkers, and only two scored their first career victories in claiming events. Pletcher does well with his firsters at Keeneland, Monmouth, Saratoga, Churchill, and Aqueduct, but he usually excels at the Belmont spring meet. Half of his 18 juvenile debut winners in 2002 ran there. In 2003, Pletcher sent out 12 of his 17 winners at either Belmont spring, or at Saratoga.

The former assistant to Hall of Fame trainer D. Wayne Lukas is one of the top young stars in the game. His debut winning percentage hovered between 24 and 30 percent in 2002–2003, and he should continue to send out well-bred runners that sold for huge amounts at auction. Be aware, however, that the public usually hammers any firster that Pletcher puts on the track.
Juvenile Debut Trainer Ranking: A+

JERRY HOLLENDORFER
2001–2003 Juvenile Debut Statistics: 73 runners, 18 winners (25%)
2001–2003 Return on Investment: $2.25
2003 Juvenile Debut Statistics: 24 runners, 5 winners (21%)
2003 Return on Investment: $1.78

They don't call him King Jerry for nothing. The perennial leading trainer in Northern California, Jerry Hollendorfer is also usually among the national leaders in wins. Therefore, it is surprising that his juvenile firsters have shown a profit in this study. Hollendorfer teamed up with Northern California's leading rider, Russell Baze, for nine of Hollendorfer's 18 juvenile debut winners, but he has also had success using Francisco Duran, Roberto Gonzalez, and Chad Schvaneveldt. Hollendorfer's live firsters usually show up at Bay Meadows, Bay Meadows Fair, Golden Gate Fields, and Solano, but he did send out a winning juvenile debut runner at Hollywood in 2003. Hollendorfer has done well with firsters owned by, or in partnership with, Marta Racing Ventures and John D. Gunther. Interestingly, none of his 2003 juvenile debut winners sold for over $50,000 at auction.

In 2001 and 2002, Hollendorfer sent a successful string of runners to Arlington Park, and it will be interesting to see if he attempts to expand his operation again in the future. Five of his 18 winning juvenile firsters graduated in maiden claiming events. All of Hollendorfer's debut winners in 2003 had between six and 10 uninterrupted (no gaps of more than 14 days) workouts before their first race with at least two of those works coming from the gate. The workouts gradually increased in distance, and four of the runners worked six furlongs as their final preparation. Only one of the five juvenile debut winners showed a bullet work on the tab. All of his 12 juvenile debut winners between 2001–2002 raced with Lasix while four wore blinkers.

Hollendorfer showed a positive ROI with his 2-year-old firsters in 2001–2002, and his winning percentage with juvenile firsters hasn't dipped below 21 percent in the study. He must be respected whenever he sends out a juvenile debut runner.

Juvenile Debut Trainer Ranking: A+

READE BAKER
2001–2003 Juvenile Debut Statistics: 46 runners, 11 winners (24%)
2001–2003 Return on Investment: $3.65
2003 Juvenile Debut Statistics: 14 runners, 3 winners (21%)
2003 Return on Investment: $1.44

Reade Baker caught my eye in 2001 when his juvenile debut runners produced a $4.03 ROI. He struck with 43 percent of his juvenile firsters the following year for a $5.36 ROI. In 2003, he maintained a winning percentage above 20 percent, and teamed up with rider James McAleney for all three of his juvenile debut winners. Baker has also had success using jockeys Laurie Gulas, David Clark, and Jake Barton. He has sent out winning juvenile firsters owned in partnership with J. Maine, and for Stronach Stable. Two of his three juvenile debut winners in 2003 were homebreds. The other sold for only $40,000 at auction.

Baker's three juvenile debut winners in 2003 came between August 2 and September 7. All had at least seven uninterrupted workouts with at least three coming from the gate. Two of them had bullet works on their tabs, and all showed workouts between five and six furlongs in their final morning outing.

All of Baker's nine juvenile debut winners in 2002–2003 raced with Lasix, and four wore blinkers. One won going seven furlongs on the turf. It seems as if only the most hard-core handicappers follow Baker, so expect to continue receiving plenty of value on his Canadian debut runners.

Juvenile Debut Trainer Ranking: A

CHAD HASSENPFLUG

2001–2003 Juvenile Debut Statistics: 21 runners, 11 winners (52%)

2001–2003 Return on Investment: $6.27

2003 Juvenile Debut Statistics: 9 runners, 5 winners (56%)

2003 Return on Investment: $6.58

Don't know this guy? You really should. His numbers with juvenile debut firsters are absolutely phenomenal. After going 0 for 3 with his 2-year-old firsters in 2001, Hassenpflug went 11 for 18 in 2002–2003 with a tremendous ROI. Hassenpflug plies his trade in Louisiana, and does most of his damage at Delta Downs. Nine of his juvenile debut winners in the study were ridden by either Carl Woodley or Kirk Leblanc. He has had two juvenile debut winners over the past two years for owner Barbara J. Wennik.

Six of his juvenile debut winners graduated with Lasix while four wore blinkers. Eight wore front bandages first time out.

Unlike the aforementioned trainers, Hassenpflug doesn't seem to train his young horses hard in the weeks leading up to their debuts. Of his five juvenile debut winners in 2003, only one had multiple uninterrupted workouts. Two winners showed no published workouts, and none had a workout at more than three furlongs as its final preparation. His 2003 winners sold at auction for between $5,500 and $13,000, so perhaps that is the reason his horses don't get much respect at the betting windows.

Thanks to the introduction of slot machines at Delta Downs, the purses at the tiny track are going through the roof. Expect more simulcast outlets to receive their signal. Therefore, Hassenpflug is a name that all handicappers need to know. His numbers speak for themselves.

Juvenile Debut Trainer Ranking: A

COLE NORMAN

2001–2003 Juvenile Debut Statistics: 72 runners, 21 winners (29%)

2001–2003 Return on Investment: $2.35

2003 Juvenile Debut Statistics: 28 runners, 9 winners (32%)

2003 Return on Investment: $2.66

Cole Norman has come a long way. In 2001 and 2002, he sent out successful juvenile firsters by sires such as Summer of Storms, Stark Ridge, A. P Jet, Marked Tree, Laabity, Hadif, Judge T C, and Devious Course. In 2003, Norman was winning first-out with progeny of Touch Gold, Cherokee Run, Silver Deputy, Cape Town, and Victory Gallop. Owners have taken notice of this excellent horseman by sending him better stock, and it's time for handicappers to recognize Norman as a dangerous debut threat.

Norman used jockey Anthony Lovato on all of his 2001 juvenile debut winners, but recently has had success teaming up with Jamie Theriot, Carlos Gonzalez, Roman Chapa, and Gerard Melancon. His winning juvenile firsters usually make their debuts at Lone Star Park or Louisiana Downs, but since he is gaining attention, it won't be surprising if he branches out to some larger circuits in the future. Norman has sent out multiple juvenile debut winners for owners Turf Express Inc., Gary and Mary West, J. Phillip Mote, Kalarikkal and Vilasini Jayaraman, and Earl Bellamy. All 15 of Norman's juvenile debut winners between 2002–2003 used Lasix. Thirteen of the 15 were equipped with blinkers. A common theme with Norman is that he likes to give his young horses multiple gate workouts before they make their debuts. Of his nine winners in 2003, six of them had at least two morning drills from the gate. He usually gives his runners between two and five uninterrupted workouts before they are unveiled to the betting public, although the $150,000 purchase Kangaroo Jack had a big gap between his last work and his successful career debut. Seven of Norman's juvenile debut winners in 2003 had multiple works at five furlongs, while three sported at least one bullet drill.

A good Norman firster can come from just about anywhere. Two of his 2003 juvenile debut winners sold for over $150,000. Three others sold for prices between $5,200 and $18,500. Norman isn't afraid to risk his live firsters for a tag. One-third of his juvenile debut winners in this study came in maiden claiming events.

A leading trainer at whatever circuit he chooses to frequent, Norman should continue to excel with his young debut runners.
Juvenile Debut Trainer Ranking: A

BENJAMIN PERKINS JR.
2001–2003 Juvenile Debut Statistics: 40 runners, 15 winners (38%)
2001–2003 Return on Investment: $1.66
2003 Juvenile Debut Statistics: 5 runners, 3 winners (60%)
2003 Return on Investment: $3.04

Ben Perkins Jr. has been a consistent source of juvenile debut winners for quite some time now. He scored with seven of 16 juvenile firsters in 2001 for a $2.06 ROI. The following season, he connected with five of his 19 2-year-old firsters.

Perkins teamed up with jockey Joe Bravo for two of his three wins in 2003 (Elvis Trujillo rode the other), but he has also done very well with Eibar Coa, Eddie King Jr., Javier Castellano, Jose Ferrer, and Tommy Turner in the irons.

All three of his 2003 wins came at Monmouth Park for owner New Farm. Perkins also has had great success with owner Raymond Dweck, and he has sent out winning firsters at The Meadowlands, Delaware Park, and Aqueduct over the past few seasons. Fifty percent of his 2002–2003 juvenile debut winners used Lasix.

Don't be alarmed if his young horses have light work tabs. None of his three debut winners in 2003 had more than four uninterrupted workouts leading up to the first start, and none worked more than four furlongs. Two of the three winners did have a bullet work on their page, however.

All of his 15 winners in the study debuted in maiden special weight events, so I would be a bit wary if he shows up with a firster in a maiden claiming race.

His youngsters usually heat up in the midsummer months. Expect Perkins to continue to receive precociously bred runners with win-early pedigrees.

Juvenile Debut Trainer Ranking: A

WESLEY WARD

2001–2003 Juvenile Debut Statistics: 69 runners, 17 winners (25%)
2001–2003 Return on Investment: $2.70
2003 Juvenile Debut Statistics: 21 runners, 4 winners (19%)
2003 Return on Investment: $2.13

With so many top trainers in California, it's easy for a "smaller" stable to slip through the cracks. Perhaps that's why Wesley Ward's juvenile firsters consistently produce profits for his followers. In 2001, Ward connected at a 21 percent clip for an ROI of $3.08. He won with 26 percent of his debuting 2-year-olds the following season for a $2.84 ROI.

Whether it is a two-furlong dash in March at Santa Anita, or a five-eighths race at Fresno in October, Ward's firsters are almost always live. Seven of Ward's 17 winners in the study were ridden by Martin Pedroza. Tyler Baze also rode multiple winners for Ward, and the trainer has also reached the winner's circle with Francisco Duran, Jason Lumpkins, Russell Baze, Macario Rodriguez, Frank Alvarado, and Antonio Castanon.

Ward has done well for a variety of owners in this study including Golden Eagle Farm, D. Chadwick Calvert, David F. Kegley,

Triple Crown Bloodstock, and the partnership of Butler, Cassells, and Moore. He also owns or co-owns many of his successful juvenile firsters. Handicappers should also respect Ward firsters that are owned by, or in partnership with, Dennis Ward. All of Ward's winners in the 2002–2003 study started with Butazolidin. Four wore blinkers while seven raced with Lasix.

His firsters are spread out around California. He wins at major tracks such as Hollywood, Santa Anita, and Bay Meadows, and at smaller venues like Fresno and Santa Rosa.

Of Ward's four juvenile debut winners of 2003, three had five uninterrupted works prior to their first start. None of the four had a workout over a half-mile, but all had at least one gate work. Two of them showed bullet speed in the mornings. While he did send out a $72,000 purchase to win first-out, the other three sold for between $3,500 and $12,000.

Nine of Ward's 17 wins in the study came in the maiden claiming ranks, so don't be afraid to take the plunge when his runners debut for a tag.

Ward's juvenile firsters have shown a flat-bet profit in each year since 2001, but his ROI and winning percentage are slowly decreasing. He should continue to have excellent years with his debut runners, but it will be interesting to see if the public is finally starting to catch on.

Juvenile Debut Trainer Ranking: A

WILLIAM WHITE

2001–2003 Juvenile Debut Statistics: 122 runners, 29 winners (24%)

2001–2003 Return on Investment: $2.95

2003 Juvenile Debut Statistics: 34 runners, 8 winners (24%)

2003 Return on Investment: $3.11

Based year-round in South Florida, William White is one of the most underrated trainers in the country. In 2001, White was successful with eight of 44 juvenile firsters for an ROI of $2.96. The following year, he improved to a 30 percent strike rate as 13 of his 44 juvenile debut runners reached the wire first.

White's main go-to riders are Cornelio Velasquez, Cecilio Penalba, and Gary Boulanger. He has also used Eibar Coa, Manuel Cruz, and Manuel Aguilar on juvenile debut winners. While White does send a healthy string of runners to Gulfstream at the start of every racing season, he saves his best youngsters for Calder. Twenty-eight of his 29 winners in the study ran at Calder; the other raced at now-defunct Hialeah.

White's notable owners include John B. Penn, Eugene and Laura Melnyk, Oxbow Racing, Kalarikkal and Vilasini Jayaraman, R. Dianne Waldron, Live Oak Plantation, and Donald Dizney.

Like Cole Norman, White loves to give his horses plenty of experience in the gate before they make their first start. All eight of White's 2003 juvenile debut winners had multiple gate works. The winning firster True Moments had nine uninterrupted workouts leading up to her debut. Eight of them came from the gate. All of White's successful 2-year-old firsters had between two and 12 uninterrupted workouts. Six of them had at least one five-furlong drill while two showed bullet works. Five of his winners sold at public auction. French Village was purchased for $100,000, but the other four sold in the $13,000 to $32,000 range.

Eighteen of White's 29 winners graduated from the maiden claiming ranks. Only five of White's 21 debut winners in 2002–2003 used Lasix. Six wore blinkers.

The dominant debut trainer in South Florida, White should continue to connect at a high percentage rate.

Juvenile Debut Trainer Ranking: A

JUVENILE DEBUT TRAINER RANKING: A-

Bob Baffert
Sends out multiple juvenile debut winners each year
William Bret Calhoun
Three-year juvenile debut winning percentage of 21%
31% juvenile debut winning percentage in 2003
Eoin Harty
35% juvenile debut winning percentage in 2003
Tim McCanna
Three-year juvenile debut ROI of $2.06
25% juvenile debut winning percentage in 2003
$3.96 juvenile debut ROI in 2003
John Servis
Three-year juvenile debut winning percentage of 24%
41% juvenile debut winning percentage in 2003
$2.85 juvenile debut ROI in 2003

JUVENILE DEBUT TRAINER RANKING: B+

Jeff Bonde
23% juvenile debut winning percentage in 2001
23% juvenile debut winning percentage in 2003
Mark Casse
20% juvenile debut winning percentage in 2003
$2.30 juvenile debut ROI in 2003
Anthony Dutrow
33% juvenile debut winning percentage in 2001
$3.28 juvenile debut ROI in 2001
Doug O'Neill
22% juvenile debut winning percentage in 2003
$2.63 juvenile debut winning ROI in 2003

Ronny Werner
31% juvenile debut winning percentage in 2001
$3.63 juvenile debut ROI in 2001

JUVENILE DEBUT TRAINER RANKING: B

Edward Plesa Jr.
$3.40 juvenile debut ROI in 2003
Angel Salinas
$2.24 juvenile debut ROI in 2001
John Salzman
21% juvenile winning percentage in 2002
Hamilton Smith
$2.20 juvenile debut ROI in 2001
Emanuel Tortora
$2.48 juvenile debut ROI in 2003

Handicappers are always worried about change. Will the trainer or sire that they have been meticulously studying suddenly cool off? It's nice to see that things have remained fairly stable in 2004. Not surprisingly, Pletcher and Asmussen dominated by sheer number of winners. The others had acceptable years. Continue to watch them in the future.

2

WHAT THE FUTURE HOLDS:
Young Stallions to Watch and the Next Great Sire of Sires

NOW THAT WE have established the current trainer and sire standouts, it is time to gaze into the future. I always enjoy poring through the various stallion registers that are published each winter. It's fun and often profitable to familiarize oneself with the incoming sires. Many handicappers only consider a sire's race record when predicting his stud chances, and that can be very hazardous to the wallet.

Holy Bull and Skip Away were outstanding runners. While they have proven to be decent sires, they haven't exactly set the world on fire. Why? My guess is that Holy Bull and Skip Away were overachievers on the racetrack. They outran their pedigrees every time they broke from a starting gate. In the breeding shed, genetics might be the most important factor. Remember, breeders aren't just sending their mares to Holy Bull or Skip Away, but to their respective families as well. Holy Bull is by the average stallion Great Above, and the first three dams in his pedigree failed to achieve black type (win or place in an added-money or stakes event) on the track. Skip Away's sire, Skip Trial, was a leading regional stallion, but never enjoyed national success before or after "Skippy."

When I scout the young sires, I look for a horse that won early in his career, hails from a sire line that produces good stallions, and boasts a classy female family. I'm proud to say that I "discovered" Rahy, El Prado, and Dynaformer when they first retired to stud. Then again, I thought that Dayjur, Eastern Echo, and Dumaani would make a significant impact. It's not an exact science, but it is very useful to make educated guesses on young sires before their runners hit the track.

Handicapping is about being one step ahead of the competition. Most horseplayers search for winning percentage information when considering whether to wager on a certain stallion's debut runners. Since first-crop sires start with a clean slate, pedigree handicappers will have an edge. And that's where the prices start getting juicy. Which stallions will dazzle the pedigree experts in the years to come?

FIRST-CROP SIRES OF 2004

LION HEARTED
Pedigree: Storm Cat—Cadillacing, by Alydar
Race Record and Earnings: 18 starts, 4 wins, 6 seconds,
   3 thirds, $191,630
2004 Stud Fee: $5,000
2004 Stud Farm: Northview Stallion Station (MD)

On paper, Lion Hearted parallels successful debut sires Not For Love and Mutakddim. Not one of them lived up to his sparkling bloodlines as a racehorse, but all three descend from ultra-classy Ogden Phipps families, and have the necessary pedigrees and conformation to succeed at stud. Phipps-family stallions always seem to do well at Northview Stallion Station. Polish Numbers got his start in Maryland, and Not For Love has been a staple of the Mid-Atlantic breeding scene for quite a while now. Lion Hearted looks poised to make an impact with his debut runners.

He reached the winner's circle in his third start, going six furlongs at Aqueduct, but never turned into a consistent stakes horse. It took him 10 races to break through his N1X condition, but he earned a 101 Beyer Speed Figure when second in the Grade 2 Riva Ridge Stakes at Belmont, and a 107 in his N1X triumph. Lion Hearted also finished second in the Grade 3 Amsterdam Stakes at Saratoga, and received a 101 Beyer for his N3X allowance win as a 4-year-old.

Lion Hearted's pedigree makes him a fascinating prospect. A son of the fantastic sire of sires Storm Cat, Lion Hearted is a half-brother to Grade 1 winner Strolling Along and Grade 2 winner Cat Cay. His dam, Cadillacing, was a Grade 1-winning full sister to the great Easy Goer and a half to Grade 1 winner Easy Now. Lion Hearted's second dam is champion Relaxing, while his third dam won the Acorn Stakes. Fourth dam Allemande was an unraced half-sister to the foundation broodmare Searching. A direct descendant of La Troienne, Lion Hearted already has sired a quick stakes winner in Chocolate Brown.

GIANT'S CAUSEWAY
Pedigree: Storm Cat—Mariah's Storm, by Rahy
Race Record and Earnings: 13 starts, 9 wins, 4 seconds,
    0 thirds, $3,078,989
2004 Stud Fee: $75,000
2004 Stud Farm: Ashford Stud (KY)

Although Giant's Causeway is by the great juvenile debut sire Storm Cat, and was an undefeated Group 1 winner as a 2-year-old, I'm going to classify him as a "Late 2" or "Early 3" sire. The expectations are so high from breeders that many sent their stoutest mares to Giant's Causeway in the hopes of getting a future classic winner. Thus, many of Giant's Causeway's progeny may need a race or two, and perhaps a route distance before reaching the winner's circle. They may win late in their 2-year-old year, or early at 3.

Giant's Causeway was special from the very start. After the colt won his debut at Naas in Ireland by six lengths at 1-3 odds, trainer Aidan O'Brien told *The Racing Post* that "This could be a very special horse. He has everything." Giant's Causeway then went on to defeat classy stablemate Brahms in the Group 3 King of Kings Futurity over seven furlongs. In his final start at 2, Giant's Causeway shipped to France for the Group 1 Prix de la Salamandre. He made all the running that day, and cruised home "unchallenged" for the victory.

At 3, Giant's Causeway proved to be one of the toughest, classiest, and most durable horses of the last 20 years. After a solid win to kick off the season in the Group 3 Gladness Stakes at The Curragh, he finished second as the favorite in both the English and Irish 2,000 Guineas. A streak of Group 1 victories began with a front-running score in the St. James's Palace Stakes at a mile. Only 18 days later, Giant's Causeway upset older runners such as Fantastic Light and Kalanisi in the Coral-Eclipse at 10 furlongs. He became the first horse in over 60 years to complete the St. James's-Coral-Eclipse double. He then turned back to a mile to record his third Group 1 win in six weeks in the Sussex Stakes, also against older rivals. He became known as the Iron Horse after his gritty win over Kalanisi in the Juddmonte International, and then won his fifth Group 1 in a row in the Irish Champion Stakes at $1\frac{1}{4}$ miles. After being upset turning back to a mile in the Group 1 Queen Elizabeth II Stakes, Giant's Causeway ran a gallant second to Tiznow in the Breeders' Cup Classic. In the wake of his 116 Beyer effort that day were such American standouts as Albert the Great, Lemon Drop Kid, and Fusaichi Pegasus.

Although he only raced once on dirt, his pedigree is full of classy American runners. His dam was a multiple Grade 2 winner on the main track. His second dam was a Grade 3-winning half-sister to champion juvenile filly and Grade 1 Acorn winner Dearly Precious.

His first foals to reach the auction ring were greeted with enthusiasm by buyers. Giant's Causeway's dogged determination, great tactical speed, and Americanized pedigree should make him a successful sire. His pedigree is free of Raise a Native blood so he should cross well with mares by sons of Mr. Prospector and Alydar.

CAPE CANAVERAL

Pedigree: Mr. Prospector—Seaside Attraction, by Seattle Slew
Race Record and Earnings: 4 starts, 3 wins, 0 seconds,
    1 third, $128,640
2004 Stud Fee: $10,000
2004 Stud Farm: Overbrook Farm (KY)

Cape Canaveral reminds me of the top debut sire Carson City. Both are compact, athletic-looking sons of Mr. Prospector that raced as homebreds for the late W. T. Young. Cape Canaveral showed brilliant speed from the moment he stepped onto a racetrack, and certainly has a top-class pedigree.

He earned a 97 Beyer Speed Figure going $6^{1}/_{2}$ furlongs in his lone start at 2, a winning effort at Santa Anita in which he set fractions of 21.20 seconds, 43.77, 1:09.04, and 1:15.68. Trainer D. Wayne Lukas wheeled Cape Canaveral back in two weeks, and the colt responded by winning the Grade 3 San Miguel Stakes as the 1-5 betting favorite. Sadly, Cape Canaveral was put on the shelf for most of his 3-year-old season, and only raced twice more in his career. He finished on a high note, however, earning a 111 Beyer in an optional claiming victory at Santa Anita.

A half-brother to Florida Derby winner and solid sire Cape Town, Cape Canaveral is a full brother to British Group 3-winning juvenile Red Carnival. He is out of Kentucky Oaks winner Seaside Attraction, and his second dam was Canadian champion Kamar. Familiar names such as Canadian champion Key to the Moon, millionaire Gorgeous, European Horse of the Year Fantastic Light, and multiple British champion Swain are only some of the top-flight runners produced by Cape Canaveral's female family.

Cape Canaveral boasts a potent combination of speed and pedigree, and should get plenty of precocious juveniles ready to fire at first asking.

CROWD PLEASER
Pedigree: A.P. Indy—Creaking Board (GB), by Night Shift
Race Record and Earnings: 24 starts, 9 wins, 1 second,
    3 thirds, $605,150
2004 Stud Fee: $3,500
2004 Stud Farm: Northview Stallion Station (MD)

A physically imposing son of the great A.P. Indy, Crowd Pleaser is another sire that should be classified as a Late 2, or Early 3. Bred and owned by George Strawbridge Jr.'s Augustin Stable, Crowd Pleaser broke his maiden in his second start at 2 over a mile and a sixteenth. He then showed his quality by coming right back to win the Valley Forge Stakes at Delaware at the same distance.

He had his best year at 3, winning three consecutive stakes on the turf between nine and 10 furlongs. First, Crowd Pleaser took the Grade 3 Saranac Handicap at Saratoga by four lengths. He then shipped to Colonial Downs to win the Virginia Derby, and followed that up with a 102 Beyer victory in the Calder Derby in South Florida.

After a difficult 4-year-old campaign, Crowd Pleaser ended his career in style at 5 with a nose win in the 13-furlong Sycamore Stakes at Keeneland with a 101 Beyer.

Although Crowd Pleaser has been perceived as nothing more than a turf and stamina influence, he may prove to be a bargain for Mid-Atlantic breeders. His dam, Creaking Board, won the Grade 1 Hollywood Starlet on dirt at 2 for Bobby Frankel, and there are some solid class influences deep in her family. I believe that A.P. Indy will be an important sire of sires, and Crowd Pleaser may surprise a few people.

CRIMSON CLASSIC

Pedigree: Sky Classic—Marianna's Girl, by Dewan
Race Record and Earnings: 55 starts, 10 wins, 12 seconds,
    7 thirds, $559,286
2004 Stud Fee: $1,500
2004 Stud Farm: Illinois Stud (IL)

He doesn't come from a fancy sire line, needed five tries to score his first victory, and never won a graded stakes. So how the heck has Crimson Classic made this list? First of all, he was an extremely durable runner who was capable on both turf and dirt. He could throw out a 105-plus Beyer on his best day, and was a multiple stakes winner at the "sire's distance" of one mile. While I'm not expecting any Eclipse Award winners from him, he may be a nice Late 2-Early 3 sire in the Midwest.

A $175,000 yearling, Crimson Classic is a half-brother to Grade 2-placed Christine's Outlaw and Grade 3-winning turfer Marastani. He is also kin to two other black-type earners, and to the dam of the speedy Don't Tell the Kids. His dam is a half-sister to Oaklawn Handicap winner Bold Style.

Crimson Classic's runners should take well to both turf and dirt, and could produce some big mutuel prices.

BEHRENS

Pedigree: Pleasant Colony—Hot Novel, by Mari's Book
Race Record and Earnings: 27 starts, 9 wins, 8 seconds,
    3 thirds, $4,563,500
2004 Stud Fee: $10,000
2004 Stud Farm: Darby Dan Farm (KY)

Behrens was one of my favorite racehorses of recent years. He was a battle-tested gladiator who always gave his all, and he was capable of mid-110 Beyers at longer distances. He was durable and relentless throughout his career, but it may take a while for Behrens to become popular with breeders. He was a true stayer with a true stayer's pedigree, and that may not translate to today's speed-crazy breeding industry. Still, his stamina could make him an important sire of classic-type runners, and he should cross well with many different strains of the modern Thoroughbred.

Behrens was unraced at 2, but people forget that he won his first three starts as a 3-year-old, including the Grade 2 Dwyer Stakes. He was nosed by Deputy Commander in only his fifth lifetime start in the Travers, and earned a 118 Beyer in winning the Grade 2 Pegasus in race number six. Behrens then suffered through a seven-race losing streak, but came back to win the Gulfstream Park Handicap, Oaklawn Handicap, Massachusetts Handicap, and Suburban Handicap in rapid-fire succession at age 5. The following season, Behrens won the Gulfstream Park Handicap for the second year in a row, and placed in the Dubai World Cup, Woodward Stakes, and in the Suburban, Whitney, and Donn Handicaps.

His dam, Hot Novel, was a multiple Grade 3 winner, so there is some class in his pedigree. It looks like it will be an uphill battle for Behrens, as the Pleasant Colony sire line isn't very popular, but he deserves a shot at siring Late 2-Early 3 runners, and perhaps some solid turf horses.

WISED UP
Pedigree: Dixieland Band—Wising Up, by Smarten
Race Record and Earnings: 19 starts, 4 wins, 2 seconds,
   7 thirds, $233,537
2004 Stud Fee: $2,500
2004 Stud Farm: Rising Hill Farm (FL)

I've always liked Dixieland Band runners on both turf and dirt, and his son Wised Up has the potential to sire some versatile performers. The $225,000 yearling was unraced at 2, but won his second start as a 3-year-old. He blossomed at 4 when trainer Richard DeStasio tried Wised Up on the turf. He won his first two starts on grass, including a 31-1 upset in the Grade 3 Fort Marcy Handicap at Aqueduct. Wised Up failed to win in eight subsequent starts, but placed in four graded stakes races.

His dam, Wising Up, is a Grade 3-winning half-sister to multiple Grade 2 winner Foresta from the family of Kentucky Oaks winner Ashado.

While Wised Up looks like he'll mainly prove to be a turf sire, he has the build and the pedigree to sire precocious sprint types. He can surprise.

FIRST-CROP SIRES OF 2005

PERIGEE MOON

Pedigree: Hennessy—Lovlier Linda, by Vigors
Race Record and Earnings: 3 starts, 2 wins, 0 seconds, 0 thirds, $42,149
2004 Stud Fee: $3,500
2004 Stud Farm: Park Stud (ON)

Perigee Moon showed brilliance as an undefeated 2-year-old in Ireland, and as a half-brother to multiple Grade 2 winner Old Trieste, his pedigree leans heavily toward dirt racing. His dam, Lovlier Linda, was a Grade 1 winner in Southern California, and Perigee Moon's progeny should enjoy getting an opportunity to run on the main track.

Trainer Aidan O'Brien has a phenomenal strike rate with debut runners, and Perigee Moon proved no exception to that rule. He won "comfortably" first time out, going six furlongs at The Curragh, and then snatched the Group 3 Killavullan Stakes in similar fashion. In his lone start at 3, and what proved to be the final race of his career, Perigee Moon finished off the board in the Group 3 Gladness Stakes after disputing the pace. He seemed in distress after the finish, and never started again.

Coolmore retained an interest in Perigee Moon, and he should fit very well in the Canadian market. A grandson of the great Storm

Cat, he should cross nicely with Raise a Native- and Bold Ruler-line mares. There is plenty of European stamina and class in his pedigree, so his runners should do as well on turf as they are expected to do on the main track.

CLOUD HOPPING
Pedigree: Mr. Prospector—Skimble, by Lyphard
Race Record and Earnings: 3 starts, 1 win, 0 seconds,
   0 thirds, $6,652
2004 Stud Fee: $3,500
2004 Stud Farm: Lambholm South (FL)

Florida is a hotbed of speedy young sires, and Cloud Hopping deserves a chance to make his mark. A son of the legendary Mr. Prospector out of multiple Grade 2 winner Skimble, Cloud Hopping is a half-brother to two-time Pacific Classic winner Skimming. The Juddmonte homebred never received an opportunity to race on the main track like his more accomplished sibling, but his lone win came over firm going at Sandown Park in England, and his progeny may appreciate the harder dirt surfaces in the United States. Cloud Hopping never raced as a juvenile, but his sire line does very well with young performers, and there is plenty of class in his pedigree.

Skimble is a half-sister to Grade 1-winning juvenile filly Contredance, and another half-sister produced the solid sires Eltish and Forest Gazelle.

Cloud Hopping doesn't have much name recognition, so his debut runners might offer value at the windows.

BRAHMS
Pedigree: Danzig—Queena, by Mr. Prospector
Race Record and Earnings: 17 starts, 5 wins, 3 seconds,
   4 thirds, $843,050
2004 Stud Fee: $10,000
2004 Stud Farm: Vinery (KY)

Pedigree handicappers looking to make beautiful music at the windows may have to look no farther than Brahms. A $1 million yearling by noted sire of sires Danzig, Brahms broke his maiden at 2-5 odds in his second start at 2 for Aidan O'Brien. He then hit the board in three consecutive group stakes before finishing seventh in the Breeders' Cup Juvenile.

Brahms was transferred to Elliott Walden's barn for new owner Thomas Van Meter II, and remained in the United States for the rest of his career. He won all four of his starts at 3, including a 104 Beyer performance in the Grade 1 Hollywood Derby on turf. Although Brahms went 0 for 7 as a 4-year-old, he never ran a Beyer figure of less than 103 that year, and placed in the Grade 2 Maker's Mark Mile, the Grade 2 Stephen Foster Handicap (on dirt, 112 Beyer), the Grade 1 Shoemaker Breeders' Cup Mile, and the Grade 1 Woodford Reserve Turf Classic.

Brahms is out of champion distaffer Queena, and is a half-brother to the talented filly La Reina. His second dam was a Grade 1 winner, and his fourth dam was a champion in Europe. His pedigree is full of graded stakes winners such as Chic Shirine, Waldoboro, Tara Roma, Serra Lake, and Cappuchino.

He may do best as a Late 2-Early 3 sire, but with his pedigree and race record, he might be worth the wait.

FIRST-CROP SIRES OF 2006

PURE PRIZE
Pedigree: Storm Cat—Heavenly Prize, by Seeking the Gold
Race Record and Earnings: 17 starts, 5 wins, 5 seconds,
2 thirds, $475,459
2004 Stud Fee: $7,500
2004 Stud Farm: Vinery (KY)

Here's another Phipps homebred that showed flashes of brilliance on occasion, but failed to live up to his fantastic pedigree. Pure Prize needed three starts to win at 2, going a mile at Belmont, but he didn't break through his N2X allowance condition until race number 12. He had his best season at age 4, and the last two starts of his career were arguably his finest. Pure Prize finished second in the off-the-turf Fourstardave Handicap with a 103 Beyer, then bowed out with a lifetime-best 108 Beyer in winning the Grade 2 Kentucky Cup Classic.

Pure Prize is a son of the fantastic Storm Cat out of champion and millionaire Heavenly Prize, a full sister to Grade 1-winning juvenile filly Oh What a Windfall. Third dam Blitey was a multiple Grade 2 winner who produced millionaire Dancing Spree and graded stakes winners Furlough, Fantastic Find, and Dancing All Night. Fourth dam Lady Pitt was champion 3-year-old filly in 1966. Although it took a bit of time for Pure Prize to find his rhythm on the racetrack, it would be no surprise if his progeny are precocious, and able to win early at 2.

GRAEME HALL
Pedigree: Dehere—Win Crafty Lady, by Crafty Prospector
Race Record and Earnings: 22 starts, 7 wins, 7 seconds,
    1 third, $1,147,441
2004 Stud Fee: $7,500
2004 Stud Farm: Winding Oaks (FL)

Graeme Hall has many positive qualities that one looks for in a successful young sire. He was quick enough to break his maiden at 2 at Saratoga. He was a multiple graded winner the next two seasons, and was sound enough to race competitively at age 5. His sire is an excellent source of debut winners, and his dam is emerging as one of the top broodmares we've seen in recent years. Plus, millionaire Graeme Hall was quick enough to go gate-to-wire in the Arkansas Derby, and had excellent tactical speed.

He reached the triple-digit Beyer plateau 13 times in his career. Perhaps his most impressive victory was his 113 Beyer performance in the Grade 3 Stuyvesant Handicap, a race in which he prevailed by 6½ lengths. He followed that win up with a gallant second-place run in the Grade 1 Cigar Mile, finishing ahead of such Grade 1 winners as Red Bullet, Volponi, Affirmed Success, and Peeping Tom.

By champion juvenile Dehere, Graeme Hall is out of Grade 3 winner Win Crafty Lady. He is a half-brother to the fleet Grade 1-winning filly Harmony Lodge from the family of crack sprinter Diligence. He sold for $200,000 as a yearling in 1998, has nice conformation, and figures to be well supported by his owners, Eugene and Laura Melnyk. He should do very nicely in Florida.

FIRST-CROP SIRES OF 2007

VINDICATION

Pedigree: Seattle Slew—Strawberry Reason, by Strawberry Road

Race Record and Earnings: 4 starts, 4 wins, 0 seconds, 0 thirds, $680,950

2004 Stud Fee: $50,000

2004 Stud Farm: Hill 'n' Dale Farm (KY)

Simply brilliant! That describes Vindication. Sold for $2.15 million as a yearling, he never disappointed in his short career. Trained by Bob Baffert, Vindication won his first two starts at Del Mar with startling ease, then turned in one of the best performances that I've ever seen from a 2-year-old in the Kentucky Cup Juvenile. In only his third lifetime start, and first around two turns, Vindication broke very poorly, but made a breathtaking five-wide move on the final bend to win going away. Stretching out to nine furlongs for the Breeders' Cup Juvenile, Vindication broke cleanly, but faced race-long pressure while on the lead. He shrugged off all challengers to win easily with a 102 Beyer Speed Figure. Unfortunately, Vindication was injured, and never raced at 3, leaving fans and handicappers wondering what could have been.

By the legendary Seattle Slew, sire of numerous champions including the top sire A.P. Indy, Vindication should cross wonderfully with mares from both the Mr. Prospector and Northern Dancer lines. His dam is a Grade 3-winning half-sister to Grade 3 winner Silver Comet. Vindication brings speed, stamina, and excellence to the table. He heads a sterling group in the Class of 2007.

SKY MESA
Pedigree: Pulpit—Caress, by Storm Cat
Race Record and Earnings: 6 starts, 3 wins, 1 second,
   1 third, $633,076
2004 Stud Fee: $30,000
2004 Stud Farm: Three Chimneys Farm (KY)

Sky Mesa has black type dripping from his pedigree page, and he hails from one of my favorite female families. It won't hurt that he was an undefeated Grade 1-winning juvenile that could stretch his speed from six furlongs to a mile and a sixteenth.

A $750,000 yearling purchase, Sky Mesa earned a 92 Beyer for his $7^3/4$-length win in his debut at Saratoga. His normally cautious trainer, John Ward, opted to try the Grade 1 Hopeful for his budding star's next race, and Sky Mesa responded with a 103 Beyer effort, and a convincing triumph. Stretching out to two turns failed to pose a problem for Sky Mesa as he took the Grade 2 Breeders' Futurity at Keeneland in his final start at 2. He suffered an injury following his juvenile season, and was never really the same at 3, although he did place in the Grade 2 Dwyer and Grade 1 Haskell.

Sky Mesa is a half-brother to Grade 2-placed Monthir out of multiple Grade 3-winning turfer Caress. Third dam La Mesa produced champion 2-year-old filly Outstandingly while fifth dam Busanda dropped the awesome Buckpasser. A direct descendant of the great broodmare La Troienne, Sky Mesa is a grandson of champion sire A.P. Indy, and should cross extremely well with Raise a Native-line mares. I'm expecting Sky Mesa to be a top sire.

MINESHAFT
Pedigree: A.P. Indy—Prospectors Delite, by Mr. Prospector
Race Record and Earnings: 18 starts, 10 wins, 3 seconds,
   1 third, $2,283,402
2004 Stud Fee: $100,000
2004 Stud Farm: Lane's End Farm (KY)

Mineshaft's wonderful 4-year-old campaign propelled him to Horse of the Year honors, and his gold-plated pedigree stamps him as a sire to watch. Unraced at 2, Mineshaft broke his maiden in his second start at 3 in England. He never distinguished himself on the grass in Europe, although he did place in the Group 3 Prix Daphne at Maisons-Lafitte. Once imported to the United States, however, Mineshaft found his true calling on dirt. He won nine of 11 races on dirt, earning Beyer figures between 96 and 118 in all of his races, and took home trophies in four Grade 1 events. Mineshaft's excellent tactical speed served him very well on the track, and if he passes that trait on to his progeny, he will be a top sire.

Mineshaft's lineage is a veritable who's who of top-class racehorses. Grade 1 winners Prospectors Delite, Tomisue's Delight, Flagbird, and Runup the Colors are only some of the successful horses in his family. He is a direct descendant of La Troienne, and figures to be bred to top mares at Will Farish's Lane's End Farm.

ALDEBARAN

Pedigree: Mr. Prospector—Chimes of Freedom, by Private Account

Race Record and Earnings: 25 starts, 8 wins, 12 seconds, 3 thirds, $1,739,186

2004 Stud Fee: $50,000

2004 Stud Farm: Darby Dan Farm (KY)

It took the beautifully bred Aldebaran some time to figure the game out, but once he did, he was virtually unstoppable. The son of Mr. Prospector began his career in England, and broke his maiden on grass in his only start at 2, but he frustrated his connections with a 2-11-2 record over his next 16 starts in both England and in the United States. And while he did place in such excellent races as the Group 3 Jersey Stakes and Grade 1 Hollywood Derby on turf, and the Grade 1 Metropolitan Handicap, Grade 1 Cigar Mile, Grade 1 Vosburgh, and Grade 1 Forego on dirt, Aldebaran was beginning to get a reputation as a "hanger."

That all changed in his 5-year-old season as Aldebaran won five of eight starts, earned Beyer figures between 101 and 122 in all of those races, and won the "sire-making" Metropolitan Handicap. He also took the Grade 1 Forego and San Carlos Handicaps, and the Grade 2 Churchill Downs and Tom Fool Handicaps.

A son of English and French champion filly Chimes of Freedom, Aldebaran is a half-brother to Grade 1-winning turf miler Good Journey. Such excellent runners as Spinning World, Denon, Blush with Pride, and Malinowski are in his immediate pedigree, and he should pass on a great deal of class to his progeny. He should cross very well to the plethora of Danzig and Storm Cat mares out there.

EMPIRE MAKER

Pedigree: Unbridled—Toussaud, by El Gran Senor

Race Record and Earnings: 8 starts, 4 wins, 3 seconds, 1 third, $1,985,800

2004 Stud Fee: $100,000
2004 Stud Farm: Juddmonte Farms (KY)

Empire Maker overcame greenness and an immature personality to become a classic winner for Bobby Frankel and Juddmonte Farms. Frankel knew he had something special right from the start when he worked unraced juvenile Empire Maker in company with his older stable star Medaglia d'Oro. The colt made his long-awaited debut at Belmont in the fall of his 2-year-old year, and he responded with a facile victory at 2-5 odds. In only his second life-time start, Empire Maker stretched out around two turns for the first time, and finished a solid third behind the red-hot Toccet in the Grade 2 Remsen Stakes.

Empire Maker disappointed at low odds in his first start at 3, and Frankel put blinkers on his Kentucky Derby prospect in the hope of getting him to focus. Empire Maker responded with a $9^3/_4$-length win in the Grade 1 Florida Derby, and a 111 Beyer victory in the Grade 1 Wood Memorial. He roared into Louisville as the favorite for the Kentucky Derby, but was upset by the plucky New York-bred Funny Cide. Frankel passed on a rematch in the Preakness, and patiently waited for the Belmont Stakes, the ultimate "Test of the Champion." Empire Maker rated kindly under Jerry Bailey before taking control on the far turn. He gamely held off Ten Most Wanted to win the Belmont with a 110 Beyer. Empire Maker only started once more in his career, finishing second in the Grade 2 Jim Dandy at Saratoga. Despite his success, one can only speculate how good Empire Maker would have been if he were more professional. He often failed to change leads, and sometimes would switch back to his wrong lead in the heat of battle. Nonetheless, he was a fantastic horse with tremendous bloodlines.

His sire, Unbridled, was known for his stamina, but he was an underrated source of debut winners, and Empire Maker may inherit that trait with his juvenile runners. His dam, Toussaud, is a true blue-hen mare. Besides Empire Maker, she has dropped Arlington Million winner Chester House, Grade 1 winners Honest Lady and Chiselling, and Grade 2 winner Decarchy. Toussaud's full sister, Navarra, was a Grade 3 winner, and has produced Grade 3 winner Indygo Shiner. Empire Maker has the pedigree to produce classic performers, but he may surprise with his debut runners.

PURE PRECISION

Pedigree: Montbrook—Al's Helen, by Distinctive
Race Record and Earnings: 8 starts, 4 wins, 2 seconds,
    1 third, $633,076
2004 Stud Fee: $4,000
2004 Stud Farm: Lou-Roe Farm (FL)

Florida stallions usually are bred to quick mares, and it helps when the stallion himself had a bit of early lick. While not a household name, Pure Precision had plenty of speed. He should fit well in the Florida market.

Pure Precision won first out by over 10 lengths going five furlongs at Calder. He earned a 94 Beyer that day. After a second-place effort in the Criterium Stakes, Pure Precision showed his versatility by rating off the pace en route to his score in the Tyro Stakes at Monmouth. He then fended off race-long pace pressure to win the Grade 3 Sapling Stakes.

Injuries put Pure Precision on the shelf for over a year following the Sapling, and he was surprisingly placed in a claiming race for his 3-year-old debut. Taken by Dominic Galluscio for $50,000, Pure Precision never made it back into stakes competition, but still won a $35,000 claimer in 1:09.82 in his next-to-last race.

Pure Precision looks like a great outcross to the many Northern Dancer- and Raise a Native-line stallions. His dam, Al's Helen, was a Grade 3-winning half-sister to the brilliant Straight Man. Fourth dam Jan's Jessie won five stakes races during her career. A swift juvenile, Pure Precision should pass that trait on to his progeny.

OMMADON

Pedigree: Grindstone—Missymooiloveyou, by Turkoman
Race Record and Earnings: 14 starts, 4 wins, 1 second,
1 third, $214,650
2004 Stud Fee: $3,000
2004 Stud Farm: Metropolitan Stud (NY)

Ommadon has a fascinating pedigree. He is inbred to the speedy Raise a Native yet has plenty of stamina influences on his page. A son of Kentucky Derby winner Grindstone (he a son of Derby winner Unbridled) out of Grade 3 winner Missymooiloveyou, Ommadon hails from the female family of classy runners such as Lady d'Accord, Honorable Miss, Bailjumper, Free At Last, and Judger. He was able to combine his speed and stamina on the racetrack, and looks like an intriguing sire for the New York market.

Ommadon went gate-to-wire in his juvenile debut at Saratoga, upsetting Pure Prize at 10-1 odds. Three starts later, he won the Grade 3 Nashua going a one-turn mile at Aqueduct with a 99 Beyer. He then ran second in the Grade 2 Remsen to close out his 2-year-old campaign. Ommadon got a late start at 3, but won his first race of the year with a 98 Beyer. While never recapturing his early brilliance, Ommadon did win an allowance at 4 before being retired to stud. He should cross very well with Northern Dancer- and Bold Ruler-line mares.

MILWAUKEE BREW

Pedigree: Wild Again—Ask Anita, by Wolf Power
Race Record and Earnings: 24 starts, 8 wins, 4 seconds,
5 thirds, $2,879,612
2004 Stud Fee: $15,000
2004 Stud Farm: Adena Springs Kentucky (KY)

Millionaire Milwaukee Brew will be best remembered for winning back-to-back runnings of the Grade 1 Santa Anita Handicap, but few will recall that he won four of his first six starts at 3, including the Grade 2 Ohio Derby with a 104 Beyer Speed Figure. He earned a 110 Beyer when third in the Grade 1 Haskell in his seventh lifetime appearance. Milwaukee Brew was multiple Grade 3-placed at 4 before embarking on his huge 5-year-old campaign. He won the "Big Cap" that year with a 118 Beyer, and followed that up with a 114 Beyer score in the Grade 2 Californian. He finished third in Grade 1 events such as the Pacific Classic, Hollywood Gold Cup, and Breeders' Cup Classic that year. At age 6, he successfully defended his Santa Anita Handicap crown against such stalwarts as Congaree and Pleasantly Perfect.

Milwaukee Brew is out of Grade 3 winner Ask Anita, and there are plenty of European turf and stamina influences in his pedigree. He has the look of a "Late 3" sire, and his progeny may do surprisingly well on the lawn. He is free of Northern Dancer and Mr. Prospector blood, and should make a nice outcross. Milwaukee Brew stands at Frank Stronach's Adena Springs, and will be given every chance to make it as a sire.

DECARCHY

Pedigree: Distant View—Toussaud, by El Gran Senor
Race Record and Earnings: 19 starts, 6 wins, 4 seconds, 3 thirds, $703,862
2004 Stud Fee: $5,000
2004 Stud Farm: Magali Farms (CA)

The California breeding program is coming along very nicely, and Empire Maker's three-quarter brother Decarchy should fit in beautifully in the Golden State. Like his more famous sibling, Decarchy broke his maiden going seven furlongs in his first start at 2. He won by seven lengths at Great Yarmouth in England that day, but didn't seem to care for European racing, and failed to win again until he was imported to the United States at age 4. Decarchy hinted at his ability with a second-place finish in the Grade 2 Citation Handicap that season. He made his mark as a 5-year-old with wins in the Grade 2 Frank E. Kilroe Mile and Grade 3 Tanforan Handicap. Decarchy placed in the Grade 1 Eddie Read Handicap the following season.

He ran Beyer figures of 99 or better in 16 of his 19 starts in America, but never had a chance to show what he could do on the main track. His runners will probably do best when stretched out around a distance of ground, and they should really enjoy the grass.

THE NEXT GREAT SIRE OF SIRES

Northern Dancer or Mr. Prospector? Breeding experts will argue forever over which stallion has more influence on today's pedigrees. Let's take a look at the last 10 winners of the Kentucky Derby, and see if we can find a pattern:

2004: Smarty Jones - by Elusive Quality - Gone West - **Mr. Prospector**

2003: Funny Cide - by Distorted Humor - Forty Niner - **Mr. Prospector**

2002: War Emblem - by Our Emblem - **Mr. Prospector**

2001: Monarchos - by Maria's Mon - Wavering Monarch - Majestic Light

2000: Fusaichi Pegasus - by **Mr. Prospector**

1999: Charismatic - by Summer Squall - Storm Bird - Northern Dancer

1998: Real Quiet - by Quiet American - Fappiano - **Mr. Prospector**

1997: Silver Charm - by Silver Buck - Buckpasser - Tom Fool

1996: Grindstone - by Unbridled - Fappiano - **Mr. Prospector**

1995: Thunder Gulch - by Gulch - **Mr. Prospector**

The Mr. Prospector line has been responsible for seven of the last 10 Derby winners, and Monarchos descends from Raise a Native, the sire of Mr. Prospector. One could easily jump to conclusions of the superiority of Mr. Prospector over Northern Dancer based upon these results, but that might be premature. Let's now turn to the Breeders' Cup Juvenile winners from 1994 through 2003:

2003: Action This Day - by Kris S. - Roberto - Hail to Reason

2002: Vindication - by Seattle Slew - Bold Reasoning - Boldnesian

2001: Johannesburg - by Hennessy - Storm Cat - Storm Bird - Northern Dancer

2000: Macho Uno - by Holy Bull - Great Above - Minnesota Mac

1999: Anees - by Unbridled - Fappiano - **Mr. Prospector**

1998: Answer Lively - by Lively One - Halo - Hail to Reason

1997: Favorite Trick - by Phone Trick - Clever Trick - Icecapade

1996: Boston Harbor - by Capote - Seattle Slew - Bold Reasoning

1995: Unbridled's Song - by Unbridled - Fappiano - **Mr. Prospector**

1994: Timber Country - by Woodman - **Mr. Prospector**

Mr. Prospector again outpoints Northern Dancer, but it is interesting to note that Favorite Trick's sire line goes back to Nearctic, the sire of Northern Dancer. Amazingly, Storm Cat and Danzig, the two great descendants of Northern Dancer, are practically absent from this list; only Storm Cat appears, through his grandson Johannesburg. Perhaps that can be explained by the fact that many of the best sons and daughters of Northern Dancer, Storm Cat, and Danzig were exported to Europe and Japan in the 1980's and early 90's. Mr. Prospector became the dominant sire here, and his line saturated the market.

In recent years, however, Storm Cat and his sons have revived the Northern Dancer line in America. Storm Cat and his progeny have dominated the year-end juvenile sire lists of late, and Storm Cat has won the money title for leading sire in two of the last five seasons. While Storm Cat has proved nothing short of a phenomenon, he has been helped by the plethora of Mr. Prospector mares. Storm Cat crosses well with Mr. Prospector, and Mr. Prospector has led the broodmare-sire list for the last seven seasons.

With so many classy Storm Cat fillies out there, Storm Cat will undoubtedly lead the broodmare-sire ranks in the near future. Handicappers may benefit by trying to guess which sire line will cross well with these Storm Cat mares. Logically, I looked for a sire from the Mr. Prospector line. I found Gone West.

Gone West was a Grade 1 winner, and he has sired quality runners since 1991. He finished third on the year-end stallion list in 1995, and has given us European champions Zafonic (sire of over 30 stakes winners) and Royal Abjar, Breeders' Cup winners Da Hoss and Johar, Belmont Stakes winner Commendable, and top young sires Elusive Quality, Grand Slam, Mr. Greeley, and West by West.

Gone West himself is mostly viewed as a sire of turf runners, but his sons have added plenty of speed to the breed. Grand Slam, Elusive Quality, and Mr. Greeley are all above-average debut sires, and should continue to do well when crossed with Northern Dancer-line mares.

But how does this help with the handicapping process? We have all encountered maiden races where the firsters either fail to have precocious pedigrees, or debut for trainers that do not have high win rates with first-out runners. This is where we can look for the hidden speed and class of Gone West's sons.

Winning Expression
Own: Flying Zee Stable

Dk. b or b. c. 2 (Feb)
Sire: Western Expression (Gone West) $10,000
Dam: Miss Winning Sweep (End Sweep)
Br: Flying Zee Stables (NY)
Tr: Serpe Philip M(47 6 11 4 .13) 2004:(111 15 .14)

Life	3	1	2	0	$68,138	66	D.Fst	2	1	1	0	$47,060 66
2004	3	1	2	0	$68,138	66	Wet(346)	1	0	1	0	$21,078 64
2003	0	M	0	0	$0	-	Turf(281)	0	0	0	0	$0 -
Bel	3	1	2	0	$68,138	66	Dst(358)	3	1	2	0	$68,138 66

26Jun04-3Bel	my	5½f	$:22^2$	$:45^3$	$:58^1$ $1:04^4$	Tremont99k	64	3	4	2½	2½	1½	2^{1½}	Prado E S	L115	7.00	87- 14	GoldJy115^{1½} WnnngExprssn115^3 PrmlStrm119^7	Pressed pace, weakened	4
4Jun04-9Bel	fst	5f	:22	$:44^4$	$:57^2$	Flash-G3	62	3	3	2^{1½}	2½	2^6	2^7	Prado E S	L115	5.40	89- 14	PrimlStorm116^7 WnnngExprsson115^{3¾} *GoldJoy*115^4	Bump, in tight, check	5
6May04-3Bel	fst	5f	:22	$:46^1$	:59	Md Sp Wt 43k	66	6	4	2½	2^{hd}	1^6	1^5	Castellano J J	114	12.20	88- 18	Winning Expression114^5 *Killenaule*117^{3½} Tip City117^{1½}	Bumped after start	7

WORKS: Jun21 Bel 4f fst :49 B *23/59* May30 Bel 4f fst $:48^2$ B *47/113* ●May23 Bel 5f fst $:59^1$ H *1/12* May17 Bel 4f fst $:50^2$ B *47/65* May1 Bel 5f fst $1:02^4$ B *21/34* ●Apr18 Bel tr.t 4f fst $:47^2$ Hg *1/44*

THIRD RACE
Belmont
MAY 6, 2004

5 FURLONGS. (.55^3) MAIDEN SPECIAL WEIGHT . Purse $43,000 (UP TO $8,170 NYSBFOA) FOR MAIDENS, TWO YEAR OLDS. Weight, 117 lbs.

Value of Race: $43,000 Winner $25,800; second $8,600; third $4,300; fourth $2,150; fifth $1,290; sixth $430; seventh $430. Mutuel Pool $239,280.00 Exacta Pool $254,373.00 Trifecta Pool $169,904.00

Last Raced	Horse	M/Eqt.	A.	Wt	PP	St	3/16	3/8	Str	Fin	Jockey	Odds $1
	Winning Expression		2	114	6	4	2^{2½}	2^3	1^6	1^5	Castellano J J	12.20
15Apr04 2Kee2	Killenaule		2	117	4	6	5^5	5^{4½}	3^7	2^{3½}	Velazquez J R	0.65
	Tip City	L b	2	117	2	1	7	7	4½	3^{1½}	Luzzi M J	a- 12.20
	Go Fernando Go		2	114	7	5	4½	3½	2½	4^{14}	Fernandez V	39.00
	Smoking Ember		2	114	5	7	6^6	6^{5½}	6½	5no	Prado E S	3.65
22Apr04 3Aqu4	Downthehill	L	2	114	3	3	3½	4^{1½}	5^1	6^{10½}	Bridgmohan S X	a- 12.20
	Defy the Odds	L b	2	117	1	2	1½	1^{hd}	7	7	Bailey J D	4.70

a-Coupled: Tip City and Downthehill.

OFF AT 2:02 Start Good. Won driving. Track fast.
TIME :22, $:46^1$, :59 (:22.05, :46.23, :59.06)

$2 Mutuel Prices:				
	5 – WINNING EXPRESSION	26.40	5.20	2.60
	3 – KILLENAULE		2.40	2.10
	1 – TIP CITY(a-entry)			2.50

$2 EXACTA 5–3 PAID $51.50 $2 TRIFECTA 5–3–1 PAID $245.00

Dk. b or br. c, (Feb), by Western Expression - Miss Winning Sweep , by End Sweep . Trainer Serpe Philip M. Bred by Flying Zee Stables (NY).

WINNING EXPRESSION was bumped after the start, pressed the pace from the outside, drew off in upper stretch and remained well clear under a drive. KILLENAULE was bumped after the start, chased the pace while between rivals, dropped back on the turn, came wide into the stretch and finished well. TIP CITY was outrun early while racing greenly, came wide into the stretch and was going well late outside. GO FERNANDO GO was hustled outside, chased the pace and tired in the final furlong. SMOKING EMBER broke slowly, raced inside and tired. DOWNTHEHILL chased the pace along the inside and tired. DEFY THE ODDS set the pace along the inside and tired in the stretch.

Owners– 1, Flying Zee Stable; 2, Tabor Michael B; 3, Taylor Kenneth and Salzman Sr John E; 4, Perez Robert; 5, Karches Peter F; 6, Taylor Kenneth and Salzman Sr John E; 7, Lewis Robert B and Beverly J

Trainers– 1, Serpe Philip M; 2, Pletcher Todd A; 3, Salzman John E; 4, Callejas Alfredo; 5, Clement Christophe; 6, Salzman John E; 7, Lukas D Wayne

Scratched– Schiloh

Winning Expression, a grandson of Gone West, made a successful debut at the expense of Todd Pletcher-trained second-time starter Killenaule. The other firsters in the race had flaws. Third-place finisher Tip City was bred to appreciate longer distances, and was dead on the tote board. Go Fernando Go made his debut for the low-percentage Alfredo Callejas barn. Smoking Ember took money, but his trainer, Christophe Clement, usually does best with turf runners at route distances. Defy the Odds attracted Jerry Bailey, but trainer D. Wayne Lukas was in a major slump at the time, and Defy the Odds had to overcome an intimidating inside post position. That left the favorite, Killenaule, who failed to win his debut even though he is trained by one of the top first-out barns in the country, and Winning Expression. The son of Western Expression showed good speed from the get-go, and was never threatened. It was a perfect example of fans ignoring an unproven sire, even though he was by an excellent sire of sires.

It should also be useful to look for the Bold Ruler line to make a major comeback, as these horses provide brilliant outcrosses for the Mr. Prospector- and Northern Dancer-line mares. A.P. Indy (by Seattle Slew) has become one of the top sires in the world, and he should continue to have great success. His classy young sons are beginning to retire to stud, and should also make an impact.

I have always been a big fan of the Roberto line, and his son Dynaformer seems to sire nothing but stone-cold runners. Keep an eye out for Dynaformer, since he crosses well with just about any mare.

The Valid Appeal strain of the In Reality line has always been known for its precocity. Valid Appeal must be respected as a top juvenile broodmare sire, and his sons are getting quick youngsters. Look out for Successful Appeal and Valid Expectations. They should be perennial leaders of the juvenile sire standings.

Let's not forget about Storm Cat. It seems as if another son of Storm Cat retires to stud every day, and they should continue to pass on speed. Here is a look at one of his unheralded sons, Tiger Ridge, sire of June the Tiger.

June the Tiger
Own: Peachtree Stable

B. c. 2 (Feb) FTKJUL03 $200,000
Sire: Tiger Ridge (Storm Cat) $7,500
Dam: Artic Experience (Slewpy)
Br: Steve Tucker (Fla)
Tr: Pletcher Todd A(117 27 22 20 .23) 2004:(472 118 .25)

	Life	2 1 0 0	$31,094	81	D.Fst	1 1 0 0	$25,800	81
	2004	2 1 0 0	$31,094	81	Wet(367)	1 0 0 0	$5,294	36
	2003	0 M 0 0	$0	–	Turf(328)	0 0 0 0	$0	–
	Bel	2 1 0 0	$31,094	81	Dst(384)	2 1 0 0	$31,094	81

26Jun04– 3Bel my 5½f :222 :453 :581 1:044 Tremont99k 36 1 3 3² 31½ 45½ 411½ Velazquez J R L115 1.65 77– 14 GoldJoy1151½ WinnngExprsson1153 PrmlStorm1197 Bumped start, inside 4
6Jun04– 3Bel fst 5f :22 :444 :57 Md Sp Wt 43k 81 5 4 1½ 11½ 13½ 16½ Velazquez J R L118 2.55 98– 09 JunthTigr186½ GoFrnndoGo115½ BrothrScott1151½ Widened under drive 8
WORKS: Jun20Bel 5f fst :594 H 10/44 May30Bel 4f fst :49 Bg 75/113 May24Bel 5f fst 1:011 B 10/23 May17Bel 4f fst :484 B 15/65 Apr25Kee 4f gd :492 B 9/20 Apr16Kee 4f fst :491 B 19/55

THIRD RACE
Belmont
JUNE 6, 2004

5 FURLONGS. (.55³) MAIDEN SPECIAL WEIGHT . Purse $43,000 (UP TO $8,170 NYSBFOA) FOR MAIDENS, TWO YEAR OLDS. Weight, 118 lbs.

Value of Race: $43,000 Winner $25,800; second $8,600; third $4,300; fourth $2,150; fifth $1,290; sixth $287; seventh $287; eighth $286. Mutuel Pool $382,038.00 Exacta Pool $384,847.00 Trifecta Pool $257,489.00

Last Raced	Horse	M/Eqt.	A.	Wt	PP	St	¾₁₆	⅜	Str	Fin	Jockey	Odds $1
	June the Tiger	L	2	118	5	4	1½	1¹½	13½	16½	Velazquez J R	2.55
21May04 3Bel³	Go Fernando Go	L	2	115	4	3	2½	2hd	2hd	2¾	Fernandez V	8.60
	Brother Scott	L f	2	115	8	5	3²	3²	3²	3¹¼	Santos J A	13.40
22Apr04 2Kee⁴	Rey de Cafe	L	2	118	1	2	4hd	55	41½	44½	Castellano J J	4.80
	Leo Getz	L bf	2	118	7	7	5½	4hd	58	5¹	Bailey J D	1.45
	Midas Gold	L f	2	118	3	6	8	8	6½	65¾	Gryder A T	20.20
	Space Watch	L	2	118	6	8	7½	7hd	76	78¼	Chavez J F	12.00
21May04 3Bel⁶	Nazareth		2	108	2	1	615	68	8	8	Maragh R⁷	62.25

OFF AT 2:05 Start Good . Won driving. Track fast.

TIME :22, :44⁴, :57 (:22.03, :44.89, :57.12)

$2 Mutuel Prices:	5 – JUNE THE TIGER...................	7.10	4.50	4.00
	4 – GO FERNANDO GO...................		6.30	4.30
	8 – BROTHER SCOTT.....................			7.40

$2 EXACTA 5–4 PAID $61.50 $2 TRIFECTA 5–4–8 PAID $300.00

B. c, (Feb), by Tiger Ridge – Artic Experience , by Slewpy . Trainer Pletcher Todd A. Bred by Steve Tucker (Fla).

JUNE THE TIGER was hustled to the front, set the pace along the inside, drew clear and widened under a drive. GO FERNANDO GO bobbled at the start, chased the pace along the inside and dug in gamely on the rail to earn the place award. BROTHER SCOTT stumbled at the start, chased the pace while three wide and weakened in deep stretch. REY DE CAFE raced in hand inside early, came wide for the drive, raced greenly in the stretch and had no rally. LEO GETZ was bumped soundly after the start, raced greenly and tired. MIDAS GOLD was outrun early and had no rally. SPACE WATCH was bumped soundly after the start and tired. NAZARETH chased inside and tired.

Owners– 1, Peachtree Stable; 2, Perez Robert; 3, Schwartz Barry K; 4, Humphrey G Watts Jr; 5, Giordano Mark Pesci Joe and Ward Wesley A; 6, Robsham Mrs E P; 7, Overbrook Farm; 8, Polese Jeanne T

Trainers– 1, Pletcher Todd A; 2, Callejas Alfredo; 3, Hushion Michael E; 4, Arnold George R II; 5, Ward Wesley A; 6, Hough Stanley M; 7, Lukas D Wayne; 8, Polese Ralph

June the Tiger made his debut for Todd Pletcher and John Velazquez, a phenomenally successful debut trainer-and-jockey combination. Surprisingly, he was sent off as a tepid 5-2 second choice. None of the youngsters that had previously raced had shown much ability, and aside from Leo Getz, none of the firsters took much betting action. Leo Getz looked to be the one to beat on paper as top debut trainer Wesley Ward pegged Jerry Bailey to ride, but the colt showed up in the paddock with front wraps on, and none of Ward's 2003 juvenile debut winners wore bandages. That left June the Tiger. But why wasn't he being bet off the board? Perhaps it was because few handicappers had stats on his first-crop sire. Tiger Ridge was winless on the racetrack, but he is kin to A.P. Indy, Summer Squall, and numerous other classy runners. More importantly, he is by Storm Cat, and pedigree handicappers should expect sons of Storm Cat to sire quick juveniles.

Back to Gone West. Here is a list of some of his sons. Don't ignore them when playing maiden races.

Authenticate
Came Home (Expect big things)
Changeintheweather
Civilisation
Commendable
Covered Wagon
Dance Master
Elusive Quality
Go for Four
Gone Hollywood
Gone for Real
Grand Slam
Macabe
Mr. Greeley
Muqtarib
Pembroke
Perfect Mandate
Performing Magic
Predicta
Proud Citizen
Really Honest
Rodeo
Supremo
Torrey Canyon
Tracker
Trajectory
Way West
Western Borders
Western Expression
Winning Fame
Winning Bid

3

THE DAM FACTOR AND AUCTION ANGLES

WE'VE SPENT PLENTY of time discussing the sires, but what about the dams? What do they provide to the pedigree of the precocious first-time starter? How do we analyze a dam's race record? How can we spot a quality female family? All excellent questions, and there aren't any easy answers. Here is one theory, however.

I concur with many pedigree analysts that the dam and her female family are responsible for the "class" of her offspring, while the sire and his male line pass on their own distance, surface, and precocity traits.

There are different classifications of dams. There are dams that were unraced on the track, dams that failed to win, stakes-placed or stakes-winning dams, and graded stakes-placed or graded stakes-winning dams. Logic would dictate that the best runners would become the best producers, but that has not always proven to be the case. Still, while a good horse can come from any kind of dam, handicappers can feel much more secure knowing that a debut runner has class on the bottom (dam's) side of his or her pedigree.

When studying a maiden's pedigree, I look for four distinct traits in the dam. Did she earn black type (win or place in an added-money or stakes event)? Is she a half- or full sibling to stakes-quality runners? Does she descend from a blue-hen or dominant broodmare? Has she already thrown a classy runner? Serious pedigree handicappers can research this information themselves, and *Daily Racing Form*'s "A Closer Look" analyses also provide helpful data.

Ravine Rose				B. f. 4 (May) KEEJUL01 $300,000					Life	3	1	0	2	$19,860	69	D.Fst	3	1	0	2	$19,860	69
Own: Stronach Stable				Sire: Gulch (Mr. Prospector) $50,000					2004	1	0	0	1	$2,750	65	Wet(398)	0	0	0	0	$0	–
				Dam: Lotka (Danzig)					2003	2	1	0	1	$17,110	69	Turf(337)	0	0	0	0	$0	–
				Br: Calumet Farm (Ky)					Lrl	3	1	0	2	$19,860	69	Dst(402)	3	1	0	2	$19,860	69
				Tr: Nixon Justin J(0 0 0 0 .00) 2004:(83 21 .25)																		

19Jan04–8Lrl fst 6f	:22² :46	:58⁴1:11	ⓅAlw 25000N1x	65 5 2 3² 2hd 34¼ 34¾ Garcia Luis⁵	L114 f	*.40	82– 18 Wallop1173¾ Debbie'sGone117¹ RavineRose114¹	Bumped,bid btw,outfnsh 7
20Dec03–7Lrl fst 6f	:22 :45¹	:58³1:11⁴	3↑ⓅAlw 26000N1x	64 4 5 5⁴ 45 33¼ 31 Garcia Luis⁵	118 f	2.70	79– 16 Last Verse118ⁿᵏ Storm Hen120¾ Ravine Rose118²	Wide,needed more 11
16Nov03–5Lrl fst 6f	:22³ :46	:58²1:11¹	3↑ⓇMd Sp Wt 25k	69 7 2 2¹ 1hd 11¼ 12¼ Garcia Luis⁵	118 f	7.10	83– 13 Ravine Rose118²¼ Polish Virtues123³ Mark Me Special123³¾	2wd, driving 9

WORKS: Jly3 AdS 3f gd :37² H 1/2 Jun26 AdS ⓉgF 3f gd :38² H 1/2

I first became acquainted with Ravine Rose while leafing through the 2001 Keeneland July yearling sale catalogue. She was by a solid sire in Gulch, but what really drew me to the filly was her dam. Lotka, a daughter of standout sire Danzig, won the Grade 1 Acorn Stakes in 1986. She is a full sister to millionaire Stephen's Odyssey, and is also a full sibling to Grade 2-placed juvenile Walesa. Ravine Rose's winning second dam was a half-sister to Kentucky Derby winner Cannonade. Her third dam was a winning half-sister to influential sire Halo, while her fourth dam a juvenile stakes-winning half-sister to the dam of the great Northern Dancer. The fact that Lotka had already thrown Grade 3 winner Lotta Dancing as well as a multiple stakes winner in Japan was icing on the cake. Class was just oozing off Ravine Rose's pedigree page, and if I'd had 300 grand to throw around, I would have invested in her. I must have left my wallet at home that day, though, and the head honcho of Magna Entertainment, Frank Stronach, took Ravine Rose home with him.

I had Ravine Rose in my DRF StableMail (now called Horse Watch) thanks to that catalogue, but handicappers with access to the American Produce Records were able to deduce Lotka's class. Ravine Rose made her debut late in her 3-year-old year, and to many that was a negative sign. To me, however, it showed that Stronach thought she could run. If Ravine Rose were simply slow, or prone to injury, then she surely would have been retired by then. With her classy pedigree, she had great value as a broodmare prospect. Fortunately, I was proven right as Ravine Rose showed good speed, and scored a mild 7-1 upset.

Smarty Jones
Own: Someday Farm

Ch. c. 3 (Feb)
Sire: Elusive Quality (Gone West) $41,294
Dam: I'll Get Along (Smile)
Br: Someday Farm (Pa)
Tr: Servis John C(76 17 12 12 .22) 2004:(146 33 .23)

Life	9	8	1	0	$7,613,155	118	D.Fst	7	6	1	0	$1,128,355	118
2004	7	6	1	0	$7,563,535	118	Wet(316)	2	2	0	0	$6,484,800	107
2003	2	2	0	0	$49,620	105	Turf(286)	0	0	0	0	$0	-
Pha	2	2	0	0	$49,620	105	Dst(427)	1	1	0	0	$15,960	84

5Jun04-11Bel	fst	1½		:483 1:113 2:002 2:272	Belmont-G1	100	9	31	1½	13½	11½	21	Elliott S	L126 f	*.35	94-10	Birdstone1261 Smarty Jones1268 Royal Assault1263	Vied, clear, gamely 9
15May04-12Pim	fst	1 3/16		:471 1:112 1:362 1:552	Preaknes-G1	118	6	21½	22½	21	15	111½	Elliott S	L126 f	*.70	100-13	SmrtyJons12611½ RockHrdTn1262 Eddington126hd	3-4w,angled in,driving 10
1May04-10CD	sly	1¼		:463 1:114 1:371 2:04	KyDerby-G1	107	13	42½	21½	2hd	1hd	12¾	Elliott S	L126 f	*4.10	79-21	*Smarty Jones*1262¾ Lion Heart1263¼ Imperialism1262	Stalked,bid,clear 18
10Apr04-9OP	my	1⅛		:464 1:113 1:364 1:492	ArkDerby-G2	107	11	2½	2½	1hd	13	11½	Elliott S	122 f	*1.00	91-17	*Smarty Jones*1221½ Borrego1181½ Pro Prado1223½	Cleared at will,drivng 11
20Mar04-10OP	fst	1 1/16		:232 :473 1:12 1:42	Rebel200k	108	7	21	21	2½	11	13¼	Elliott S	122 f	3.50	100-16	*Smarty Jones*1223¼ Purge1173¾ Pro Prado1173¾	Kicked strongly clear 9
28Feb04-9OP	fst	1		:224 :454 1:111 1:372	Southwest100k	95	6	21½	22½	2hd	12	1¾	Elliott S	122 f	*.50	97-18	*SmrtyJons*122¾ *TwoDownAtomtc*112½ ProPrd1177¼	Chased,took over,drvng 9
3Jan04-8Aqu	fst	170	⊡	:231 :47 1:113 1:412	CountFleet81k	97	7	31	31	2hd	1½	15	Elliott S	116 f	*.40	91-21	*Smarty Jones*1165 Risky Trick1166 Mr. Spock116½	Stumbled start, 3 wide 7
22Nov03-9Pha	fst	7f		:214 :441 1:083 1:214	Ⓢ PennaNurse56k	105	1	10	12	12½	18	115	Elliott S	117 f	*.70	98-17	*SmartyJones*11715 SaltyPunch1172¼ IsleofMirth1171½	Off slow, dominated 11
9Nov03-6Pha	fst	6f		:221 :451 :574 1:11	Md Sp Wt 23k	84	8	4	2hd	15	16	17¾	Elliott S	118 f	*1.10	84-22	*Smarty Jones*1187¾ *Deputy Rummy*1132¾ Speedwell Beau1186	Handy score 10

WORKS: May28 Pha 7f fst 1:291 B *1/1* ●Apr24 CD 5f gd :58 B *1/34*

Pedigree handicappers didn't need the odds board to tell them that Smarty Jones was a live first-time starter. Not only was he by the top debut sire Elusive Quality, and conditioned by an excellent first-out trainer in John Servis, but his dam was a multiple stakes-winning half-sister to the fleet Grade 3 winner Cowboy Cop. If that wasn't enough to convince punters of the class in his female family, they could simply have looked in the American Produce Records and found that Smarty Jones was a direct descendant of foundation broodmare La Troienne. All that class in the pedigree figured to be enough to handle maiden special weights at Philadelphia Park, and Smarty Jones romped by over seven lengths. It could be argued that the class in his female family helped him conquer his supposed distance limitations as he rose to the occasion in the Kentucky Derby and Preakness Stakes.

FIFTH RACE

Delaware

JUNE 6, 2004

1¹⁄₁₆ MILES. (1.41²) MAIDEN CLAIMING . Purse $22,000 (plus $300 Starters Bonus) FOR MAIDENS, THREE YEAR OLDS AND UPWARD. Three Year Olds, 116 lbs.; Older, 122 lbs. Claiming Price $50,000, For Each $2,500 To $45,000 1 lb.

Value of Race: $22,300 Winner $13,200; second $4,400; third $2,420; fourth $1,320; fifth $660; sixth $300. Mutuel Pool $36,981.00 Exacta Pool $39,804.00 Trifecta Pool $30,393.00

Last Raced	Horse	M/Eqt. A. Wt	PP	St	¼	½	¾	Str	Fin	Jockey	Cl'g Pr	Odds $1
	Hawking	L f 3 116	3	3	6	6	5⁴	12½	1¹⁰	Caraballo J C	50000	4.10
23May04 6Pha⁷	Bruceybruceybrucy	L 3 116	1	1	1²	1¹	11½	2³	2¹½	Potts C L	50000	6.80
8May04 3Del²	Jack of Clubs	L b 3 116	4	4	5½	4hd	3½	3½	32½	Pino M G	50000	0.80
22May04 2Del³	Marigot Red	L bf 5 120	5	6	4¹	3¹	2½	4⁷	415½	Madrigal R Jr	45000	3.80
12Mar04 8GP⁶	My Mystery Man	L f 4 122	6	5	2²	2¹	4hd	5⁵	53½	Valdes R A	50000	11.60
24Apr04 7GP¹¹	DiamondPossession	L f 3 116	2	2	3hd	51½	6	6	6	Castillo O O	50000	21.80

OFF AT 2:33 Start Good . Won ridden out. Track wet fast.

TIME :23, :47³, 1:13, 1:39⁴, 1:46¹ (:23.09, :47.67, 1:13.14, 1:39.86, 1:46.35)

$2 Mutuel Prices:

3 – HAWKING.	10.20	5.20	2.20
1 – BRUCEYBRUCEYBRUCEY.		6.40	2.60
4 – JACK OF CLUBS.			2.10

$2 EXACTA 3–1 PAID $49.60 $2 TRIFECTA 3–1–4 PAID $76.60

Dk. b or br. c, (Mar), by Defrere – Rare Fling , by Kris S. . Trainer Dickinson Michael W. Bred by Liberation Farm & Oratis Thoroughbreds (Ky).

HAWKING was unhurried early, rallied leaving the far turn and gained the lead in upper stretch to win going away while being ridden out. BRUCEYBRUCEYBRUCEY broke alertly, saved ground setting the pace to the stretch then was no match for the winner. JACK OF CLUBS moved up menacingly on the far turn then lacked a closing response. MARIGOT RED moved closer into the far turn then flattened out in the drive. MY MYSTERY MAN stalked the pace to the far turn then offered little response. DIAMOND POSSESSION showed early speed along the inside then tired.

Owners– 1, Winchell Thoroughbreds LLC; 2, Barberino John S Sr; 3, Win and Place Stable; 4, Smart Start Stables LLC; 5, Knight Cynthia; 6, Centennial Farms

Trainers– 1, Dickinson Michael W; 2, Ritchey Tim F; 3, Dutrow Anthony W; 4, Moran William E; 5, Morales Carlos J; 6, Matz Michael R

Scratched– Mr. B's Diamond (22May04 2Del²)

Let's take a look at Hawking. Michael Dickinson has a good winning percentage with debut runners, and Defrere is an above-average first-out sire. So why was Hawking let go at 4-1 in a weak-looking maiden claimer at Delaware? The heavy favorite, Jack of Clubs, had competitive Beyer Speed Figures (between 47 and 79 in all of his six lifetime starts), but he had already failed at odds of 7-2 or less in five of his races. When watching Jack of Clubs's past races, one could see a horse that lacked the requisite killer instinct to reach the winner's circle. Second choice Marigot Red was making his ninth career start, and had failed in weaker races at Tampa Bay Downs. As you can see, both of the public's choices had holes in their form. Why didn't Hawking take a bigger hit at the windows? Perhaps the fans were leery of playing a firster in a maiden claiming race (we'll discuss the maiden claiming myth later on), or the route distance dissuaded them. Most likely, they saw that his dam was unraced, and hadn't thrown a stakes-winner from three previous foals to race.

As stated in the sire section, breeders are not only mating to the individual, but also to the entire family. Industrious handicappers who took time to analyze Hawking's pedigree saw that his dam, Rare Fling, was a half-sister to stakes winner Dr. Arne and multiple stakes-placed Star Pride. While the pedigree wouldn't make Ogden Phipps or Khalid Abdullah jealous, it certainly was enough to compete at this $50,000 maiden claiming level. Hawking made a big move from last to win by 10 lengths

Remember that class can be defined in many different ways. Race record, immediate family, and long-term pedigree should always be considered when attempting to determine the class of the dam.

AT THE SALES

Daily Racing Form readers are privy to exclusive auction information. The breeding industry is the engine that makes this great game go, and handicappers of maiden races can benefit from the sales prices provided by the *Form*.

There are three major types of auctions that horseplayers should recognize. Most horses sell as weanlings (foals that are no longer getting milk from their dams), as yearlings, or as 2-year-olds in training. The top weanling auction in the United States is the Keeneland November Breeding Stock Sale (which also includes broodmares, horses of other ages, stallion shares, and seasons). The Keeneland July Selected Yearling Sale used to be the priciest of all the yearling auctions, but it has been phased out in recent years, and has given way to the Fasig-Tipton Saratoga Selected Yearlings Sale in August, and the bulky Keeneland September Yearling Sale. Important 2-year-olds in training sales include Ocala Breeders' Sales February, Fasig-Tipton at Calder February, Barretts March, and Keeneland April.

From a handicapping standpoint, there is reason to be wary of horses that were sold as 2-year-olds in training. First of all, these babies, some still months away from legitimately turning 2, are asked to work a blazing eighth or quarter of a mile under tack. In order to be ready to work in front of the public, these youngsters have already been training hard for weeks or months on the farm, and one has to wonder if a growing Thoroughbred is emotionally and physically ready to handle such demanding workouts. Still, speed sells, and 2-year-olds in training sales are arguably the most popular in the world.

Between 1980 and 2003, there have been four 2-year-olds in training in North America that sold for $2 million or more at public auction. Let's take a look at how they did on the racetrack.

Gotham City
Own: Fog City Stable
Dk. b or b. c. 4 (May) BARMAR00 $2,000,000
Sire: Saint Ballado (Halo) $125,000
Dam: What a Reality (In Reality)
Br: F. Carl Schwietert (Fla)
Tr: Hess R B Jr(0 0 0 0 .00) 2004:(89 16 .18)

Life	2	M	0	0	$2,880	75	D.Fst	2	0	0	0	$2,880 75
2002	1	M	0	0	$2,880	75	Wet(343)	0	0	0	0	$0 -
2001	1	M	0	0	$0	21	Turf(281)	0	0	0	0	$0 -
Bel	0	0	0	0	$0	-	Dst(390)	2	0	0	0	$2,880 75

23Mar02-10SA fst 6f :211 :441 :5611:091 3↑Md Sp Wt 48k 75 4 3 42 32½ 24½ 49½ Desormeaux K J LB124 4.40 82-12 HevenlySerch1247 MrPowerful117½ Grenlnd1242 Stalked pace, weakened 8
1Sep01-9Dmr fst 6f :214 :443 :5641:092 3↑Md Sp Wt 47k 21 9 5 2½ 33 1014 1128½ Nakatani C S LB118 4.70e 64-12 *Swept Clean*1181 *No Socks Doc*1183 A. J.'s Band1182 5wd to turn, gave way 11

La Salle Street
Own: Tabor Michael B
Dk. b or b. c. 3 (May)
Sire: Not For Love (Mr. Prospector) $20,000
Dam: Three Grand (Assert*Ire)
Br: Katherine Willson (Md)
Tr: Lukas D. W(34 4 4 3 .12) 2004:(307 34 .11)
KEE APR 99
$2 MILLION

Life	3	M	1	0	$3,420	73	D.Fst	3	0	1	0	$3,420 73
2000	3	M	1	0	$3,420	73	Wet(411)	0	0	0	0	$0 -
1999	0	M	0	0	$0	-	Turf(310)	0	0	0	0	$0 -
Bel	0	0	0	0	$0	-	Dst(359)	1	0	0	0	$0 41

13Sep00-1TP fst 1 :224 :464 1:1231:401 3↑Md Sp Wt 19k 73 3 31½ 21½ 21 21½ 22 Borel C H L118 f 3.00 69-38 Indeed I Hope1182 La Salle Street1188 Dominus1186 Drifted in start 10
20Aug00-4Sar fst 7f :222 :461 1:1131:243 3↑Md Sp Wt 41k 53 3 5 53½ 86¾ 69 614¼ Day P L118 7.50 68-14 Panner1184 Foolish Lover118½ Kipperscope1183¼ Inside trip, tired 9
27Jly00-4Sar fst 6f :22 :454 :58 1:102 3↑Md Sp Wt 41k 41 4 10 51½ 76¼ 1013 920½ Day P L117 f 5.40 72-09 Graze1173 *Night Flight*117½ Toredown1171¾ Green between rivals 12

Diamond Fury
Own: Fipke Charles E
Ch. g. 3 (Apr) BARMAR03 $2,700,000
Sire: Sea of Secrets (Storm Cat) $6,500
Dam: Swift Spirit (Tasso)
Br: John T. L. Jones Jr. (Ky)
Tr: Baffert Bob(9 2 1 2 .22) 2004:(320 59 .18)

Life	4	M	0	2	$10,560	78	D.Fst	4	0	0	2	$10,560 78
2004	2	M	0	0	$0	58	Wet(264)	0	0	0	0	$0 -
2003	2	M	0	2	$10,560	78	Turf(317*)	0	0	0	0	$0 -
Bel	0	0	0	0	$0	-	Dst(315)	1	0	0	1	$4,680 78

14Feb04-4SA fst 1 1/16 :221 :453 1:1031:443 Md Sp Wt 46k 33 11 41½ 52 76¾ 1013 1028½ Baze T C LB120 b 19.00 53-15 Hippocrates1204 GrandWrrior120no D *SintChrisjon*120½ 5wd,4wd,gave way 11
18Jan04-4SA fst 6½f :213 :44 1:0911:153 Md Sp Wt 47k 58 5 6 62¼ 53½ 56½ 711¾ Nakatani C S LB120 4.00 82-06 Gamblin1201¼ CorondosPride1204 HickoryPete1201 3wd into lane,no rally 12
16Nov03-5Hol fst 6f :214 :444 :5711:094 Md Sp Wt 39k 78 2 8 42½ 1½ 1hd 31¾ Fogelsonger R LB120 2.70 89-10 *Saint Afleet*1201¼ Gamblin120½ Diamond Fury1203 Squeezed start,inside 8
30Aug03-3Dmr fst 5½f :214 :451 :5731:041 Md Sp Wt 49k 58 3 3 31 21 22 38½ Smith M E LB120 b 1.60 85-13 Consecrte1206 Wimplstiltskin1202½ DimondFury1202 Bid 3wd,led,wkened 6
WORKS: Jly8 SA 3f fst :361 H *5/16*

Morocco
Own: Barber Don and DeLima, Jose
Ch. h. 7 (May)
Sire: Brocco (Kris S.) $874
Dam: Roll Over Baby (Rollin On Over)
Br: Kenneth Roberts, Brenda Roberts & Taylor Made Farm (Ky)
Tr: DeLima Jose E(0 0 0 0 .00) 2004:(31 1 .03)
BAR MAR 99
$2 MILLION

Life	16	4	0	1	$133,640	95	D.Fst	10	2	0	1	$67,460 95
2004	1	0	0	0	$0	32	Wet(271)	0	0	0	0	$0 -
2003	2	0	0	0	$3,900	93	Turf(204)	6	2	0	0	$66,180 95
Bel	0	0	0	0	$0	-	Dst(251)	4	1	0	0	$25,800 94

12May04-5Hol fst 6f :214 :451 :5721:10 4↑Clm 8000 32 3 10 1111 1112 1114 919¾ Linares M G LB118 f 10.00 67-11 *Greenbaypcker*118¾ *SenstionlGuy*1185½ NturlStyle1202½ Lame after,vanned 11
Previously trained by Mandella Richard
21Feb03-7SA fm *6½f ⓣ :21 :43 1:06 1:122 4↑RebsPlicyH81k 91 2 9 812 710 76 65 Espinoza V LB115 b *2.20e 90-05 Grandiser1163 Kachamandi1161 Ecstatic117no Off bit slow,mild bid 9
16Jan03-2SA fm *6½f ⓣ :211 :43 1:0511:112 4↑OC 125k/N$Y-N 93 1 6 610 67¼ 64 42½ Espinoza V LB117 b *2.00e 97 - Cayoke117hd Kachamandi1171½ Ecstatic1161 Slow into stride 6
2Dec01-8Hol fst 6f :22 :441 :5611:09 3↑VOUndrwd-G3 94 5 6 69½ 67 64¾ 63¼ Stevens G L LB122 b 9.40 92-12 Men's Exclusive120½ Tavasco114nk *Caller One*1241½ Gaining lane,no threat 7
12Oct01-5SA fm *6½f ⓣ :211 :43 1:0631:124 3↑OC 100k/N3x-N 95 6 7 79¾ 78¾ 41¾ 14 Espinoza V LB118 b 8.20 96-06 Morocco1184 Martel1182 *Lebontempsroulet*118hd 4w bid,lugged in,clear 7
27Sep01-7SA fst 7f :22 :442 1:0911:212 3↑OC 100k/N3x-N 95 7 9 918 912 76¼ 57¾ Espinoza V LB118 b 6.50 90-15 ImpressiveGrdes118nk ILovSilvr1183½ *RbsGold*1182 No speed,imp position 9
17Aug01-5Dmr fst 6f :213 :442 :5641:094 3↑OC 100k/N3x-N 85 6 9 915 98¼ 64 63 Espinoza V LB120 b 6.00 88-13 LoveAllthWy1181 *ThMorrisMonro*118½ RockyBr116½ Stdied,blkd final 1/16 9
28Jly01-8Dmr fst 6½f :22 :444 1:0931:16 3↑OC 62k/N2x-N 95 5 12 1216 105½ 77 1no Espinoza V LB119 b 8.70e 93-08 Morocco119no El Curioso1191½ *Love All the Way*1191½ 6 wide rally,up wire 12
14Jun01-5Hol fst 1 1/16 :231 :461 1:1011:421 3↑OC 80k/N2x-N 83 4 65 75¾ 75¼ 87¼ 86 Espinoza V LB119 b 5.50e 86-13 Eye Pea Oh119nk Timber Baron114½ Kaiser So Say119½ Came out,no rally 9
30Aug00-6Dmr fst 1 :22 :451 1:0941:362 3↑OC 62k/N2x-N - 3 43 36 811 818 - Desormeaux K J LB117 b 12.60 - 11 LethalInstrument1171 KiserSoSy1191 MilkWood117½ 3wd,gave way,eased 8
26Jly00-5Dmr fm 1 ⓣ :223 :46 1:1031:352 Ⓡ Oceanside86k 71 7 812 811 97¼ 1010 1013¼ Espinoza V LB118 b 9.60 75-13 DukeofGreen115½ *DesignedforLuck*1172 Safarndo1141 Off bit slow,wkened 10
Run in divisions
24Jun00-3Hol fm 1 ⓣ :234 :48 1:1141:344 Alw 54000N2x 84 7 66½ 67 64 64¾ 55 Espinoza V LB119 2.40 84-11 Gnrtions1221½ DsigndforLuck118½ LostinPrdis1172½ 3wd 2nd turn,no rally 7
4Jun00-7Hol fm 1 ⓣ :233 :471 1:1021:343 Alw 51000N1x 88 7 56 76 44 31 11 Espinoza V LB120 6.00 90-09 Morocco1201 Credit Call1181 *Pizza N Beer*122nk Rallied, up late 8
6May00-4Hol fst 6f :22 :453 :58 1:102 3↑Md Sp Wt 43k 89 1 8 75¾ 76 54½ 1nk Espinoza V LB116 6.50 85-16 *Morocco*116nk Trampus Too111nk Retro Fever1161½ 4wd into lane,up late 8
14Aug99-6Dmr fst 6½f :22 :45 1:1031:172 Md Sp Wt 46k 66 4 11 77½ 77¾ 46 56¼ McCarron C J LB118 2.30 78-13 Commendable1184 Silver Axe118nk Ronton118no Stdied strt,tight late 11
24Jly99-6Dmr fst 5f :23 :46 :58 Md Sp Wt 45k 70 2 4 43 41½ 32 33½ McCarron C J B118 2.50 90-12 Magical Dragon1182¾ *Joopy Doopy*118¾ Morocco1187 Off bit slow, cut off 4
WORKS: May6 SA 5f fst 1:023 H *26/39* Apr25 SA 5f fst 1:021 H *43/49* Apr18 SA 5f fst 1:03 H *29/30*

Not very promising, to say the least. Gotham City and La Salle Street didn't even make their career debuts until late in their 3-year-old seasons. Diamond Fury was purchased for $2.7 million in March 2003 after working an eighth of a mile in 10.20 seconds and a quarter mile in 21.60. He didn't start until late August, and was immediately banished to the bench for a couple of months. Morocco actually made two unsuccessful attempts as a juvenile before being sent to the sidelines. It could be argued that all of these runners were knocked out from their training leading up to their respective sales, and had to be turned out before even making their career debuts. None of them has run as fast as the day he worked at the sales.

Fans of these juvenile sales do have some grounds for optimism, however. There have been 30 purchases of $1 million or more at these events between 1980 and 2003. Twelve of the expensive runners earned black type, with five winning Grade 1 races. How can the horseplayer separate the potential winners from the flops? Let's look at three quality horses to exit 2-year-olds in training sales.

Yonaguska
Own: Tabor Michael B

Dk. b or b. c. 4 (Apr) FTFFEB00 $1,950,000
Sire: Cherokee Run (Runaway Groom) $40,000
Dam: Marital Spook (Silver Ghost)
Br: Edward P. Evans (Ky)
Tr: Lukas D. W(34 4 4 3 .12) 2004:(307 34 .11)

Life	18	6	1	5	$536,355	107	D.Fst	17	6	1	5	$536,355	107
2002	4	0	0	0	$15,000	100	Wet(394)	0	0	0	0	$0	-
2001	7	3	0	3	$278,060	107	Turf(252)	1	0	0	0	$0	74
Bel	5	2	0	2	$212,610	107	Dst(350)	5	1	1	1	$131,560	106

27Jly02-8Sar	fst	6½f	:221	:444	1:093	1:16	4↑Alw 56000N$Y	**81**	6	4	42½	41½	73¾	710	Santos J A	L124 b	3.50	85-09	*WildSummer*117nk DaytonFlyer1171¼ StormCrft1212¼	Chased 4 wide, tired	7
6Jly02-9Pha	fst	6f	:22	:452	:573	1:103	3↑PhaBCH-G3	**83**	3	6	31½	2hd	42¼	78¼	Castillo H Jr	L122 b	*1.70	78-24	TruePassion1152¼ LteCrson118nk RellyIrish114nk	Step slow,bid3w, empty	7
8Jun02-6Bel	fst	6f	:221	:45	:57	1:094	3↑TrNthBCH-G2	**100**	4	1	1hd	2hd	2½	41¾	Smith M E	L118 b	4.50	87-10	Explicit1191 Entepreneur115½ Late Carson114nk	Vied inside, tired	7
26Jan02-5SA	fm	1	Ⓣ:231	:463	1:102	1:332	4↑Alw 65000N$MY	**74**	4	1hd	1hd	3nk	96½	1013	Stevens G L	LB116 b	8.00	82-08	Designed for Luck117no El Cielo119½ Sarafan1231	Dueled,btwn,wkened	10
26Dec01-6SA	fst	7f	:221	:444	1:092	1:22	Malibu-G1	**87**	1	9	64¼	52½	53¼	68¾	Stevens G L	LB119 b	4.40	86-12	*MizzenMst*1172½ GintGentlemn115nk ILoveSilvr1172½	Came out,no late bid	13
22Nov01-9Aqu	fst	6f	:222	:451	:571	1:093	3↑FallHwtH-G2	**103**	1	8	31	2hd	1hd	1¾	Santos J A	L131 b	*1.95	89-18	Yonaguska131¾ Big E E1291 Voodoo1231¼	Vied 3 wide, driving	8
27Oct01-2Bel	fst	6½f	:23	:46	1:092	1:152	3↑SportPgH-G3	**107**	6	4	51¼	3nk	11½	11½	McCarron C J	L116 b	*1.55	98-03	*Yonaguska*1161½ Silky Sweep1164 Big E E1141	4 wide move, lugged in	6
7Oct01-9Bel	fst	6f	:23	:46	:572	1:092	3↑FrstHlsH-G2	**106**	3	5	41½	52¼	42½	33½	Prado E S	L113 b	8.40	87-21	DelwrTownship1183¼ HookndLddr114nk *Yongusk*1131½	Inside, good finish	5
11Apr01-8Kee	fst	7f	:222	:45	1:093	1:223	Lafayett-G3	**100**	2	6	2½	1hd	2½	31¾	Bailey J D	L123 b	*1.30	87-15	Griffinite116no SmLordsCstle1181¾ Yongusk1237¼	Pressed,led,weakened	7
10Mar01-8GP	fst	7f	:221	:442	1:092	1:221	Swale-G3	**83**	5	3	3½	2hd	33	312¼	Bailey J D	L122 fb	*.90	83-10	D'wildcat11610½ Tarek1121¾ Yonaguska1222¼	Vied 3 wide, tired	6
27Jan01-10GP	fst	7f	:221	:444	1:091	1:223	Hutchesn-G2	**95**	10	4	31½	2½	14	1½	Bailey J D	L119 b	*1.90	93-11	Yonaguska119½ City Zip1226½ Sparkling Sabre1122	Drew clear, lasted	11
19Nov00-8Hol	fst	7f	:22	:444	1:092	1:23	HolPrevu-G3	**88**	7	3	41¼	41½	32½	33	McCarron C J	LB122 b	*1.40	81-19	*Proud Tower*1221 Chinook Cat1162 *Yonaguska*122¾	4wd to turn,held 3rd	8
4Nov00-8CD	fst	1 1/16	:232	:464	1:111	1:42	BCJuven-G1	**70**	11	52¼	31	31½	1218	1216¼	Day P	L122 b	9.80	84 -	Macho Uno122no *Point Given*1221½ *Street Cry*122½	4-5 trip, tired	14
14Oct00-9Bel	fst	1 1/16	:223	:45	1:092	1:412	Champagn-G1	**94**	4	82¼	61¼	4nk	1hd	32½	Bailey J D	122 b	7.60	87-09	A P Valentine1221¾ Point Given122¾ Yonaguska1221	4 wide move, gamely	10
2Sep00-9Sar	fst	7f	:223	:461	1:111	1:242	Hopeful-G1	**86**	2	7	4¾	1hd	11½	1nk	♦Bailey J D	122 b	3.55	83-14	DH Yonaguska122 DH City Zip122nk *Macho Uno*1227¼	Pace, clear, driving	11
27Jly00-9Sar	fst	6f	:21	:451	:571	1:103	Sanford-G2	**81**	4	4	41½	11	1½	23½	Bailey J D	119 b	*.55	88-09	*City Zip*1193½ *Yonaguska*119½ Scorpion1143¼	Speed outside, gamely	7
9Jun00-7Bel	fst	5f	:214	:444		:574	Flash82k	**97**	7	5	2hd	1hd	13½	12½	Bailey J D	115 b	*.95	93-17	Yonaguska1152½ The Goo1151¼ *City Zip*115no	Bumped start, driving	7
3May00-4CD	fst	4½f	:222	:451		:511	Md Sp Wt 38k	**84**	6	2	11		13	19¼	Bailey J D	118 b	*1.50	99-07	*Yongusk*1189¼ DivineProvidnc118nk TwoWinnrsLong1181¼	Easily, on own	11

Chapel Royal
Own: Smith Derrick and Tabor, Michael

Dk. b or b. (Mar) OBSFEB03 $1,200,000
Sire: Montbrook (Buckaroo) $20,000
Dam: Cut Class Leanne (Cutlass)
Br: Ocala Stud Farm (Fla)
Tr: Pletcher Todd A(128 30 24 21 .23) 2004:(488 123 .25)

Life	7	3	2	1	$493,755	100	D.Fst	6	2	2	1	$403,755	99
2004	1	0	0	0	$9,000	84	Wet(374)	1	1	0	0	$90,000	100
2003	6	3	2	1	$484,755	100	Turf(247)	0	0	0	0	$0	-
Bel	3	2	1	0	$189,755	99	Dst(397)	1	1	0	0	$90,000	100

13Mar04-10GP	fst	7f	:22	:443	1:092	1:224	Swale-G3	**84**	1	5	1½	1hd	21½	45¼	Velazquez J R	L122	1.30	83-13	WynnDotComm120hd Euroslvr1204¼ DshbordDrmmr1201	Inside, faltered	5
25Oct03-7SA	fst	1 1/16	:221	:45	1:094	1:433	BCJuvnle-G1	**79**	10	3½	2hd	11	11½	37¼	Velazquez J R	LB122	5.70	79-07	ActionThisDy1222¼ MinistrEric1225 ChplRoyl122no	Clear turn, weakened	12
4Oct03-7Bel	fst	1 1/16	:234	:481	1:133	1:44	Champagn-G1	**90**	7	1hd	1½	1½	2hd	22½	Velazquez J R	L122	*1.55	77-26	*Birdstone*1222½ ChpelRoyl1226¾ DshbordDrummr1222	Set pace, weakened	7
30Aug03-8Sar	fst	7f	:222	:452	1:102	1:232	Hopeful-G1	**83**	7	5	4¾	3nk	1½	24	Velazquez J R	L122	*.65	86-11	SilverWagon1224 ChpelRoyl1221½ NotoriousRogue1221	4 wide, held place	7
24Jly03-8Sar	sly	6f	:212	:444	:572	1:103	Sanford-G2	**100**	2	4	41	31½	12	15¾	Velazquez J R	L122	*1.00	89-12	ChplRyl1225¾ BlshngIndn1183½ *FlshngMdws*1181¼	Jumped puddles stretch	7
6Jun03-7Bel	fst	5f	:214	:442		:57	Flash-G3	**99**	3	2	2hd	1½	11½	15¼	Velazquez J R	L114	*.30	98-12	*Chapel Royal*1145¼ Hasslefree1142¼ *Juventus*1144¼	When asked, ridden out	4
15May03-2Bel	fst	5f	:22	:451		:58	Md Sp Wt 43k	**81**	7	7	2hd	2hd	13½	19¼	Velazquez J R	L118	*.65	93-12	*Chapel Royal*1189¼ *Snow Eagle*1183 Golden Diamond118¾	Ducked out start	7

WORKS: Apr20 CD 4f fst :492 B *14/32*

Songandaprayer
Own: Hurley Leslie and R. and D. J. Stable

B. c. 3 (Mar) FTFFEB00 $1,000,000
Sire: Unbridled's Song (Unbridled) $125,000
Dam: Alizea (Premiership)
Br: Donna M. Wormser (Ky)
Tr: Dowd John F(4 0 0 0 .00) 2004:(74 10 .14)

Life	8	3	1	1	$380,480	105	D.Fst	5	1	1	1	$311,000 105
2001	6	1	1	1	$314,000	105	Wet(359)	3	2	0	0	$69,480 94
2000	2	2	0	0	$66,480	94	Turf(289)	0	0	0	0	$0 -
Bel	0	0	0	0	$0	-	Dst(372)	2	1	0	1	$61,880 94

4Jly01-3Mth	fst	6f	:213	:44	:562	1:09	JerShrBC-G3	88	5	2	31½	1½	21	35½	Bravo J	L122 f	*.80	88- 11	*City Zip*1194¼ *Sea of Green*1171¼ Songandaprayer1222	3-deep bid,led,tired	5
5May01-8CD	fst	1¼	:444	1:091	1:35	1:594	KyDerby-G1	75	1	11½	11½	41¾	1212	1327	Gryder A T	L126 f	35.90	77 -	Monarchos1264¾ Invisible Ink126no Congaree1264	Hustled inside,faded	17
14Apr01-9Kee	fst	1⅛	:462	1:102	1:352	1:481	BlueGras-G1	105	6	21½	21	2hd	21½	25¼	Prado E S	L123 f	6.50	89- 14	MllnnmWnd1235¼ Songndpryr1231¾ DollrBll1231½	Pressed, no match late	7
10Mar01-11GP	fst	1⅛	:464	1:112	1:37	1:494	FlaDerby-G1	88	9	52	3½	3nk	32	510¼	Prado E S	L122 f	4.80	78- 13	Monarchos1224½ Outofthebox1222½ InvisibleInk122½	Wide trip, weakened	13
17Feb01-10GP	fst	1 1/16	:234	:464	1:104	1:432	FntnOYth-G1	101	3	11½	14	12½	13	12½	Prado E S	L117 f	18.00	91- 14	Songandaprayer1172½ Outofthebox114¾ City Zip1174½	Inside, driving	11
20Jan01-10GP	gd	1 1/16	:222	:454	1:121	1:46	HolyBull-G3	81	4	2½	11½	2hd	41¾	55	Day P	L117 f	3.10	73- 23	Radical Riley119hd Buckle Down Ben119½ Cee Dee1174	Off rail, tired	8
26Nov00-8Aqu	sly	6f	:214	:443	:572	1:102	Huntington84k	94	5					1nk	Gryder A T	L116 f	10.80	85- 22	Songandaprayer116nk Native Heir1182½ *Voodoo*1161	Dense fog, driving	10
15Jun00-5Mth	gd	5f	:213	:442		:573	Md Sp Wt 26k	78	1	6	12	14	15	1½	Bravo J	118 f	*.20	92- 09	*Songandpryer*118½ *Strbury*11810¾ UndercoverCper118½	Clear,widened,held	7

Yonaguska, Chapel Royal, and Songandaprayer all sold for princely sums, and all won at first asking early on in the juvenile season. That indicates that they were tough enough to handle the rigors of pre-sale and then pre-race training. When looking at auction prices in maiden races, I really like to see horses that sold for 12 times the stud fees of their respective sires (up to $80,000 or so). In juvenile maiden races, I give the edge to the 2-year-olds in training sales graduates early in the season (between April and July). As summer turns into fall, I tend to view these high-priced juvenile purchases in a negative light. Why did it take them so long to make it to the track? Was there a physical setback? Buyers at 2-year-olds in training sales are purchasing speed, and are looking for a quick return on their investment. If I don't see these types early on in the year, then I'm assuming that all hasn't gone according to plan.

While I focused on juvenile colts in the above examples, I must stress that I have more confidence backing debuting fillies early in the season. I believe that they mature quicker than the boys, and can handle the demanding training better than their male counterparts.

Juvenile sales buyers are looking for speed. I've always believed that traders in the weanling market are looking for well-bred individuals, especially fillies that could bolster their breeding operations in the future. Let's look at the four top-priced weanlings sold in North America between 1980 and 2003.

$2,500,000 (1985): Magic of Life (filly by Seattle Slew—Larida)

Group 1 winner with blueblood pedigree. Dam of French stakes-winner From Beyond and British Group 2 winner Enthused.

$2,400,000 (2003): Unnamed (colt by Storm Cat—Spain)

Beautiful pedigree. Now a yearling.

$2,300,000 (1987): Ghashtah (filly by Nijinsky II—My Charmer)

Unraced half-sister to Seattle Slew.

$1,500,000 (1998): King Charlemagne (colt by Nureyev—Race the Wild Wind)

Group 1 winner.

To show how much weight pedigree carries in these sales, nine of the 25 weanlings that sold for over $1 million in North America between 1980 and 2003 were sired by Storm Cat. Sixteen of them were fillies, and most of them had impeccable pedigrees.

Buying weanlings is also a risky proposition. These horses are true babies, and it's difficult to gauge how they'll look conformation-wise as grown-ups. When handicapping maiden races that feature high-priced weanlings that sold for over 12 times the stud fee, stick to the fillies. They stand out in the auction ring as weanlings because of their maturity edge over the boys at that age, and thus give buyers a chance to surmise how they will grow into their bodies.

Call me old-fashioned, but I prefer the yearling sales above all others. Buyers at yearling sales get the perfect balance between pedigree and conformation. These horses are old enough for horsemen to make educated guesses on how they'll look once they get to the racetrack, and they're still young enough for pedigree to play a major role. While there have been such high-priced flops as Seattle Dancer and Snaafi Dancer, remember that Fusaichi Pegasus sold for $4 million as a yearling, and he went on to win the Kentucky Derby. A.P. Indy was purchased for $2.9 million, and he won the Belmont and Breeders' Cup Classic on his way to being a top stallion. Vindication was bought for $2.15 million, and he was undefeated in a career that included a sparkling triumph in the Breeders' Cup Juvenile.

Most of these high-priced purchases offer little value when they make their career debuts, however. I prefer to look for horses with modest stud fees that sell surprisingly well. Take On the Porch, for example.

On the Porch				
Own: Brodsky Alan				

Dk. b or b. c. 2 (Mar) SARAUG03 $40,000
Sire: Accelerator (A.P. Indy) $1,500
Dam: Northern Eyes (Valet de Pied*Fr)
Br: Dr. Patricia Staskowski Purdy (NY)
Tr: Hennig Mark A(0 0 0 0 .00) 2004:(276 39 .14)

Life	1 1 0 0	$24,600	47	D.Fst	1 1 0 0 $24,600 47
2004	1 1 0 0	$24,600	47	Wet(228)	0 0 0 0 $0 –
2003	0 M 0 0	$0	–	Turf(195)	0 0 0 0 $0 –
Sar	0 0 0 0	$0	–	Dst(221)	1 1 0 0 $24,600 47

2Jly04–3Bel fst 5f :231 :473 1:001 ⑤Md Sp Wt 41k 47 4 2 4³ 4½ 1½ 11½ Fragoso P L118 6.70 82– 19 OnthePorch118¹¼ Wonforjodi118¹¼ ChncuxVous113¹¼ Greenly, drew clear 8

WORKS: Jun24 Sar tr.t 4f fst :52⁴ Bg 10/14 Jun17 Sar tr.t 4f fst :50 B 4/28 Jun10 Sar tr.t 4f fst :52 B 8/18 Jun3 Sar tr.t 3f fst :37¹ B 7/32 May27 Sar tr.t 3f gd :37¹ B 2/15 May19 Sar tr.t 3f fst :39 B 9/15

On the Porch's sire, Accelerator, was a graded winner at 2, finished third in the Metropolitan Mile, and hails from an exceptional female family, but his initial foals did not sell well, and many pedigree experts had written him off. On the Porch's dam was a minor winner, and had produced a stakes-placed runner. A solid pedigree, but nothing that would get the heart rate pounding. Nonetheless, On the Porch sold for over 26 times his sire's stud fee, and was making his debut for a very capable barn in a weak statebred maiden special weight. He certainly should have been played in multi-race wagers based on these angles, and was worth a win bet at a solid 6-1 price.

I Love a Tru Saint				
Own: Freitag Timothy				

B. c. 3 (Apr) KEESEP02 $4,000
Sire: Saint Ballado (Halo) $125,000
Dam: True Love (Affirmed)
Br: Robert Berger (Ky)
Tr: Hobbs Kyle A(0 0 0 0 .00) 2004:(5 0 .00)

Life	5 1 1 2	$11,716	63	D.Fst	4 0 1 2 $7,596 63
2004	5 1 1 2	$11,716	63	Wet(354)	1 1 0 0 $4,820 47
2003	0 M 0 0	$0	–	Turf(298)	0 0 0 0 $0 –
Aqu□	1 0 0 0	$272	28	Dst(348)	1 0 0 0 $272 20

5Sep04–8CT fst 7f :22³ :474 1:152 1:29³ Alw 29000n3L 54 10 7 3³ 42½ 33½ 36½ Carmouche K L116 f 10.70 66– 27 EdtorsPg116³ SprtofMontri119³³½ ILovTruSnt116²½ Lacked late response 10
26Aug04–4CT fst 1¼ :49³ 1:16¹ 1:43¹ 1:58 3↑ Clm c–(5-4.5)n2L 63 3 2² 2¹ 1½ 1hd 2nk Cora D L116 f *1.50 64– 33 Ameribrill116nk ILovTruSint116⁷½ MountSuribchi121½ Very game effort 8
Claimed from Chen Danny J. for $5,000, Thompson Harry F Jr Trainer 2004(as of 8/26): (63³ 94 97 83 0.15)
11Aug04–5Pen fst 5½f :22² :46¹ :59³ 1:05⁴ 3↑ Clm 7500k2L 47 1 1 4² 6½ 55½ 3³ Rodriguez E L117 f 9.70 84– 11 Alghero119hd Third Gear119³ I Love a Tru Saint117nk Inside, some gain 11
23Jly04–4Pen gd 5½f :22¹ :46³ :59³ 1:05² Md 7500 47 5 3 2½ 1¹ 1hd 1³ Perez E R L122 f 5.10 84– 15 ILovTruSnt122³ AutomtcDpost122²¼ Stcktothprogrm122³ 2 wide, driving 8
4Jun04–6Aqu fst 6f □:23² :474 1:00³ 1:14 Md Sp Wt 41k 20 6 5 6⁷ 7¹⁰ 7²⁰ 8²² Espinoza J L 120 30.25 47– 32 Goodin120¹½ National Legend120⁵½ Torun120⁴½ Tired after a half 8

WORKS: Aug7 Pen 3f fst :39¹ B 34/47 Jly20 Pen 3f fst :38³ B 7/11 Jly9 Pen 5f fst 1:01³ H 2/9 Jun30 Pen 4f fst :50 H 10/16 Jun21 Pen 3f fst :38² B 8/10

But what should you do when a horse by an expensive sire shows up with a meager auction price on the past performances? You don't make the same mistake that I made at Aqueduct on January 4, 2004. I Love a Tru Saint made his debut in a maiden special weight over the inner track. He showed an excellent pedigree. His sire, Saint Ballado, had six debut winners in 2003, and the female family was full of quality. His dam is from the immediate family of successful sire Halo, as well as Natalma, the dam of Northern Dancer.

Trainer Harry Thompson Jr. is usually among the leaders at Penn National, and I found it interesting that he sent this colt up to the major leagues when a seemingly easy payday was on the horizon at his local oval. New York maidens in the winter are usually slow, and this looked like a great opportunity for an invader to steal a juicy purse. But how could I explain the sales price? Here was a son of a $125,000 stallion that sold for only $4,000 as a yearling. Red flags flashed before my eyes. Sirens, whistles, and bells boomed in my ears. But I didn't listen.

I rationalized that the Keeneland September Yearling Sale annually features thousands of horses. It seemed reasonable that one or two good ones could fall through the cracks. I loaded up on I Love a Tru Saint to win and place and in multi-race wagers. The past-performance line speaks for itself. Nothing is given away in the breeding business. Either I Love a Tru Saint had horrible conformation, or was unable to "vet out" at the sale, and the result was a "bargain" price. Beware low-priced horses with high stud fees in maiden special weights. There is usually a reason why they didn't sell well. Of course, I Love a Tru Saint returned to Penn National after a six-month layoff, and immediately won a $7,500 maiden claimer at 5-1. He hasn't been off the board since, racing at Penn National and Charles Town. Every horse has a proper class level. Maybe these high-priced sires/low-priced yearlings could be useful in weaker maiden claimers.

Pay attention to the auction prices in the *Form*. When a difficult maiden race rears its ugly head, the auction angle may pay off nicely.

4

TRIPS, PROFESSIONALISM, AND LOTS OF EARLY SPEED

I LOVE BEYER Speed Figures. Unfortunately, so does everyone else. The value isn't there like it was years ago. So in 2000, I decided to switch my tack to trip handicapping. It has opened a whole new world to me in terms of analyzing maiden races. Now, I wasn't going to enter this new venture halfheartedly. I was going to watch every stride of every horse in every race. If a horse jumped a shadow on the backstretch, I would know. If a horse was rank in race after race after race, I would know. I would delve into the mind of the Thoroughbred. I would understand each horse's personality, his strengths and his weaknesses.

And I was getting results. Trip handicapping helps you spot underlays that look great on paper, but are underachievers on the racetrack. After one meet at Belmont, however, I was totally exhausted. After coming home from work, I was faced with nine or 10 replays of full fields. There is not time for sleep if you are a serious trip handicapper. When I started cursing the trees at Saratoga for blocking my view of the first four strides of some races, I decided that I either needed serious therapy, or to make a change. So I compromised. I would only do maiden races and turf races. And while I cringe when the New York Racing Association cards four maiden races, and five turf races, I feel that it's well worth the sleep sacrifice.

Trip handicapping is helpful in selecting next-out winners, but it may be most useful in projecting the long-term quality of a racehorse. One of my favorite examples is the first race at Belmont on June 28, 2001. Proud Citizen went off at 1-5 for Wayne Lukas and Jerry Bailey after a good second in his debut. Here were my notes after all was said and done.

THIRD RACE
Belmont
JUNE 28, 2001

5½ FURLONGS. (1.02¹) MAIDEN SPECIAL WEIGHT. Purse $41,000 (Up To $7,954 NYSBFOA) For Maiden Two Year Olds. Weight 117 lbs.

Value of Race: $41,000 Winner $24,600; second $8,200; third $4,510; fourth $2,460; fifth $1,230. Mutuel Pool $233,483.00 Exacta Pool $245,661.00 Trifecta Pool $176,850.00

Last Raced	Horse	M/Eqt.	A.	Wt	PP	St	¼	⅜	Str	Fin	Jockey	Odds $1
2Jun01 ^{3}Bel^{2}	Proud Citizen		2	117	1	1	1^{1}	$1^{1\frac{1}{2}}$	1^{6}	$1^{9\frac{1}{4}}$	Bailey J D	0.30
	My Cousin Matt		2	117	3	5	4^{hd}	$4^{2\frac{1}{2}}$	3^{hd}	$2^{1\frac{1}{2}}$	Luzzi M J	50.00
	Fine and Dandy		2	117	2	3	$2^{\frac{1}{2}}$	2^{hd}	$2^{\frac{1}{2}}$	3^{2}	Gryder A T	25.75
8Jun01 ^{6}Bel^{5}	Deeliteful Guy		2	117	4	2	$3^{1\frac{1}{2}}$	3^{hd}	$4^{3\frac{1}{2}}$	$4^{1\frac{3}{4}}$	Samyn J L	8.00
10Jun01 ^{3}Bel^{3}	Dr. Rockett		2	117	6	6	$6^{1\frac{1}{2}}$	5^{2}	$5^{1\frac{1}{2}}$	$5^{1\frac{1}{4}}$	Arroyo N Jr	26.75
	Copywriter	L	2	117	7	8	$8^{\frac{1}{2}}$	$6^{\frac{1}{2}}$	$6^{1\frac{1}{2}}$	6^{3}	Castellano J J	26.00
	Pitbull		2	117	8	7	$7^{3\frac{1}{2}}$	7^{hd}	$7^{\frac{1}{2}}$	$7^{\frac{3}{4}}$	Migliore R	13.60
	The Chauffeur		2	117	5	4	5^{hd}	8^{1}	$8^{2\frac{1}{2}}$	$8^{\frac{3}{4}}$	Prado E S	14.40
	Flyman Fly		2	117	9	9	9	9	9	9	Bridgmohan S X	24.75

OFF AT 2:03 Start Good. Won ridden out. Track fast.
TIME :22¹, :45², :57¹, 1:02⁴ (:22.22, :45.45, :57.25, 1:02.99)

$2 Mutuel Prices:				
	2 – PROUD CITIZEN	2.60	2.30	2.10
	4 – MY COUSIN MATT		9.90	2.50
	3 – FINE AND DANDY			2.30

$2 EXACTA 2–4 PAID $69.00 $2 TRIFECTA 2–4–3 PAID $455.00

B. h, (Mar), by Gone West – Drums Of Freedom, by Green Forest. Trainer Lukas D Wayne. Bred by Edmund J Loder (Ky).

PROUD CITIZEN was bumped after the start, quickly showed in front, set the pace and drew away under a hand ride. MY COUSIN MATT was hustled along inside, came wide into the stretch and finished gamely outside to earn the place award. FINE AND DANDY was bumped after the start, chased the pace along the inside and tired in the final furlong. DEELITEFUL GUY chased the pace along the rail and tired in the stretch. DR. ROCKETT chased the pace while three wide and tired. COPYWRITER raced very greenly while wide throughout. PITBULL chased four wide and tired. THE CHAUFFEUR tired after showing brief speed. FLYMAN FLY raced greenly while wide and tired.

Owners– 1, Baker Robert C Cornstein David and Mack William L; 2, Lunar Stables; 3, Stonerside Stable LLC; 4, Karches Peter and Rankowitz Michael; 5, Grant Mary and Joseph and Kelly Thomas J; 6, Dogwood Stable; 7, Streicher Judson L; 8, Goldfarb Sanford J; 9, Valando Elizabeth J

Trainers– 1, Lukas D Wayne; 2, Ribaudo Robert J; 3, Mott William I; 4, Clement Christophe; 5, Kelly Patrick J; 6, Alexander Frank A; 7, Russo Sal; 8, Dutrow Richard E Jr; 9, Nafzger Carl A

Scratched– Be Bop Alula

Proud Citizen: Made easy lead, set fast pace, nice acceleration, never hit (+).

My Cousin Matt: Career debut, shuffled back early, made midmove on rail, had to wait a bit on turn, angled three-wide at quarter pole, okay late kick, faced sharp winner (+).

Fine and Dandy: Career debut, stalked nice winner, simply no match, not terrible (+).

Deelightful Guy: Steadied slightly, ended up in the pocket, finished evenly behind nice winner (+).

Dr. Rockett: Liked his nice low running action, was green weaving a bit in midstretch (?).

Copywriter: Career debut, off a length slow, was roguishly rank, made an okay wide midmove, tired (?).

Pitbull: Career debut, raced wide, no real impact.

The Chauffeur: Career debut, raced in between horses throughout, steadied twice quarter pole, has a poor up-and-down stride (?).

Flyman Fly: Career debut, showed no speed, fair wide midmove, still green changing leads.

The horses that I gave the plus sign to were immediately put on my horses-to-watch list, not only for next time, but for the future. The question marks were ones to watch down the road with some potential, but I wasn't going to invest in them. The others seemed run-of-the-mill. Whenever I give a horse a minus sign, then he goes on the bet-against list. In the past, I would keep all these horses in alphabetical order in my notebook. Now, I simply go to Horse Watch at *www.drf.com.* Let's see how the horses coming out of the Proud Citizen race did in their careers.

Proud Citizen: Ran fifth at 6-5 next time out in the Sanford. In fact, he didn't win again until the Lexington Stakes at 8-1 odds the following season. He followed that up with a runner-up effort in the Kentucky Derby, and a third-place finish in the Preakness.

My Cousin Matt: Finished second in his next two starts. He broke his maiden in his sixth career start at 11-1 odds. After being claimed by Scott Lake, My Cousin Matt eventually untapped his potential. He won the Grade 2 General George Handicap with a 114 Beyer Speed Figure.

Fine and Dandy: Won his next start on grass at Saratoga, and then finished second in the Continental Mile on the grass at Monmouth.

Deeliteful Guy: Won next start at Belmont, became Grade 3-placed.

Dr. Rockett: Finished third and second in his next two starts. Eventually graduated, but remained a nibbler throughout his career.

Copywriter: Never broke his maiden.

Pitbull: Ran off the board in next start, then won turf debut at Saratoga at 59-1 odds.

The Chauffeur: Went on long hiatus. Ran poorly off the layoff, then won next two starts.

Flyman Fly: Never broke his maiden.

Now, I don't expect most handicappers to obsess about watching trips. For those of you that still want to maintain a normal social life, here are some things to look for when watching the races:

LEAD CHANGES

Horses aren't machines. They get tired. When they need a break, they switch leads. In a perfect world, all Thoroughbreds would lead with their left foreleg on the turns, and change to their right foreleg in the straightaway. Try hopping on one foot for an elongated period of time. When you get tired, simply switch to the other foot. You'll get a new boost of energy, and will be able to continue hopping. Okay, stop hopping. When horses switch leads, they get a boost, and are able to finish more powerfully. Beware of horses that fail to change leads. It is often either a sign that the horse is green or unsound. I can forgive a baby that doesn't change leads in the first or second career race, but I usually toss out horses that haven't learned this important lesson once they have racing experience.

The best lead changes are ones that are done smoothly and at the right time. I will give a horse about seven strides to change leads once he turns for home before wondering if something is amiss. Some horses really hit the ground hard, and that can be damaging to their fragile legs. Because of conformation, horses change leads in different ways. The good ones are very smooth. Others will plant the immediate lead change on the ground as if they were hammering a nail. That has to be very tough on a young horse's bones.

THE RAIL RALLY

When watching races involving babies, keep an eye out for youngsters that are pinned down on the rail for most of the running. These horses are getting a real education. Not only are they stuck between the inner railing and other horses, but they are probably getting dirt kicked back into their faces for the first time in their lives. If one of these horses then makes a serious late move, he or she is certainly one to follow next time out.

Eddington
Own: Willmott Stables Inc

Ch. c. 3 (Mar) KEEJUL02 $450,000
Sire: Unbridled (Fappiano) $200,000
Dam: Fashion Star (Chief's Crown)
Br: Carl Rosen Associates (Ky)
Tr: Hennig Mark A(0 0 0 0 .00) 2004:(376 53 .14)

Life	10	2	2	4	$434,560	101	D.Fst	9	2	2	3	$414,560	101
2004	9	2	1	4	$425,360	101	Wet(408)	1	0	0	1	$20,000	90
2003	1	M	1	0	$9,200	75	Turf(285)	0	0	0	0	$0	-
Aqu	3	0	1	2	$104,200	97	Dst(323)	0	0	0	0	$0	-

28Aug04-11Sar	fst	1¼	:49 1:124 1:37 2:022	Travers-G1	99	1	32½	31	42	44	36	Migliore R	L126 b	9.70	89-05	Birdstone1262½ TheCliff'sEdge1263½ Eddington126nk	Chased inside, tired	7
8Aug04-9Sar	fst	1⅛	:453 1:093 1:343 1:472	JimDandy-G2	101	5	511	512	58	37	35	Migliore R	L115 b	7.00	93-02	Purge1214½ The Cliff's Edge123½ [D]Eddington1157½	Lugged in, bumped	6
Disqualified and placed 4th																		
5Jun04-11Bel	fst	1½	:483 1:113 2:002 2:272	Belmont-G1	86	8	41½	31½	47	410	412	Bailey J D	L126 b	14.20	83-10	*Birdstone*1261 Smarty Jones1268 Royal Assault1263	Chased 5 wide, tired	9
15May04-12Pim	fst	1 3/16	:471 1:112 1:362 1:552	Preaknes-G1	97	8	63½	65¼	85¾	712	313½	Bailey J D	L126 b	13.20	86-13	SmrtyJons12611½ RockHrdTn1262 Eddington126hd	4-5wd,altered crse 1/8	10
10Apr04-8Aqu	fst	1⅛	:47 1:112 1:37 1:493	WoodMem-G1	97	8	52	42	3nk	2hd	3½	Bailey J D	L123 b	3.20	90-12	Tapit123½ Master David123no Eddington1231½	3 wide move, gamely	11
20Mar04-7Aqu	gd	1	:214 :433 1:08 1:352	Gotham-G3	90	2	75¼	74½	53	43½	33	Prado E S	L116 b	*1.35	85-14	Saratoga County1162¼ Pomeroy116¾ Eddington1165¼	Bumped after start	8
28Feb04-1GP	fst	1 1/16	:234 :474 1:114 1:43	Alw 34000n1x	101	5	21	21	2hd	11	15½	Bailey J D	L122 b	*.30	94-14	Eddington1225½ *Tiger Heart*1186¾ Capias1225½	Greenly, drew off	6
7Feb04-6GP	fst	1 1/16	:233 :473 1:112 1:423	Md Sp Wt 32k	97	6	21	2½	2hd	1½	14¾	Bailey J D	L122 b	*1.20	96-09	*Eddington*1224¾ *Forty Five*1225¼ Shots122½	Drew away, driving	12
8Jan04-6GP	fst	1 1/16	:241 :491 1:14 1:444	Md Sp Wt 32k	77	10	43½	53¼	42	33½	26¾	Bailey J D	L122	*2.10	78-18	Shaniko1226¾ *Eddington*1222½ Radiant Cat1221½	3 wide, 2nd best	11
28Nov03-4Aqu	fst	1	:232 :461 1:113 1:39	Md Sp Wt 46k	75	4					2no	Migliore R	120	7.10	70-29	OneToughDude120no Eddington12010½ *PesoPorBso*1201¾	Game on rail, fog	9

WORKS: Aug23 Sar 4f fst :48 B *16/64* Aug2 Sar 5f fst 1:002 H *7/38* Jly25 Bel 5f gd 1:011 B *2/13* Jly18 Bel 6f fst 1:13 B *2/2* Jly10 Bel 5f fst :594 H *3/25* Jly3 Bel 4f fst :473 B *3/42*

Eddington made his debut under a shroud of fog at Aqueduct. The son of Unbridled emerged in the stretch buried down on the inside, and was still fearlessly charging at the winner. The fact that he was unfazed by being where he was showed a certain professionalism and will to win. While the inside didn't bother this horse, the fact that he was often unwilling or unable to change leads as a 3-year-old certainly didn't help his Triple Crown chances. We didn't know that after his debut, however. All we knew was that he was a baby with potential.

Also watch horses that are willing to barrel through a narrow opening from between horses. They aren't afraid of that tight spot, and should be considered tough enough to eventually reach the winner's circle.

THE GALLOP-OUT

For trip handicappers, the race isn't over when the winner hits the wire. In some baby races, that's when the real analyzing begins. Did the winner stop to a walk when being pulled up? Was he passed by every horse in the field? Who was that hard-charging baby that ended up 10 lengths clear of everyone as his rider tried his best to gather him?

Babies are often very green in their first or second races. Who can blame them? They're babies. When the bell goes off, and the gate opens, it may take a second or two for the brain to register what they have to do. Many juveniles will break slowly from the gate, and at sprint distances that is often the determining factor in whether a horse is going to win or not. The slow-breakers that trip handicappers want to follow are the ones that pin their ears back and take off after their rivals with a sharp move entering the turn. The ones to follow are the horses that sustain their move into the stretch, and gallop out powerfully past the line, often passing a few horses that finished ahead of them.

Mark down the name of that late-running fifth-place finisher that was pulled up just off the runaway winner's flanks. He likely needed the race, will probably want to go longer distances, and showed he can run. Analyzing the gallop-out gives the trip handicapper an edge over bettors that only pore over past performances.

WON SPEED DUEL, LOST RACE BATTLE

Early speed is so important in maiden races. Trip handicappers should be mindful of speed horses that get caught up in pace battles, and are thus unable to respond when the closers start charging. Let's say Horse A duels with Horse B for a half-mile of a six-furlong race. Horse A finally puts Horse B away at the top of the stretch, but is collared by a fresh Horse C at the eighth pole. Horse A finishes third, beaten five lengths, while Horse B finishes eighth, beaten 18.

When this scenario occurs, I immediately put Horse A on my Horse Watch list. In my opinion, Horse A was the best horse in that race. He did all the hard running, discouraged another speed horse, and set the table for the closers. What will happen if there is no other speed in Horse A's next start? Speed is so dangerous, and horses that won speed duels, but didn't reach the winner's circle, are very good plays in their next outings.

IT'S NOT EASY BEING GREEN

Juvenile racehorses are learning with every start. They are going to be green at times. What kinds of immaturity can the trip handicapper put up with?

Horses that flash their tails when being asked for their best run are ones that I immediately put on my nonrunner list. They are being obstinate, and often quit when they don't get their way. European handicappers absolutely loathe tail-swishers. They call it one of the worst flaws a horse can have.

Youngsters that are "climbing" on the backstretch don't have their mind on their business. They aren't handling the track, and one could even argue that they are playing out there. This may be corrected with the addition of blinkers, but I am generally not thrilled about playing these types of runners.

Horses that lug in or out are not favorites of mine.

Thunder Ridge
Own: Overbrook Farm

Ch. c. 2 (Mar)		
Sire: Storm Cat (Storm Bird) $500,000		
Dam: City Band (Carson City)		
Br: Overbrook Farm (Ky)		
Tr: Lukas D. W(0 0 0 0 .00) 2004:(425 48 .11)		

Life	2 M 0 0	$2,379	45	D.Fst	2 0 0 0	$2,379	45
2004	2 M 0 0	$2,379	45	Wet(432)	0 0 0 0	$0	-
2003	0 M 0 0	$0	-	Turf(333)	0 0 0 0	$0	-
Sar	2 0 0 0	$2,379	45	Dst(443)	1 0 0 0	$129	42

6Sep04– 2Sar fst 5½f :22³ :46³ :59 11:05⁴ Md Sp Wt 45k 42 2 5 2½ 2ʰᵈ 3¾½ 9 11¼ Castillo H Jr L119 b 9.20 75– 17 GetWild119½ BiloxiPlce119½½ IllustriousKiss119¼½ Bumped start, between 12
7Aug04– 2Sar fst 6f :22⁴ :46¹ :59 1:12⁴ Md Sp Wt 45k 45 8 1 2½ 1ʰᵈ 2½ 4 6¼ Bailey J D L118 b 2.35 72– 13 Funk118⁵½ Lion Cat118½ One Fein Dad118⁶⁰ Erratic stretch 8
WORKS: Sep1 Sar tr.t 4f fst :48⁴ B 3/30 Aug22 Sar tr.t 4f my :52 B 4/9 ●Aug15 Sar tr.t 4f fst :47⁴ H 1/30 Jly19 CD 4f fst :47¹ B 2/57 Jly12 CD 4f fst :47⁴ B 4/51 Jly4 CD 4f fst :48² B 7/19

Thunder Ridge had a beautiful pedigree. By Storm Cat out of a Grade 1-winning juvenile filly, he was bred for stardom. He took lots of money for his debut at Saratoga, and pressed the pace from the get-go. Just as he was getting to the eventual winner, Funk, he started doing a little dance. He weaved all the way out. Then he wandered all the way in. Then he started doing it all over again. Was this simply the sign of a tired horse that needed the race, or had he become discouraged? Until proven otherwise, I'll consider Thunder Ridge the kind of runner that needs every break possible in order to reach the winner's circle.

Babies that are rank or uncontrollable are hard to count on. Trip handicappers can spot these horses by watching their heads. A rank runner will be fighting his rider, straining and shaking his head in an effort to escape the bit. Obviously, this horse doesn't have his mind on racing, and until he learns to relax, he can't be played with any confidence.

Avoid horses with a paddling running style, or who have an up-and-down circular stride. Paddlers may have conformation flaws. Runners with an up-and-down stride have usually proven to be hangers. The same can be said about horses that have their head turned to the side when they run. Often this kind makes the lead, and thinks that the race is over. They begin to lose their focus, gear themselves down, and are often overtaken.

I'm willing to forgive babies that fail to change leads for a start or two. I will also forgive most green runners if they return for their next starts with Lasix and/or blinkers. This shows to me that the trainer is aware of the problem, and is taking steps to correct it. If the horse showed at least some ability while green, I'm willing to give him another chance.

Don't be discouraged when a horse on your Watch List returns to run poorly. Take the case of Sissay.

Sissay
Own: Baker Charlton and Frankel, Richard

Dk. b or b. f. 3 (May)
Sire: Personal Flag (Private Account) $3,000
Dam: Hush Sister (Alwuhush)
Br: Michael Anchel & Raylene Anchel (NY)
Tr: Baker Charlton(2 0 2 0 .00) 2004:(263 64 .24)

Life	7	1	1	1	$15,647	59	D.Fst	6	1	1	1	$14,795	59
2004	7	1	1	1	$15,647	59	Wet(322)	1	0	0	0	$852	35
2003	0	M	0	0	$0	-	Turf(260)	0	0	0	0	$0	-
Bel	1	0	0	0	$140	-	Dst(309)	1	0	1	0	$1,920	-

13Sep04-4FL	fst	6f	:23¹	:47³	1:00¹	1:13²	3↑ⒻClm 10000(10-8)N2L	–	3	6	6 4½	6 3¾	7 4½	2 2	Rojas Ruben7	L109 b	*2.00	80– 16	Ancient Beauty120² Sissay109 1½ She's Got Style116¹	Rallied	7
6Sep04-2FL	fst	1 70	:23²	:47⁴	1:13²	1:45²	3↑ⒻAlw 14900N2L	29	8	7 9	9 7	8 9	8 13	9 16	Rojas Ruben7	L111 fb	5.00	70– 08	Sunnytown118 6½ HourglssFgur120¹ FortuntSwng120hd	6-w trip, no factor	10
8Aug04-4FL	fst	1 70	:24²	:48³	1:13³	1:45¹	3↑ⒻAlw 14900N2L	45	5	1½	1hd	1hd	2 1½	4 3½	Lee K10	L109 b	*1.85	83– 12	GoldenGlowTwo124 1½ FortuntSwing120 1¾ HourglssFigur120nk	Weakened	6
24Jly04-7FL	fst	1 70	:23	:47¹	1:12¹	1:44²	3↑ⒻAlw 14900N2L	43	3	6 8½	5 4¾	5 12	6 15	3 12½	Lee K10	L109 b	*2.15e	78– 12	Raf's Society Girl119 8¼ Fortunate Swing120 3¼ Sissay109 1½	Finished well	8
11Jly04-6FL	fst	1 70	:24	:48²	1:14	1:45	3↑ⒻⓈMd Sp Wt 17k	59	5	7 4¼	5 3¼	3 1½	2hd	1 2	Lee K10	L109 b	11.00	88– 15	Sissay109² Emblem's Glory119½ Moel124 1½	5-w trip, driving	10
30Jun04-5Bel	fst	1	:23³	:47²	1:13²	1:38⁴	3↑ⒻⓈMd Sp Wt 42k	–0	7	5 2¾	9 7½	10 14	11 33	11 52	Luzzi M J	L117	3.65	15– 21	*Shady Lane*117 17 Secret Troika117 1½ Contenders Emotion117 2¼	Tired	11
1Jun04-3FL	gd	5½f	:22²	:46⁴	1:00²	1:07³	3↑ⒻⓈMd Sp Wt 14k	35	2	6	7 9¾	7 10	7 9¼	4 5	Lee K10	109	13.30	72– 14	BreezeEsy124 2¼ RgingRuby119½ BrssyShirley119 2¼	5 wide turn, mild gain	9

WORKS:	Sep1 FL 5f fst 1:03¹ B *3/12*	Aug23 FL 4f fst :52 B *20/26*	●Jun25 FL 5f fst 1:01⁴ H *1/4*	Jun19 FL 7f gd 1:30² H *1/1*

Sissay was a 3-year-old maiden that had an awful trip in her debut at Finger Lakes. Ridden by a 10-pound apprentice, Katie Lee, Sissay fell way out of it in the early stages of the 5½-furlong test. She angled very wide turning for home, and passed several runners late. When Sissay showed up at Belmont for the high-percentage Charlton Baker barn, I was ready to pounce. All systems seemed ready to go as Sissay switched to Mike Luzzi, and took a great deal of early money. She didn't run a step, and was beaten over 50 lengths.

As I was tearing up my tickets, I wondered if I should take her off my Watch List. Nah! It's a free service. Maybe this race was simply an anomaly. Sure enough, Sissay returned to Finger Lakes 11 days later, was reunited with Katie Lee, and graduated at 11-1 odds. Trip horses sometimes disappoint in their first race back after the horrible journey. Give them a couple of chances before you dispose of them.

On the other hand, you do want to follow horses that have a nice low stride. They are reaching out for ground, and giving it their all. Also, follow horses that do things very easily, even when pressured by rivals. When Raging Fever broke her maiden at Belmont as a 2-year-old, it looked like she was flying over the track with the greatest of ease. Most of these types haven't even scratched the surface of their ability.

PACE MAKES THE RACE

Why is early speed so important in maiden races? Take these stats, for example. At the 2004 Keeneland spring meet, nine juvenile races were carded. Of those nine, eight were won by runners that were within a length of the lead at the pace call. I know what you're thinking. Keeneland is a notoriously speed-favoring track, so that stat can be misleading. Good point. So how do you explain that at the 2004 Saratoga meet, 37 of the 48 (77 percent) juvenile maiden winners were within a length of the lead after the first two calls? Speed is deadly in maiden races. But why?

Is it because horses are herd animals, and most youngsters need a start or two to figure out that this game is about racing, not staying with the herd? Is it all about pedigree? Does that Carson City or Valid Appeal gene give a horse the advantage over the runner with the Go for Gin or Old Trieste blood? Is it the fact that most horses make their debuts at sprint distances? Does that work against the late-runners? Perhaps babies are spooked by all the hubbub surrounding their first start. They have to face the crowd in the paddock, then are loaded into the gate amid the shoutings of the gate crew, side by side with other keyed-up horses. Are they confused when that bell goes off, and the riders start hooting and hollering? The ones that can handle all these distractions often find themselves on the lead, and they aren't the ones getting dirt or mud kicked back in their faces.

Whatever the reason, speed is dominant, and handicappers need to pick out the pace horse(s) in maiden races. But what should you do when there are only a handful of proven runners, and the others are first-time starters?

It didn't take an expert handicapper to see that Iron Wall was the speed of the ninth race at Calder on August 21, 2004. He was the only horse that had even sniffed the lead in his previous races, and he had an excuse for why he didn't show better speed in his career debut. I

9 Calder Race Course 5½ Furlongs (1:04^{1}) Md Sp Wt 29k Purse $29,000

(include $6,000 FOA – Florida Owners Awards) For Maidens, Two Year Olds. Weight, 118 lbs.

START ▼ 5½ FURLONGS ▲ FINISH

1 Rascal Ralph Own: Jack W Jones
Red Blue, Blue J In White Ball, Blue Dots
AGUILAR M (468 65 63 62 .14) 2004: (720 87 .12)
Dk. b or br c. 2 (Feb)
Sire: Abaginone (Devil's Bag) $3,000
Dam: Known Lova (Known Fact)
Br: R Farm (NY)
Tr: Richardson Susan G(1 0 0 0 .00) 2004:(6 0 .00)
118

Life	0	M	0	0	$0	–	D.Fst	0	0	0	0	$0	–
2004	0	M	0	0	$0	–	Wet(308)	0	0	0	0	$0	–
2003	0	M	0	0	$0	–	Turf(132)	0	0	0	0	$0	–
Crc	0	0	0	0	$0	–	Dst(342)	0	0	0	0	$0	–

WORKS: Aug7 NJF 5f fst 1:02^{4} B 3/4 Jly31 NJF 3f fst :36^{1} Bg 1/2 Jly3 NJF 4f fst :49^{3} B 4/6 Jun26 NJF 3f fst :35^{2} B 1/1
TRAINER: Dirt(7 .00 $0.00) Sprint(4 .00 $0.00) MdnSpWt(2 .00 $0.00)

2 Iron Wall Own: Half Moon Racing Stable & Janet Raffa
White Pink, Black Star, Black Stars On
BOULANGER G (237 41 36 36 .17) 2004: (550 66 .12)
Dk. b or br c. 2 (Apr) OBSAPR04 $20,000
Sire: Western Borders (Gone West) $2,500
Dam: Syrian Tricks (Clever Trick)
Br: Lucy de Yarhi (Fla)
Tr: McDonald Michael K(41 3 8 4 .07) 2004:(85 7 .08)
(471)
L 118

Life	2	M	1	0	$4,600	55	D.Fst	2	0	1	0	$4,600	55
2004	2	M	1	0	$4,600	55	Wet(333*)	0	0	0	0	$0	–
2003	0	M	0	0	$0	–	Turf(303*)	0	0	0	0	$0	–
Crc	2	0	1	0	$4,600	55	Dst(264)	0	0	0	0	$0	–

7Aug04-10Crc fst 7f :22^{3} :47^{1} 1:14^{1} 1:28^{2} Md Sp Wt 29k 55 3 3½ 1½ 13½ 2nk Boulanger G L118 b *1.50 74– 19 Coyoteshighstcll118nk IronWll1184¼ SimplySupr1183¾ Poor st, just failed 8
17Jly04-10Crc fst 6f :22^{4} :47^{2} 1:00 1:13^{2} Md Sp Wt 29k 49 5 63¼ 5^{2} 4^{6} 49¾ Boulanger G L118 b 3.00 72– 18 CptinLindsy118^{3} LermTime1185¾ MgicAlphbt118^{1} Slow st, bumped bkstr 8
Disqualified and placed 7th
WORKS: Aug1 Crc 4f fst :48^{3} Bg 5/54 Jly6 Crc 5f gd 1:02^{2} Bg 3/17 Jun30 Crc 4f fst :49^{1} B 4/33 Jun22 Crc 4f gd :50^{2} Bg 11/31 Jun15 Crc 4f fst :50^{1} Bg 13/42 Jun7 Crc 4f fst :50^{2} B 19/29
TRAINER: 2YO(58 .14 $1.55) Dirt(182 .13 $1.62) Sprint(119 .11 $0.95) MdnSpWt(22 .09 $1.69)

3 Stormy Thrill Own: Sally & Macy Pike
Blue Red, Red P On White Diamond, Red
CAMEJO O (66 3 1 8 .05) 2004: (77 3 .04)
B. c. 2 (Mar) OBSJUN04 $19,000
Sire: Stormy Atlantic (Storm Cat) $12,500
Dam: License to Thrill (Unzipped)
Br: Horses of Course Inc (Fla)
Tr: Warren Fred G(103 17 13 13 .17) 2004:(169 23 .14)
L 118

Life	1	M	0	0	$170	37	D.Fst	1	0	0	0	$170	37
2004	1	M	0	0	$170	37	Wet(373)	0	0	0	0	$0	–
2003	0	M	0	0	$0	–	Turf(278)	0	0	0	0	$0	–
Crc	1	0	0	0	$170	37	Dst(403)	1	0	0	0	$170	37

31Jly04- 3Crc fst 5½f :23 :47^{3} 1:00^{3} 1:07^{3} Md 40000(40-35) 37 8 73½ 5^{5} 7^{10} 79¾ Judice J C L118 7.80 73– 19 ModestGuy118no Rocktightyight1181¼ HillbillyBndit1113¼ 4 wide, faltered 8
WORKS: Aug18 Crc 4f fst :50^{1} B 13/24 Aug12 Crc 5f fst 1:03^{4} B 5/9 Jly24 Crc 5f fst 1:04^{4} Bg 34/42 ●Jly16 Crc 4f fst :48^{3} H 1/29 Jly11 Crc 4f fst :50^{4} B 15/31 Jly2 Crc 4f fst :50^{4} B 13/20
TRAINER: 2ndStart(21 .10 $0.75) 2YO(110 .09 $1.06) Dirt(450 .10 $1.56) Sprint(302 .10 $1.45) MdnSpWt(38 .11 $0.77)

4 Ice Skating Own: Michael H Sherman
Yellow Turquoise, Turquoise 'S' On Pink Ball
LOPEZ J E (185 21 19 25 .11) 2004: (358 40 .11)
B. g. 2 (Feb)
Sire: Fortunate Prospect (Northern Prospect) $5,000
Dam: Over Ice (Desert Wine)
Br: Farnsworth Farms (Fla)
Tr: Salinas Angel(105 13 12 15 .12) 2004:(158 16 .10)
118

Life	1	M	0	0	$850	51	D.Fst	1	0	0	0	$850	51
2004	1	M	0	0	$850	51	Wet(330)	0	0	0	0	$0	–
2003	0	M	0	0	$0	–	Turf(168)	0	0	0	0	$0	–
Crc	1	0	0	0	$850	51	Dst(351)	1	0	0	0	$850	51

31Jly04- 3Crc fst 5½f :23 :47^{3} 1:00^{3} 1:07^{3} Md 40000(40-35) 51 2 2½ 3½ 23½ 44½ Lopez J E 118 b *1.00e 78– 19 ModstGuy118no Rocktightyight1181¼ HillbllyBndt1113¼ Chased, gave way 8
WORKS: Aug12 Crc 3f fst :38^{4} B 12/15 Jly29 Crc 3f sly :37 B 7/18 Jly19 Crc 4f fst :49^{1} Bg 10/23 Jly16 Crc 4f fst :50^{1} B 15/29 Jly12 Crc 3f fst :38 Bg 10/13 Jly1 Crc 3f fst :37^{2} B 6/11
TRAINER: 2ndStart(69 .19 $1.32) 2YO(297 .14 $1.50) Dirt(479 .14 $1.47) Sprint(435 .15 $1.54) MdnSpWt(31 .10 $4.94)

5 Silly Savage Own: Jacks or Better Farm Inc
Green Purple, Gold Dots, Gold Cap
HOMEISTER R B JR (313 38 41 49 .12) 2004: (426 51 .12)
Ch. c. 2 (Mar)
Sire: Hunting Hard (Seeking the Gold) $1,500
Dam: Ej's Honey (Honey Jay)
Br: Jacks or Better Farm Inc (Fla)
Tr: Hatchett James(66 9 8 5 .14) 2004:(91 9 .10)
(L) 118

Life	0	M	0	0	$0	–	D.Fst	0	0	0	0	$0	–
2004	0	M	0	0	$0	–	Wet(261)	0	0	0	0	$0	–
2003	0	M	0	0	$0	–	Turf(216)	0	0	0	0	$0	–
Crc	0	0	0	0	$0	–	Dst(290)	0	0	0	0	$0	–

WORKS: Aug14 NJF 4f fst :50^{1} B 1/1 Aug7 NJF 5f fst 1:03^{2} B 4/4 Jly16 Crc 4f fst :53^{3} Bg 29/29 Jly9 Crc 5f fst 1:05^{3} B 11/14 Jun26 Crc 5f fst 1:06^{3} Bg 33/33
TRAINER: 1stStart(48 .10 $0.63) 1stLasix(7 .00 $0.00) 2YO(99 .14 $1.20) Dirt(284 .15 $1.39) Sprint(176 .15 $1.24) MdnSpWt(83 .14 $1.56)

6 Its All Good Babe Own: Miguel A Nieves
Black Fuchsia & Hunter Green, Hunter Green Cap
TORIBIO A JR (300 40 40 30 .13) 2004: (482 53 .11)
Ch. f. 2 (Apr) OBSMAR04 $37,000
Sire: Honor Grades (Danzig) $15,000
Dam: Princess Clef (His Majesty)
Br: Bradyleigh Farms Inc (Ky)
Tr: Catanese Joseph C III(24 3 2 2 .12) 2004:(39 4 .10)
(L) 118

Life	0	M	0	0	$0	–	D.Fst	0	0	0	0	$0	–
2004	0	M	0	0	$0	–	Wet(348)	0	0	0	0	$0	–
2003	0	M	0	0	$0	–	Turf(284)	0	0	0	0	$0	–
Crc	0	0	0	0	$0	–	Dst(323)	0	0	0	0	$0	–

WORKS: Aug15 Crc 4f fst :50 Bg 9/32 Aug8 Crc 4f fst :49^{4} Bg 14/37
TRAINER: 1stStart(22 .27 $2.15) 1stLasix(1 1.00 $12.00) 2YO(47 .23 $1.79) Dirt(98 .16 $1.39) Sprint(80 .15 $1.33) MdnSpWt(22 .32 $2.42)

7 Gallant Bandit Own: K K & V D Jayaraman
Orange Blue, White T On Red Ball, Blue Cap
TORIBIO A R (296 54 43 42 .18) 2004: (296 54 .18)
Ch. c. 2 (Mar)
Sire: Time Bandit (Time for a Change) $1,500
Dam: Dearest Juliet (Lyphard's Ridge)
Br: Dr K K Jayaraman & Dr Vilasini Jayaraman (Fla)
Tr: White William P(123 37 20 18 .30) 2004:(214 48 .22)
(L) 118

Life	0	M	0	0	$0	–	D.Fst	0	0	0	0	$0	–
2004	0	M	0	0	$0	–	Wet(306*)	0	0	0	0	$0	–
2003	0	M	0	0	$0	–	Turf(215*)	0	0	0	0	$0	–
Crc	0	0	0	0	$0	–	Dst(398)	0	0	0	0	$0	–

WORKS: Aug16 Crc 5f fst 1:03 Bg 7/18 Aug9 Crc 5f fst 1:03 Bg 4/14 Aug3 Crc 4f gd :49^{3} B(d)g 5/35 Jly25 Crc 4f fst :50^{3} Bg 42/71 Jly20 Crc 3f gd :39 Bg 23/25 Jly10 Crc 4f fst :52 B 56/59
Jly4 Crc 3f fst :37^{3} Bg 11/22 Jun28 Crc 3f fst :39^{3} B 12/14 Jun23 Crc 3f fst :39 B 16/20 Apr23 Crc 3f fst :38^{4} Bg 14/26 Apr16 Crc 3f fst :37^{2} Bg 10/19 Apr10 Crc 3f fst :37 Bg 8/40
TRAINER: 1stStart(94 .21 $2.40) 1stLasix(45 .36 $1.97) 2YO(127 .30 $2.36) Dirt(468 .22 $1.62) Sprint(321 .24 $1.77) MdnSpWt(129 .22 $1.83)

8 Here Comes the Man Own: Vinery Stables
Pink Green, White Yoke, Green Stripes On
CASTRO E (475 92 84 80 .19) 2004: (850 126 .15)
Dk. b or br c. 2 (Apr) OBSAUG03 $105,000
Sire: Straight Man (Saint Ballado) $6,000
Dam: Aberdeen Gate (Known Fact)
Br: Sugar Knoll Farm (Fla)
Tr: Plesa Edward Jr(127 24 22 18 .19) 2004:(226 36 .16)
118

Life	0	M	0	0	$0	–	D.Fst	0	0	0	0	$0	–
2004	0	M	0	0	$0	–	Wet(360*)	0	0	0	0	$0	–
2003	0	M	0	0	$0	–	Turf(258)	0	0	0	0	$0	–
Crc	0	0	0	0	$0	–	Dst(351)	0	0	0	0	$0	–

WORKS: Aug10 Crc 5f fst 1:03 B 5/17 Jly24 Crc 4f fst :49 B 5/53 Jly17 Crc 4f gd :50 B 22/65 Jly9 Crc 4f fst :50 B 10/26
TRAINER: 1stStart(67 .16 $2.52) 2YO(172 .16 $1.62) Dirt(541 .17 $1.68) Sprint(438 .18 $1.79) MdnSpWt(116 .16 $1.60)

marked down his 47 1/5 half-mile time for his last race, and was ready to compare it to any other horse that had shown speed (within one length of the lead at the pace call) in at least 50 percent of its races. There wasn't really any need. Stormy Thrill couldn't keep up in his debut. Ice Skating showed stalking speed against claimers, but was now stepping up to face maiden special weights. Its All Good Babe and Here Comes the Man both showed slow works.

The only runner that scared me a bit was Gallant Bandit. The son of Time Bandit was trained by top debut conditioner William White, and the August 3 workout told me that he had some speed. The workout rankings in *Daily Racing Form* can be very helpful assessing debut runners. I usually put a circle around workouts that are in the top 17 percent of the day (1-6, 2-12, 3-18, etc.). Gallant Bandit's workout was the fifth of 35 workouts at four furlongs at Calder on August 3. Unfortunately, his other works didn't show the same zip. He could beat me, but Iron Wall looked like the horse in multi-race wagers (he would be too short to play to win).

NINTH RACE
Calder
AUGUST 21, 2004

5½ FURLONGS. (1.04¹) MAIDEN SPECIAL WEIGHT . Purse $29,000 (includes $6,000 FOA – Florida Owners Awards) FOR MAIDENS, TWO YEAR OLDS. Weight, 118 lbs.

Value of Race: $29,000 Winner $19,000; second $4,600; third $2,990; fourth $1,150; fifth $230; sixth $230. Mutuel Pool $96,166.00 Exacta Pool $84,003.00 Trifecta Pool $64,945.00 Superfecta Pool $29,826.00

Last Raced	Horse	M/Eqt.	A.	Wt	PP	St	¼	¾	Str	Fin	Jockey	Odds $1
7Aug04 ¹⁰Crc²	Iron Wall	L b	2	118	1	3	1¹	1²	1⁴	1⁵	Boulanger G	1.00
31Jly04 ³Crc⁷	Stormy Thrill	L	2	118	2	5	5¹	4²	2¹	2⁶	Camejo O	27.40
	Gallant Bandit	L b	2	118	5	1	6	6	5²½	3ⁿᵒ	Toribio A R	2.10
	Here ComestheMan		2	118	6	4	3¹½	2¹½	3¹½	4⁴¾	Castro E	5.80
31Jly04 ³Crc⁴	Ice Skating	b	2	118	3	2	2½	3¹½	4²	5³½	Lopez J E	5.80
	Its All Good Babe	L b	2	118	4	6	4²	5²	6	6	Toribio A Jr	12.00

OFF AT 4:34 Start Good . Won ridden out. Track fast.

TIME :22³, :46², :59, 1:05³ (:22.67, :46.52, :59.05, 1:05.75)

$2 Mutuel Prices:

2 – IRON WALL	4.00	2.80	2.20
3 – STORMY THRILL		11.60	4.20
7 – GALLANT BANDIT			2.80

$2 EXACTA 2–3 PAID $40.40 $2 TRIFECTA 2–3–7 PAID $132.80
$2 SUPERFECTA 2–3–7–8 PAID $439.80

Dk. b or br. c, (Apr), by Western Borders – Syrian Tricks , by Clever Trick . Trainer McDonald Michael K. Bred by Lucy de Yarhi (Fla).

IRON WALL set the pace along the inside into the stretch, then drew off under a hand ride. STORMY THRILL reserved early, angled out on the turn and closed to prove second best. GALLANT BANDIT outrun early, passed tired rivals to be up for the show. HERE COMES THE MAN chased the pace around the turn and tired. ICE SKATING chased the pace along the inside, then faltered in the drive. ITS ALL GOOD BABE was through early.

Owners– 1, Half Moon Racing Stable and Raffa Janet; 2, Pike Sally and Macy; 3, Jayaraman Kalarikkal K and Vilasini D; 4, Vinery Stables; 5, Sherman Michael H; 6, Nieves Miguel A

Trainers– 1, McDonald Michael K; 2, Warren Fred G; 3, White William P; 4, Plesa Edward Jr; 5, Salinas Angel; 6, Catanese Joseph C III

Scratched– Rascal Ralph , Silly Savage

If a horse is wearing blinkers for the first time, I usually give him a + 25 percent speed rating. If a horse is stretching out a quarter of a mile or more, I give him a +25 percent speed rating. Runners removing blinkers and horses turning back a quarter of a mile or more get a –25 percent. When there are several horses that show the magic 50 percent or higher speed number, I try to narrow them down by the fractional calls. Now, this is risky business. What if the track was extremely fast that day? What if it was dead? That would certainly affect the fractional times of races. I understand that, and reluctantly accept that the theory could be flawed. For newcomers to the pace game, however, I think it is a simple yet effective way of finding runners that will be on or near the lead.

Storied Cat looked like a short-priced single in Race 5 at Saratoga on August 21, 2004.

5 Saratoga 6 Furlongs (1:08) **Md Sp Wt 45k** Purse $45,000 (UP TO $8,550 NYSBFOA) For Maidens, Two Year Olds. Weight, 118 lbs.

1 Interpatation
Own: Mavorah Elliot
Black, White Blocks, Black Cap
VELASQUEZ C (94 12 18 10 .13) 2004: (945 138 .15)

2 Better Than Bonds
Own: Abbo Robert D
Fuchsia Pink, Orange Chevrons, Orange
MIGLIORE R (89 13 10 10 .15) 2004: (594 100 .17)

3 Susanne's Honor
Own: RC Hill Stable
Mistral Blue, Titanium 'Rch,' Titanium
DOMINGUEZ R A (17 5 3 2 .29) 2004: (890 241 .27)

4 Maharishi
Own: Mount Joy Stables
Forest Green, Gold Diamond, Gold
ALBARADO R J (86 7 8 9 .08) 2004: (921 158 .17)

5 Duty Yeoman
Own: Kenneth L and Sarah K Ramsey
White, Red 'R,' Red Sleeves, White Hoop
PRADO E S (126 19 25 18 .15) 2004: (987 197 .20)

6 Remuneration
Own: Dogwood Stable
Green, Yellow Dots And Collar, Yellow
VELAZQUEZ J R (121 33 17 12 .27) 2004: (865 216 .25)

7 Datsyuk
Own: Reddam J Paul
White, Purple Hoop, Purple Sleeves
FRAGOSO P (86 7 12 10 .08) 2004: (646 102 .16)

(45.3)

8 Storied Cat
Own: Atkins Clinton C Atkins Susan A
Pink White, Red Saratoga Emblem And Cap
BAILEY J D (90 19 14 16 .21) 2004: (535 122 .23)

B. c. 2 (Mar) FTSAUG03 $400,000
Sire: Tale of the Cat (Storm Cat) $16,518
Dam: Celestial Crown (Holy Bull)
Br: Third Street Partners (Ky)
Tr: Lukas D Wayne(46 3 9 6 .07) 2004:(377 41 .11)

L 118

Life	2	M	2	0	$18,080	80	D.Fst	2	0	2	0	$18,080	80
2004	2	M	2	0	$18,080	80	Wet(383)	0	0	0	0	$0	-
2003	0	M	0	0	$0	-	Turf(290)	0	0	0	0	$0	-
Sar	1	0	1	0	$9,000	80	Dst(413)	0	0	0	0	$0	-

4Aug04-3Sar fst 5f :22^{1} :45^{3} :58^{3} Md Sp Wt 45k **80** 8 8 4$^{\frac{3}{4}}$ 2^{hd} 2^{hd} 2^{hd} Bailey J D L118 *.80 94- 10 Upscaled118^{hd} Storied Cat118^{9} Tani Maru118$^{1\frac{1}{2}}$ Vied outside, gamely 8
23Jun04-4CD fst 4½f :22^{4} :45^{3} :51^{3} Md Sp Wt 44k **74** 6 5 2½ 2^{2} 2^{1} Day P 119 3.40 96- 10 Toliver119^{1} Storied Cat119$^{2\frac{1}{4}}$ *More Than Wild*119$^{1\frac{1}{2}}$ Chased 4w,2ndbest 8
WORKS: ●Aug12 Sar tr.t 4f fst :48^{2} B *1/8* ●Jly29 Sar tr.t 4f my :48 B *1/9* ●Jly19 CD 5f fst :59^{4} B *1/30* Jly10 CD 5f fst 1:02^{1} B *9/11* ●Jly1 CD 4f fst :46^{4} B *1/30* Jun15 CD 4f fst :47^{3} B *4/27*
TRAINER: 2YO(297 .12 $1.01) Dirt(905 .11 $1.13) Sprint(632 .11 $1.01) MdnSpWt(451 .11 $0.95)

---

9 Silver Vista
Own: Fulton Stan E
Turqse Lime Green, Blue Ball, White 'F,' Green
DAY P (48 8 9 5 .17) 2004: (522 111 .21)

Dk. b or br c. 2 (Jan) KEESEP03 $150,000
Sire: Silver Deputy (Deputy Minister) $40,000
Dam: Canadian Vista (St. Jovite)
Br: Dell Ridge Farm (Ky)
Tr: Walden W Elliott(13 0 0 1 .00) 2004:(117 21 .18)

Ⓛ 118

Life	0	M	0	0	$0	-	D.Fst	0	0	0	0	$0	-
2004	0	M	0	0	$0	-	Wet(338)	0	0	0	0	$0	-
2003	0	M	0	0	$0	-	Turf(271)	0	0	0	0	$0	-
Sar	0	0	0	0	$0	-	Dst(335)	0	0	0	0	$0	-

WORKS: Aug18 Sar tr.t 4f fst :51 B *24/31* Aug11 Sar 5f fst 1:03^{2} B *17/30* Aug6 Sar tr.t 5f fst 1:05 B *9/10* ●Jly30 Sar 4f fst :46^{3} Hg *1/151* Jly26 Sar 3f fst :37 Bg *7/15* Jly21 Sar 4f fst :50^{2} B *20/29* Jly9 CD 4f fst :49^{1} B *20/41* Jly1 CD 3f fst :38^{1} B *14/18* Jun11 CD 4f fst :49 B *8/35* Jun4 CD 3f fst :38^{2} B *12/13* May29 CD 3f fst :38^{2} B *12/13*
TRAINER: 1stStart(47 .09 $2.11) 1stLasix(11 .09 $0.25) 2YO(58 .19 $2.18) Dirt(271 .23 $1.76) Sprint(138 .24 $2.09) MdnSpWt(110 .22 $2.19)

---

10 Tampa's Big City
Own: Dee Conway and Fam Stable Cornacchia
Purple Bright Green, Black Shamrock, Black Hoop
SELLERS S J (58 7 5 5 .12) 2004: (640 142 .22)

Dk. b or br c. 2 (Apr) KEESEP03 $125,000
Sire: Old Trieste (A.P. Indy) $25,000
Dam: Coral Sea (Rubiano)
Br: W S Farish EJ Hudson Jr Irrevocable Trust et a (Ky)
Tr: Zito Nicholas P(32 5 3 2 .16) 2004:(291 47 .16)

Ⓛ 118

Life	0	M	0	0	$0	-	D.Fst	0	0	0	0	$0	-
2004	0	M	0	0	$0	-	Wet(385)	0	0	0	0	$0	-
2003	0	M	0	0	$0	-	Turf(235)	0	0	0	0	$0	-
Sar	0	0	0	0	$0	-	Dst(331)	0	0	0	0	$0	-

WORKS: Aug7 Bel 5f fst 1:02^{2} Bg *13/25* Jly31 Bel 5f fst 1:03^{1} B *17/21* Jly23 Bel 4f fst :48 B *4/50* Jly16 Bel 5f fst 1:02 B *26/46* Jly1 Bel 4f fst :51 B *24/28* Jun24 Bel 4f fst :52^{3} B *47/48* May30 Bel 3f fst :38 B *28/43*
TRAINER: 1stStart(72 .12 $2.75) 1stLasix(14 .29 $3.94) 2YO(119 .22 $3.06) Dirt(727 .16 $2.12) Sprint(345 .16 $2.25) MdnSpWt(252 .15 $2.23)

FIFTH RACE
Saratoga
AUGUST 21, 2004

6 FURLONGS. (1.08) MAIDEN SPECIAL WEIGHT . Purse $45,000 (UP TO $8,550 NYSBFOA) FOR MAIDENS, TWO YEAR OLDS. Weight, 118 lbs.

Value of Race: $45,000 Winner $27,000; second $9,000; third $4,500; fourth $2,250; fifth $1,350; sixth $300; seventh $300; eighth $300. Mutuel Pool $663,643.00 Exacta Pool $619,074.00 Trifecta Pool $420,811.00

Last Raced	Horse	M/Eqt.	A.	Wt	PP	St	¼	½	Str	Fin	Jockey	Odds $1
4Aug04 ^{3}Sar^{2}	Storied Cat	L	2	118	6	1	1^{1}	1^{1}	1$^{1\frac{1}{2}}$	1$^{3\frac{1}{4}}$	Bailey J D	0.85
	Remuneration	L	2	118	4	3	2^{hd}	2$^{1\frac{1}{2}}$	2^{2}	2$^{\frac{1}{2}}$	Velazquez J R	4.90
28Jly04 ^{5}Sar^{4}	Datsyuk	L	2	118	5	2	5$^{1\frac{1}{2}}$	3$^{1\frac{1}{2}}$	3^{5}	3$^{6\frac{1}{4}}$	Fragoso P	6.70
	Susanne's Honor	L b	2	118	2	8	8	7$^{2\frac{1}{2}}$	6^{1}	4^{1}	Dominguez R A	18.10
	Silver Vista	L	2	118	7	7	6$^{\frac{1}{2}}$	6^{hd}	7$^{3\frac{1}{2}}$	5$^{1\frac{1}{4}}$	Day P	5.30
	Better Than Bonds	b	2	118	1	6	4$^{\frac{1}{2}}$	5^{6}	5$^{\frac{1}{2}}$	6$^{3\frac{1}{4}}$	Migliore R	31.75
	Maharishi	L b	2	118	3	4	3$^{5\frac{1}{2}}$	4$^{1\frac{1}{2}}$	4$^{1\frac{1}{2}}$	7$^{1\frac{1}{2}}$	Albarado R J	17.90
	Tampa's Big City	L	2	118	8	5	7^{8}	8	8	8	Sellers S J	27.75

OFF AT 3:09 Start Good . Won driving. Track sloppy.
TIME :22^{2}, :45^{4}, :58, 1:10^{4} (:22.42, :45.90, :58.10, 1:10.98)

$2 Mutuel Prices:

8 – STORIED CAT	3.70	2.70	2.30
6 – REMUNERATION		3.70	2.80
7 – DATSYUK			2.90

$2 EXACTA 8–6 PAID $15.20 $2 TRIFECTA 8–6–7 PAID $33.00

B. c, (Mar), by Tale of the Cat – Celestial Crown , by Holy Bull . Trainer Lukas D Wayne. Bred by Third Street Partners (Ky).

STORIED CAT stumbled at the start, moved up swiftly to gain a clear early advantage, set the pace in hand to the turn, shook off REMUNERATION to get clear in upper stretch, drifted out in midstretch then drew away under strong left hand urging. REMUNERATION pressed the pace outside the winner into upper stretch but was no match for that one while holding well for the place. DATSYUK bumped at the start, raced in the middle of the pack along the backstretch, launched a bid four wide to reach contention on the turn and finished willingly to gain a share. SUSANNE'S HONOR raced far back while trailing to the then then finished with interest along the inside. SILVER VISTA failed to mount a serious rally while three wide. BETTER THAN BONDS raced in the middle of the pack while three wide, angled four wide leaving the turn then lacked a strong closing bid. MAHARISHI bobbled after the start, chased the leaders along the rail to the top of the stretch and steadily tired thereafter. TAMPA'S BIG CITY never reached contention while racing four wide throughout.

Owners– 1, Atkins Clinton C and Susan A; 2, Dogwood Stable; 3, Reddam J Paul; 4, RC Hill Stable; 5, Fulton Stan E; 6, Abbo Robert D; 7, Mount Joy Stables Inc; 8, Conway Dee Family Stable Cornacchia Joseph M and Evans Bruce

Trainers– 1, Lukas D Wayne; 2, Pletcher Todd A; 3, Hennig Mark; 4, Weaver George; 5, Walden W Elliott; 6, Reinacher Robert Jr; 7, Stewart Dallas; 8, Zito Nicholas P

Scratched– Interpatation , Duty Yeoman

He had shown speed in both of his starts, and although it looked like he had a bit of an up-and-down stride, I couldn't avoid his pace advantage, the dearth of speed shown by his opponents, and his 80 Beyer Speed Figure. Interpatation looked like he might have some speed, as over 50 percent of his workouts were in the upper echelon of ranked morning drills. Once Interpatation scratched, I was confident that Storied Cat could handle the rest.

Finding the speed horses is a very important part in the handicapping process. Those interested in pursuing it further should consider the more sophisticated pace analysis of such handicappers as Tom Brohamer and James Quinn. Hopefully, novice handicappers will find this quick-and-dirty method helpful.

5

HOW BIG IS THAT FIG?
Speed Figures vs. Visual Impressions; Firsters vs. Experienced Maidens; Know Thy Beyer Par Times

*T*HE DATE WAS Friday, July 27, 1999. I visited my friend Ken Band, one of the best harness handicappers I know. As he pored over torts and *"res ipsa loquitur"* in preparation for the bar exam, I analyzed the next day's feature race at Saratoga. The Schuylerville looked like a tough race on paper so I threw him the past performances and asked his opinion. He stared at the page for a few minutes, tossed back the paper, and said, "Circle of Life. Can't beat that 91 Beyer."

It made sense. Circle of Life had won a maiden race by over eight lengths at Belmont for Todd Pletcher and Jerry Bailey. That Beyer dwarfed anything that her six Schuylerville rivals had earned in their previous races. You would think that she had at least 10 points of improvement in the tank, and she wasn't asked for her best when she won her maiden race. Something didn't seem right, however. It just looked too simple. Circle of Life had made the lead so easily in her debut that she didn't have to face any sort of pace pressure. There looked to be a lot of speed in the Schuylerville. What would happen if she got hooked early? Would she be able to run back to that 91 Beyer? What if she had to rate and pass horses? Who would benefit if she got involved in a speed duel?

Gilded Diablo had showed good speed in her previous race, but tired badly in the stretch, and now had to stretch out in distance. She figured to keep Circle of Life busy on the front end. Regally Appealing was impressive earning an 85 Beyer in her debut, but she didn't run too hard to the pace call that day, and would have to go much faster in this spot. Cecilia's Crown was third behind Chilukki in her last start at Churchill Downs, but was 34-1 in that race, and looked exhausted in the last furlong. Finder's Fee seemed interesting. She had run down Gilded Diablo to win the Astoria at Belmont, and figured to appreciate the added distance. I'm infatuated with

NINTH RACE
Saratoga
JULY 28, 1999

6 FURLONGS. (1.08) SCHUYLERVILLE S. Grade II. Purse $100,000 (Up to $19,400 NYSBFOA) FOR FILLIES TWO YEARS OLD. By subscription of $100 each, which should accompany the nomination; $500 to pass the entry box; $500 to start, with $100,000 added. The added money and all fees to be divided 60% to the winner, 20% to second, 11% to third, 6% to fourth and 3% to fifth. 122 lbs. Non-winners of $30,000 twice allowed 3 lbs.; $30,000, 5 lbs.; a race other than claiming, 8 lbs. Trophies will be presented to the winning ownerphies will be presented to the winning owner,trainer and jockey.Closed Saturday, July 17 with 25 nominations.

Value of Race: $109,500 Winner $65,700; second $21,900; third $12,045; fourth $6,570; fifth $3,285. Mutuel Pool $518,291.00 Exacta Pool $466,012.00 Trifecta Pool $328,158.00

Last Raced	Horse	M/Eqt.	A.	Wt	PP	St	¼	½	Str	Fin	Jockey	Odds $1
5Jly99 ³Hol¹	Magicalmysterycat	L b	2	122	6	1	2²	1hd	1hd	1¾	Day P	3.60
8Jly99 ⁶Bel¹	Circle of Life		2	114	3	6	4³	3²	32½	2no	Bailey J D	1.40
1Jly99 ²Bel¹	Regally Appealing		2	114	2	4	1hd	2hd	2¹	3¹	Prado E S	7.30
2Jly99 ⁸Bel¹	Finder's Fee		2	119	5	5	65½	52½	4²	46	Smith M E	3.30
10Jly99 ⁶EIP²	Silk Sails		2	114	7	2	7	7	66	52¾	Chavez J F	34.75
26Jun99 ⁷CD³	Cecilia's Crown		2	114	4	7	5³	41½	52½	620½	Sellers S J	11.10
2Jly99 ⁸Bel³	Gilded Diablo		2	119	1	3	3hd	6hd	7	7	Velazquez J R	10.70

OFF AT 5:15 Start Good For All But. Won . Track fast.
TIME :21³, :45, :57³, 1:10⁴ (:21.71, :45.19, :57.65, 1:10.91)

$2 Mutuel Prices:	6 – MAGICALMYSTERYCAT	9.20	3.90	3.30
	3 – CIRCLE OF LIFE		3.30	2.60
	2 – REGALLY APPEALING			4.60

$2 EXACTA 6–3 PAID $30.60 $2 TRIFECTA 6–3–5 PAID $146.50

Ch. m, (Feb), by Storm Cat – Nanneri, by Valid Appeal. Trainer Lukas D Wayne. Bred by Katsuhiko Hirai (Ky).

MAGICALMYSTERYCAT flashed good speed from the outside, gained a short lead turning for home, dug in resolutely in the stretch and prevailed under a steady drive. CIRCLE OF LIFE, close up early, put in a three wide run approaching the stretch and continued on gamely from the outside and got the nod for the place award. REGALLY APPEALING showed good speed along the rail and dug in gamely on the rail through the stretch. FINDER'S FEE, hustled along early, came wide for the drive and finished well from the outside. SILK SAILS, outrun early, came wide into the stretch but had no response when roused. CECILIA'S CROWN, outrun early, put in an inside run on the turn but had nothing left for the stretch drive. GILDED DIABLO chased the pace on the rail and tired badly in the stretch.

Owners– 1, Padua Stables and Iracane Joseph; 2, Tabor Michael B; 3, Heiligbrodt Racing Stable; 4, Phipps Ogden; 5, McKee Stables Inc; 6, Polydoros Nick Abt Martin Derybowski Greg and McDermott Tom; 7, Diamond A Racing Corporation

Trainers– 1, Lukas D Wayne; 2, Pletcher Todd A; 3, Kimmel John C; 4, McGaughey III Claude R; 5, Romans Dale; 6, Stall Albert M Jr; 7, Hennig Mark

Scratched– Gilded Diablo (02Jul99 ⁸Bel³), Regally Appealing (01Jul99 ²Bel¹), Circle of Life (08Jul99 ⁶Bel¹), Cecilia's Crown (26Jun99 ⁷CD ³), Finder's Fee (02Jul99 ⁸Bel¹), Magicalmysterycat (05Jul99 ³Hol¹), Silk Sails (10Jul99 ⁶EIP²)

speed runners in these sprint stakes, however, and I wasn't sure if Finder's Fee could catch some quality speed horses in the stretch. Silk Sails failed to win an allowance race at Ellis Park in her last start.

Of all the other runners, Magicalmysterycat was the most visually impressive. She was an undefeated 3 for 3 in Southern California, and had overcome pace pressure to win every time. She had veered in at the start and drifted out a bit in the stretch in her last race. Usually I would penalize horses for drifting out, but Magicalmysterycat was getting blinkers for the first time in the Schuylerville, and she figured to show better speed and focus with her new eyewear. But what about the Beyers? Her last three figures were 73, 77, and 85. Could she run faster? Visually, she did everything well despite difficult pace scenarios. At 7-2 odds, she seemed worth the risk.

While horses with huge debut Beyers look impressive on paper, they are often terrible bets in their next races. Babies are supposed to improve their speed figures with time. If a 2-year-old runs a 100 Beyer in the debut, what should a handicapper expect in the next start? A 110? A 115? Let's be realistic. Most of these huge Beyer debut winners have easy pace scenarios, and never face any pressure. When they step up in class, the circumstances are much different. Let's look at Tugger.

Tugger
Own: Anstu Stables Inc

B. m. 5 (Mar)
Sire: Twining (Forty Niner) $11,562
Dam: Pushy (Assert*1re)
Br: Dr. Dan White (Ky)
Tr: Pletcher Todd A(0 0 0 0 .00) 2004:(838 215 .26)

Life	28	8	5	1	$414,920	111		D.Fst	21	5	4	0	$304,630	111
2002	10	1	2	0	$71,950	94		Wet(375)	5	3	1	0	$104,400	101
2001	10	4	1	1	$208,870	103		Turf(250)	2	0	0	1	$5,890	90
	0	0	0	0	$0	–		Dst①(315)	0	0	0	0	$0	–

Tugger made her debut in a 10-horse maiden special at Gulfstream for Todd Pletcher. She moved up to engage the leader after a half-mile in a quick 45³/₅, and drew off to an impressive 11¹/₂-length win. The Beyer was simply spectacular. A 111 for a debuting 3-year-old filly! Many handicappers saw the winning margin coupled with the huge Beyer and felt that they had witnessed the next coming of Ruffian. Not surprisingly, Tugger was sent off at 2-5 for her next start, a Keeneland allowance event for nonwinners of a race other than maiden, claiming, or starter.

After being bumped just a bit at the start from the far-outside post position, Tugger moved comfortably up into second after a half in 44²/₅. Note that the pace was much faster than what Tugger experienced in her debut at Gulfstream. Try as she might, Tugger couldn't reel in Emily's Angel, a filly that had earned a meager 40 Beyer in her previous start, but owned the important experience advantage against winners.

Tugger went on to a nice little career, becoming a multiple stakes winner of $414,920. After her debut, however, she only broke the 100 Beyer mark three times in her next 27 starts, and never approached the 111 Beyer of her debut again.

When babies run huge numbers in their career debuts, don't rely on the speed figure alone. Conversely, when young horses run average numbers in their debuts, don't count them out in subsequent outings. They have plenty of improvement left.

FIRSTERS VS. EXPERIENCED MAIDENS

When does an experienced runner have a significant edge over the first-time starters? Let's take a look at Storm Legacy. The second race at Belmont on June 27, 2004, initially seemed like a pretty competitive affair. Morph, a $150,000 yearling purchase by juvenile champion and Horse of the Year Favorite Trick, showed three bullet workouts, and was going out for a potent trainer-jockey combination.

All for Love, a half-brother to a $207,000 earner by the good debut sire Not For Love, was making his first start and was trained by the always dangerous Allen Jerkens. Parade Out Front had earned a 62 Beyer Speed Figure in his debut, and was getting Lasix for the first time. Gainango had hit the board in his last seven starts with Beyers between 68 and 80, and had retained the services of Jerry Bailey.

Then there was Storm Legacy. The son of Storm Cat hadn't run in over two months, but he had earned an 83 Beyer in his last start at Keeneland. Anytime I see a maiden with an 80 or higher Beyer that didn't earn the figure in California, I am impressed. That number is easily better than par for most maiden events at Belmont.

SECOND RACE	6 FURLONGS. (1.07³) MAIDEN SPECIAL WEIGHT . Purse $43,000 (UP TO $8,170 NYSBFOA) FOR
Belmont	MAIDENS, THREE YEAR OLDS AND UPWARD. Three Year Olds, 118 lbs.; Older, 124 lbs.

JUNE 27, 2004

Value of Race: $43,000 Winner $25,800; second $8,600; third $4,300; fourth $2,150; fifth $1,290; sixth $287; seventh $287; eighth $286. Mutuel Pool $320,386.00 Exacta Pool $269,060.00 Quinella Pool $27,625.00 Trifecta Pool $177,386.00

Last Raced	Horse	M/Eqt.	A.	Wt	PP	St	¼	½	Str	Fin	Jockey	Odds $1
23Apr04 ⁷Kee²	Storm Legacy	L	3	118	8	7	4½	42½	1½	15¼	Prado E S	a- 2.05
	Morph	L	3	118	1	3	1½	1hd	23½	25	Castellano J J	6.70
1Nov03 ⁶Aqu⁹	Western Territory	L b	3	118	3	2	2hd	2hd	3hd	31½	Espinoza J L	a- 2.05
	All for Love		3	118	4	4	5²	51½	52½	4½	Ganpath R	3.00
12Jun04 ⁴Bel⁶	Parade Out Front	L b	4	119	7	5	7⁶	6⁶	6⁸	5½	Jara F⁵	10.90
5May04 ⁴Bel³	Gainango	L	3	118	5	1	32½	3hd	41½	610	Bailey J D	2.55
17Sep03 ⁴Bel¹⁰	Raven Cliff Falls	L	3	118	6	6	6½	7³	7⁶	710½	Velazquez J R	9.00
	Judgement Maker	L	3	118	2	8	8	8	8	8	Day P	a- 2.05

a–Coupled: Storm Legacy and Western Territory and Judgement Maker.

OFF AT 1:33 Start Good . Won ridden out. Track fast.

TIME :22¹, :45, :56³, 1:08⁴ (:22.20, :45.03, :56.73, 1:08.80)

$2 Mutuel Prices:	1X– STORM LEGACY(a–entry)	6.10	3.40	2.70
	2 – MORPH		7.00	4.70
	1A– WESTERN TERRITORY(a–entry)	6.10	3.40	2.70

$2 EXACTA 1–2 PAID $36.40 $2 QUINELLA 1–2 PAID $20.80
$2 TRIFECTA 1–2–5 PAID $123.50

B. c, (Feb), by Storm Cat – Inca Legacy , by Saratoga Six . Trainer Zito Nicholas P. Bred by Marylou Whitney Stables & Overbrook Farm (Ky).

STORM LEGACY rated kindly during the opening stages, cruised towards the front, four wide on the turn, established command at the furlong grounds, drew off while being flashed the whip, then was given one tap of the whip when he began drifting out during the late stages. MORPH contested the early pace during the inside, quickly proved no match when the winner drew alongside in the lane but continued on with good energy to be clearly second best. WESTERN TERRITORY vied for command between rivals to the furlong marker and weakened. ALL FOR LOVE raced greenly along the inside. PARADE OUT FRONT, content to sit off the early activity during the early portion, attempted to launch a four wide rally and lacked the needed response. GAINANGO was part of the swift pace scene while three wide to upper stretch and gave way. RAVEN CLIFF FALLS, away from the gate awkwardly, raced between rivals and tired. JUDGEMENT MAKER off slowly, always trailed while saving ground.

Owners– 1, Marylou Whitney Stables and Overbrook Farm; 2, Houyhnhnm Stable; 3, Overbrook Farm; 4, Bohemia Stable; 5, Partingglass Stable; 6, Shadwell Stable; 7, Peachtree Stable; 8, Farmer Tracy

Trainers– 1, Zito Nicholas P; 2, Turner William H Jr; 3, Lukas D Wayne; 4, Jerkens H Allen; 5, Tagg Barclay; 6, Hennig Mark; 7, Pletcher Todd A; 8, Zito Nicholas P

Scratched– Togetherness , Reapply

Since Storm Legacy was lightly raced, one could easily project at least five more points of improvement. A high Beyer isn't enough, however. One has to ask how the Beyer was earned. Rifling through my back copies of *DRF Simulcast Weekly*, I noticed that front-runners had won almost all the sprint races at Keeneland on April 23. Storm Legacy chased a gate-to-wire winner throughout, against the bias. He had the speed figures, the excuse for the last race, a powerful trainer and rider, and a good outside post. The firsters took money, but could they run Storm Legacy's projected Beyer of 88? I doubted it.

Storm Legacy sat a nice trip off the pace, made the lead easily with a wide, sweeping move on the turn, and drew off to score with a whopping 99 Beyer Speed Figure.

While handicappers shouldn't rely solely on speed figures, sometimes you can't avoid picking a top Beyer runner when the number is legitimized through trip or bias handicapping. When you see those 80 or higher Beyers in maiden races on the East Coast, you can rest assured that the horse certainly fits the condition.

KNOW THY BEYER PAR TIMES

Maiden-race handicappers can be greatly helped by the presence of Beyer par times for each track in *DRF Simulcast Weekly*. By utilizing par times, a horseplayer can see if an experienced maiden towers over the field, or whether a first-time starter should be given more respect. Par times for maiden races aren't listed in *DRF Simulcast Weekly*, but an enterprising handicapper can make a solid estimation by going through the list of available conditions that a track offers.

For maiden claiming races, I like to look for the "nonwinners of two" claiming race Beyer par, and then subtract five to 10 points. For example, at Canterbury Park, the NW2 (claiming) Beyer is a 59. A 49-54 would then seem reasonable for a maiden claimer at

Canterbury. While this seems like a crude way to calculate Beyer pars, I've found it to be pretty successful at weeding out horses that don't fit the class level. Of course, if you regularly get *DRF Simulcast Weekly*, you can calculate your own Beyer pars by jotting down the winning Beyer for each level, and then find the median after collecting an acceptable amount of data. Here are some of my calculations for several tracks. Use your own judgment in finding the proper Beyers for different levels of maiden claimers as well as for statebred maiden races. You may also want to adjust for age differences.

Estimated Beyer Par Times, Dirt (Older Maidens)

Arlington
Maiden Special Weight, 71-76
Maiden Claiming, 51-56

Bay Meadows
Maiden Special Weight, 77-82
Maiden Claiming, 55-60

Calder
Maiden Special Weight, 74-79
Maiden Claiming, 53-58

Charles Town
Maiden Special Weight, 63-68
Maiden Claiming, 46-51

Delaware
Maiden Special Weight, 73-78
Maiden Claiming, 58-63

Ellis
Maiden Special Weight, 75-80
Maiden Claiming, 63-68

Emerald
Maiden Special Weight, 64-69
Maiden Claiming, 57-62

Evangeline
Maiden Special Weight, 55-60
Maiden Claiming, 45-50

Fairmount
Maiden Special Weight, 55-60
Maiden Claiming, 39-44

Finger Lakes
Maiden Special Weight, 56-61
Maiden Claiming, 40-45

Fort Erie
Maiden Special Weight, 61-66
Maiden Claiming, 50-55

Great Lakes Downs
Maiden Special Weight, 57-62
Maiden Claiming, 39-44

Hoosier
Maiden Special Weight, 66-71
Maiden Claiming, 49-54

Louisiana Downs
Maiden Special Weight, 71-76
Maiden Claiming, 56-61

Mountaineer
Maiden Special Weight, 54-59
Maiden Claiming, 42-47

Penn National
Maiden Special Weight, 55-60
Maiden Claiming, 45-50

Philadelphia
Maiden Special Weight, 68-73
Maiden Claiming, 50-55

Retama
Maiden Special Weight, 70-75
Maiden Claiming, 56-61

River Downs
Maiden Special Weight, 66-71
Maiden Claiming, 48-53

Suffolk
Maiden Special Weight, 63-68
Maiden Claiming, 43-48

Thistledown
Maiden Special Weight, 61-66
Maiden Claiming, 46-51

Woodbine
Maiden Special Weight, 75-80
Maiden Claiming, 54-59

6

WORKOUTS AND SPOTTING A STAR IN THE MAKING

I'M VERY FORTUNATE to call *Daily Racing Form* handicapper Brian Pochman a friend of mine. Not only is he one of racing's "good guys," but he is one of the best horseplayers in the world. I'll always be indebted to him, as he tipped me off to one of racing's hidden secrets: the work tab.

I had always paid attention to workouts, but really didn't know what to make of them. Was that $46^2/5$ work really faster than the $46^4/5$? What if the rider of the $46^4/5$ worker was 20 pounds heavier than the rider of the horse who went in $46^2/5$? What if the $46^4/5$ work was accomplished several paths off the rail while the $46^2/5$ runner stayed glued to the inside? Did the $46^4/5$ horse work before or after the renovation break?

Pochman always seemed to know what was going on in the tab. He wasn't clocking horses, yet he could look at the tab and give you a winner. I remember asking him how he came up with a winning firster, and he told me that the horse may have worked in company with a good runner from the same barn.

It seemed to make sense. Why do trainers work their horses in company? How do they know which horses to work together? Logically, one would think that trainers use company works to give their horses a sense of competition. They will be head and head with another rival for the majority of the work, and will get an understanding of what it feels like to be in the heat of battle.

One would think that the trainer would work horses of similar ability together. It wouldn't make sense for Fusaichi Pegasus to work in company with Zippy Chippy. Fusaichi wouldn't get anything out of the work, as he would leave Zippy in the dust after three strides. Zippy would likely get his heart broken after failing to keep up with Fusaichi.

If horses of similar ability worked together in the mornings, then perhaps we could find a live firster that was working with a horse that had already raced. I began clipping the work tabs daily and pasting them in my little marble notebook. Old-fashioned, yes. Time-consuming, absolutely. Profitable? Let's find out.

I fell in love with Medaglia d'Oro as he was finishing second in the 2002 Belmont Stakes. He dueled throughout the 12-furlong classic with War Emblem and company, and was still battling it out to the wire. I turned to DRF handicapper Paul Malecki and said, "That's the best 3-year-old in the country."

Paul, my first friend in the racing business, and a fantastic handicapper, was surprised. "Sarava?"

"No! Medaglia d'Oro."

"You feeling okay?"

I wasn't hallucinating. I felt that he was the best 3-year-old, if not the best horse in the country. I couldn't wait until he ran next. Medaglia didn't disappoint. He won the Jim Dandy by over 13 lengths with a 120 Beyer, and then gamely won the Travers with a 113. Trainer Bobby Frankel told the media that he would train Medaglia d'Oro up to the Breeders' Cup Classic. I eagerly clipped the tab every day looking for his next work. Then I saw it.

September 26, Belmont: 6 furlongs 1:13.3 - Medaglia d'Oro
1:13.3 - Empire Maker

I had enjoyed some success by matching up workouts. But this couldn't be right, could it? Who was Empire Maker, anyway? By scanning the *Daily Racing Form* database, I found that Empire Maker was a 2-year-old (!) son of Unbridled out of Toussaud. I knew it was a Juddmonte Farms pedigree, and knew that Frankel trained for Juddmonte. Could this Empire Maker really be working in company with Medaglia d'Oro? I figured it had to be some weird coincidence, but decided to keep my eye on Empire Maker. It couldn't hurt.

October 15, Belmont: 6 furlongs 1:13 - Medaglia d'Oro
1:13 - Milwaukee Brew
1:13 - Empire Maker

Milwaukee Brew was the defending Santa Anita Handicap winner. It was possible that Medaglia d'Oro and Milwaukee Brew worked together. What about Empire Maker? Frankel wouldn't work three across the track, would he? I double-checked the official times of all three works. They were exactly the same—1:13.02. I thought it was reasonable to assume that Empire Maker was good. Really good. Derby good. Future-bet good.

Well, we all know how the story turned out. Empire Maker made his debut on October 20. He went off at 2-5, won by open lengths, and became the hype horse. He won the Florida Derby and Wood Memorial, and went off as the favorite in the Run for the Roses. If it weren't for Funny Cide, he would have won the Derby. That's racing. The point of the story is that you can tell a good horse from the work tab.

It's easy to assess the ability of a horse that has raced. That's what Beyer Speed Figures are for. If I could approximate a Beyer for a debut runner, I would be able to compare that horse with the proven performers he would face in his first start.

Birdstone made his debut on August 2, 2003, and set Saratoga aflame with a 99 Beyer Speed Figure and a $12\frac{1}{2}$-length win. I missed the boat, and Birdstone paid 7-2 odds. There had to be a way to profit from Birdstone's victory even after the fact. The work tab came in handy.

June 27, Saratoga Training: 4 furlongs 50.04 - Birdstone
4 furlongs 50.04 - Eurosilver

July 14, Saratoga Training: 4 furlongs 50.10 - Birdstone
4 furlongs 50.10 - Eurosilver

Was Eurosilver just as good as Birdstone? If he was, you could make a case for singling him whenever he made his debut, hopefully at good odds. He showed up on August 8, and I was ready. I put a little 99 (Birdstone's debut Beyer) next to Eurosilver's name, and was ready to cash in. Unfortunately, Eurosilver was coupled with Silver Wagon, a horse that had run second in his debut at Calder, and was going to take money. The entry went off at a measly 3-2. Silver Wagon won easily, and went on to capture the Grade 1 Hopeful in his next start. Eurosilver dueled for the early lead, and held on for second. He won his next three starts, including the Grade 2 Breeders' Futurity at Keeneland, and was considered one of the winter-book favorites for the Kentucky Derby. Injuries would derail his Derby plans, but at least the work tab was reliable enough to spot a good horse.

Here's one more example. St. Averil earned a 102 Beyer in winning the 2004 Santa Catalina Stakes, and followed that race up with a 101 runner-up effort in the San Felipe. He disappointed in the Santa Anita Derby, but still had to be considered one of the top 3-year-olds in Southern California. His work tab looked something like this:

April 19, Santa Anita: 5 furlongs 59.2 - St. Averil
59.4 - Vencer

April 24, Santa Anita: 6 furlongs 1:11.80 - St. Averil
1:12 - Vencer

St. Averil was a pretty good horse, but Vencer was an unknown. Both were trained by Rafael Becerra and owned by Stan Fulton. I assumed that they were working in company, and was proved correct by a story in *Daily Racing Form* about St. Averil's progress. Vencer made his debut on May 15 in a six-furlong maiden special at Hollywood. He went off at 9-2, and won by four widening lengths.

Todd Pletcher often works his horses in company. Funk, a 2-year-old by Unbridled's Song, made his debut on August 7, 2004, at Saratoga. We've already discussed how successful Pletcher is with firsters, but Funk also had a positive work tab.

June 30, Saratoga: 5 furlongs 1:04.86 - Colita
                               1:04.86 - Funk

Colita, a 4-year-old, came out of that work to run on the Fourth of July at Belmont. Making his first start in eight months, Colita won a N3X allowance with a 105 Beyer. He then was a game runner-up in a conditioned allowance at the Spa on July 28 with a 101 Beyer. Here was a horse that always had great potential, and was starting to run to his hype. If Funk could keep up with him in the morning (albeit in slow time), then I was pretty sure he could handle seven other debut runners.

None of the other firsters made much of an impression on the work tab. There were some excellent pedigrees, however. Lion Cat was a $300,000 yearling by Tale of the Cat. Thunder Ridge was an Overbrook Farm homebred by Storm Cat out of a Grade 1 winner. All Trumps was kin to graded stakes winner Leelanau by top debut sire Grand Slam. Still, that "Funky" workout seemed to outshine all of those pedigrees. When Funk went off at 7-2 odds for the top trainer-jockey combination of Pletcher and John Velazquez, he was worth a significant play. (See race chart, next page.)

By clipping the work tabs in the *Daily Racing Form*, or by reviewing them daily for free on www.drf.com, you can get a feeling of

SECOND RACE

Saratoga

AUGUST 7, 2004

6 FURLONGS. (1.08) MAIDEN SPECIAL WEIGHT . Purse $45,000 (UP TO $8,550 NYSBFOA) FOR MAIDENS, TWO YEAR OLDS. Weight, 118 lbs.

Value of Race: $45,000 Winner $27,000; second $9,000; third $4,500; fourth $2,250; fifth $1,350; sixth $300; seventh $300; eighth $300. Mutuel Pool $600,978.00 Exacta Pool $562,984.00 Quinella Pool $57,799.00 Trifecta Pool $346,789.00

Last Raced	Horse	M/Eqt. A. Wt	PP	St	¼	½	Str	Fin	Jockey	Odds $1
	Funk	L 2 118	1	4	1½	2⁶	1½	1⁵¾	Velazquez J R	3.75
	Lion Cat	2 118	2	3	3ʰᵈ	4¹	3ʰᵈ	2¼	Prado E S	4.50
	One Fein Dad	2 118	3	8	5¹½	3½	6½	3ⁿᵒ	Chavez J F	23.30
	Thunder Ridge	L b 2 118	8	1	2¹	1ʰᵈ	2⁵½	4ⁿᵒ	Bailey J D	2.35
	All Trumps	2 118	4	6	6⁷	6½	5ʰᵈ	5¹	Velasquez C	2.30
	Tadreeb	L 2 118	6	7	8	7⁵	7¹⁰	6⁴	Fragoso P	25.75
	Jonathan Quick	L 2 118	5	5	4½	5½	4ʰᵈ	7⁸¾	Sellers S J	20.70
	You Are a Kris	L 2 118	7	2	7¹½	8	8	8	Migliore R	18.80

OFF AT 1:38 Start Good . Won driving. Track fast.

TIME :224, :461, :59, 1:124 (:22.93, :46.23, :59.05, 1:12.94)

$2 Mutuel Prices:				
1 – FUNK	....	9.50	5.20	4.00
2 – LION CAT	....		5.40	4.20
3 – ONE FEIN DAD	....			7.50

$2 EXACTA 1–2 PAID $33.20 $2 QUINELLA 1–2 PAID $18.60
$2 TRIFECTA 1–2–3 PAID $280.00

B. c, (Apr), by Unbridled's Song – Verbal Volley , by Oh Say . Trainer Pletcher Todd A. Bred by Formal Gold LLC (Ky).

FUNK rushed up along the inside to gain the early advantage, set the pace under pressure into upper stretch, shook off THUNDER RIDGE in midstretch and drew away under steady urging. LION CAT raced just off the pace while saving ground, launched a rally leaving the turn, drifted out and bumped with ALL TRUMPS in upper stretch and closed late to gain the place. ONE FEIN DAD was unhurried early after breaking awkwardly, circled five wide while gaining on the turn, lugged in and bumped with ALL TRUMPS in upper stretch then finished willingly to gain a share. THUNDER RIDGE pressed the pace from outside into upper stretch, steadied while lugging in nearing the furlong marker and continued to lug in while racing greenly through the final eighth. ALL TRUMPS was bumped at the start, steadied while racing greenly in the four path on the turn, bumped with rivals while moving between horses in upper stretch and lacked a strong closing bid. TADREEB steadied leaving the gate and was never close thereafter. JONATHAN QUICK bumped at the start, raced just off the pace while three wide on the turn, was bumped between horses in upper stretch then steadied in tight while tiring at the three-sixteenths pole. YOU ARE A KRIS raced greenly in the early stages and was never close thereafter.

Owners– 1, Starlight Stables Saylor Paul H and Kurtin Barbara; 2, Giacopelli Richard J; 3, Fein Scott; 4, Overbrook Farm; 5, Lazy F Ranch; 6, Shadwell Stable; 7, My Meadowview Farms; 8, Garazi Solomon and Suchliski Jaime

Trainers– 1, Pletcher Todd A; 2, Biancone Patrick L; 3, Brice Michael; 4, Lukas D Wayne; 5, Penna Angel Jr; 6, Hennig Mark; 7, Zito Nicholas P; 8, Iwinski Allen

who's working with whom. You'll notice that Pletcher, Bob Baffert, Bobby Frankel, Bill Mott, Christophe Clement, and many others will train their horses in company. Mark down horses with similar times. Use the index in *DRF Simulcast Weekly* to find out which trainer has which horse. You can guesstimate their recent Beyer Speed Figures, since *Simulcast Weekly* offers winning Beyer Speed Figures for all races. Apply those numbers to the unraced horses from the same barn, and come up with a "Beyer" for the unraced workmate.

Pletcher basically told us who he felt was his best 2-year-old when he worked Proud Accolade in company with his Kentucky Oaks winner, Ashado. Proud Accolade had won a maiden race by over seven lengths in his debut and earned a whopping 94 Beyer. This was going to be Ashado's last workout before the upcoming Alabama Stakes. Between races on August 14, 2004, Pletcher sent the two out together. Proud Accolade, under Angel Cordero Jr., raced closest to the inside while Ashado stayed in the two path. Not surprisingly, the older, more accomplished Ashado went faster. She finished her five furlongs in 58.64 while Proud Accolade was timed in 58.78. Still, it was a strong vote of confidence from Pletcher to have the juvenile colt out there with his prize filly. Ashado earned a 103 Beyer with her third-place finish in the Alabama. Proud Accolade won a N1X allowance on September 1 with an 88 Beyer, and five weeks later won the Champagne Stakes with a Beyer of 100.

Let's put this theory to the test. Nick Zito sent out a juvenile debut runner named Sun King on Travers Day 2004. The son of Charismatic sold as the $400,000 sales-topper at the 2003 Keeneland January sale, and is a half to Grade 1 winner Traitor, multiple Grade 3 turf winner Ocean Drive, and multiple stakes winner Beavers Nose. He is also a half-brother to the dam of Grade 1 winner Peeping Tom. Here's the work that made Sun King so interesting.

August 20, Saratoga: 5 furlongs   59.61 - Sir Shackleton
                                   59.64 - Sun King

Three-year-old Sir Shackleton had just won the Grade 3 West Virginia Derby with a 105 Beyer Speed Figure, and was prepping for the Travers. After seeing Sun King's workout, I was willing to gamble that he could run.

After breaking slowly from post 10 under Pat Day, Sun King raced well behind the field in the early stages. He passed several horses despite racing greenly in the stretch, and galloped out beautifully. (See chart, next page.) In his second start, Sun King rallied from off the pace with a wide move on the turn, and dug in gamely for the score. To show how babies are capable of immense improvement from

THIRD RACE

Saratoga

AUGUST 28, 2004

6½ FURLONGS. (1.14²) MAIDEN SPECIAL WEIGHT . Purse $45,000 (UP TO $8,550 NYSBFOA) FOR MAIDENS, TWO YEAR OLDS. Weight, 118 lbs.

Value of Race: $45,000 Winner $27,000; second $9,000; third $4,500; fourth $2,250; fifth $1,350; sixth $129; seventh $129; eighth $129; ninth $129; tenth $129; eleventh $129; twelfth $126. Mutuel Pool $830,639.00 Exacta Pool $819,877.00 Trifecta Pool $525,162.00

Last Raced	Horse	M/Eqt.	A.	Wt	PP	St	¼	½	Str	Fin	Jockey	Odds $1
7Aug04 5Sar2	Silver Train	L f	2	118	9	1	2hd	1hd	15	17	Bailey J D	9.20
	Commander Pat	L	2	118	1	12	41	4½	32½	2¾	Bejarano R	50.50
28Jly04 5Sar2	Malheur	L b	2	118	7	5	3hd	21½	21	31¼	Velazquez J R	0.75
	Sun King	L	2	118	10	10	12	12	106	4nk	Day P	6.90
	Survivalist		2	118	3	6	6hd	7hd	6½	51	Prado E S	5.90
	Scott's Cat	L f	2	118	11	9	10hd	102	71½	6nk	Fragoso P	70.50
4Aug04 3Sar3	Tani Maru	L	2	118	2	7	72½	62½	5½	72½	Castellano J J	28.25
	Dynawhite	L b	2	118	6	3	5hd	3hd	41	81¼	Bridgmohan S X	13.10
	Interpatation	L	2	118	12	2	1110	9½	8hd	91	Gryder A T	35.75
	Tucan	L	2	118	5	4	1hd	52½	9½	104½	Sellers S J	36.75
	Quiet Retaliation	L	2	118	4	8	8½	8½	113½	113	Velasquez C	43.25
	Student Council		2	118	8	11	92	113	12	12	Albarado R J	52.00

OFF AT 1:39 Start Good . Won driving. Track fast.

TIME :22, :45, 1:09⁴, 1:16² (:22.10, :45.01, 1:09.91, 1:16.50)

$2 Mutuel Prices:

1 – SILVER TRAIN	20.40	10.00	4.30
2 – COMMANDER PAT		37.00	8.30
8 – MALHEUR			2.50

$2 EXACTA 1–2 PAID $534.00 $2 TRIFECTA 1–2–8 PAID $1,617.00

Dk. b or br. c, (Feb), by Old Trieste – Ridden in Thestars , by Cormorant . Trainer Mikhalides George. Bred by Joe Mulholland Sr Joe Mulholland Jr & John Mulholland (Ky).

SILVER TRAIN rushed up between horses, dueled three wide to the turn, shook loose in upper stretch and drew away while being kept to the task. COMMANDER PAT settled just behind the leaders while saving ground, launched a rally along the inside leaving the turn and finished willingly to gain a share. MALHEUR bumped at the start, moved up from outside, pressed the pace outside the winner leaving the turn then weakened slightly in the final eighth. SUN KING broke awkwardly, raced far back while trailing to the turn then raced erratically while rallying belatedly through the stretch. SURVIVALIST raced in the middle of the pack from outside along the backstretch, circled five wide on the turn then failed to threaten while improving his position. SCOTT'S CAT raced far back while saving ground to the turn, steadied along the rail in upper stretch and failed to threaten thereafter. TANI MARU raced in the middle of the pack along the backstretch, steadied along the inside on the far turn, swung five wide entering the stretch then flattened out. DYNAWHITE was reserved early, made a run four wide to threaten on the turn then flattened out. INTERPATATION was never a factor. TUCAN bumped at the start, dueled along the rail to the far turn and steadily tired thereafter. QUIET RETALIATION bumped at the start, steadied in traffic on the far turn and was never close thereafter. STUDENT COUNCIL bumped at the start, raced five wide throughout.

Owners– 1, Buckram Oak Farm; 2, WinStar Farm LLC and Four Fifths Stable; 3, Jones Aaron U and Marie D; 4, Farmer Tracy; 5, Phipps Ogden Mills et al; 6, Ramsey Kenneth L and Sarah K; 7, Carrion Jaime S; 8, Guenther Scott D; 9, Mavorah Elliot; 10, Heiligbrodt Racing Stable; 11, Phillips William and Rupolo Frank; 12, Farish William S

Trainers– 1, Mikhalides George; 2, Walden W Elliott; 3, Pletcher Todd A; 4, Zito Nicholas P; 5, McGaughey III Claude R; 6, Romans Dale; 7, Plesa Edward Jr; 8, Violette Richard A Jr; 9, Barbara Robert; 10, Asmussen Steven M; 11, McLaughlin Kiaran P; 12, Howard Neil J

Scratched– High Hi , Thunder Ridge (07Aug04 2Sar4)

start to start, Sun King's Beyer increased 30 points, from a 64 to a 94. Next time out he ran third—to Proud Accolade—in the Champagne, and he finished third in the Breeders' Cup Juvenile as well.

Knowing the ins and outs of the work tab is essential, as you will have an advantage over your handicapping competition. It's a lot of work, but it will serve you well in the long run.

7

LOOKING SHARP:
Watching the Board;
Noting Body Type
and Body Language

DURING MY SUMMER break from college in 1994, I got a job as a groom at Yonkers Raceway in New York. If anything was going to wean me off this horse-racing kick, it was going to be this job. I was out the door at 4:00 a.m., at the track by 4:45, and at work by 5:00. The work was hard and dirty, and if the barn had a horse in the last race, I wouldn't be out of the track until midnight. I loved every minute of it. I kept a written list of each horse's individual quirks, kept my ears open and my mouth shut, and worked like a dog. After a couple of weeks, I earned the trainer's trust, and he unofficially named me his assistant. One afternoon, before the races, he handed me a stack of bills and a piece of paper.

"Here are the bets that the owner wants to make," he said.

"Um. Okay." Back then, I was very garrulous and well-spoken.

"Bet early. Now go."

I walked up to the grandstand with a huge wad of bills in my hand and a dilemma. Should I take the money and run? With visions of brass knuckles, cement shoes, and broken bones dancing in my head, I decided to enter the track. But why should I bet early? Why was that important? I couldn't figure that one out as I munched on a hot dog waiting for the row of happy tellers to move into line. There were all kinds of bets on that slip. Pick threes, daily doubles, and win wagers dominated. I felt embarrassed and proud as our horse opened up at 1-9 on the board in the first race. I had manipulated the tote. Obviously, there would be audible gasps of shock by the 80 or so people at the Hilltop, and they would follow the "hot" money. I looked around for the angry faces accusing me of some sort of larceny. I strained to hear the shouts of the gamblers. There were none. All that I noticed was that the horse started to drift up and up. The horse went off at 2-1, broke stride at the start, and hippity-hopped across the finish line. Well, at least it wasn't my money.

Years later, I finally came up with a theory (and this is only a theory) as to why I was instructed to bet early. What would be the point of waiting until three minutes to post? If my horse was 5-1 at that point in time, and I lowered him to 2-1, then surely the public would react to the "smart money," and might make the horse even shorter on the board. Since I bet early, I slipped one past the public. They probably thought some boob (true enough) had just bet his savings on a hunch.

I've kept a keen eye on the wagering patterns of maiden races, and am amazed at how many "live" horses open at short odds and then drift upward to acceptable prices. These horses usually run very well and often win. Let's take the case of E. Ticket.

E. Ticket made her debut in a weak New York-bred maiden special weight on May 22, 2004, at Belmont. She was trained by Joe Aquilino, a horseman who didn't have very promising statistics with first-time starters at the time. E. Ticket had gaps in her published work tab, and although she had a nice pedigree, she wasn't expected to take a ton of money. She opened up at 2-5. I rushed down to the paddock to get a look at this "wunderhorse." She looked good, but the most interesting thing I noticed was that Patrick Biancone, trainer of Lion Heart and many other stakes horses, was down in the paddock, chatting with Aquilino, and giving E. Ticket the eye.

Biancone didn't have a horse entered until the next race, so it was interesting that he was there. What connection did he have with Aquilino? Was he merely an old buddy looking for a chat, or a prospective buyer of the horse? I knew that Biancone had privately purchased New York-breds for Flying Zee Stable, and it was possible that he was looking to add to his collection. Based on the early money, the Biancone presence, and the fact that her opposition looked terrible on paper, I was ready to make E. Ticket the key on all of my tickets. If only she weren't so short. Before long, she wasn't. E. Ticket kept drifting up and ended up at 1.70-1. She showed no interest in the early stages of the race, lagged 18 lengths behind the leader on the turn, and was last turning for home. She began to kick in at the eighth pole, but there was no way she could catch the winner, could she?

THIRD RACE
Belmont
MAY 22, 2004

6 FURLONGS. (1.07³) MAIDEN SPECIAL WEIGHT . Purse $41,000 FOR MAIDENS, FILLIES AND MARES THREE YEARS OLD AND UPWARD FOALED IN NEW YORK STATE AND APPROVED BY THE NEW YORK STATE–BRED REGISTRY. Three Year Olds, 118 lbs.; Older, 124 lbs.

Value of Race: $41,000 Winner $24,600; second $8,200; third $4,100; fourth $2,050; fifth $1,230; sixth $820. Mutuel Pool $433,716.00 Exacta Pool $408,845.00 Trifecta Pool $253,787.00

Last Raced	Horse	M/Eqt. A. Wt	PP	St	¼	½	Str	Fin	Jockey	Odds $1
	E. Ticket	L	3 118	2	5	6	6	4⁵	1ʰᵈ	Chavez J F	1.70
2May04 9Aqu⁵	Maidez	L b	3 113	6	4	1⁷	13½	1³	2¹	Cotto P L Jr⁵	2.80
2May04 9Aqu⁶	Mystical Sea	L	3 118	1	2	3½½	25½	2⁶	32¾	Espinoza J L	5.10
9Apr04 4Aqu⁸	Mistress Hemming	L f	3 118	4	6	4½½	3³	3½	48½	Bridgmohan S X	3.30
15Apr04 1Aqu⁹	Let's Get Personal	L b	4 119	5	3	5⁷	5½	53½	5⁸	Jara F⁵	8.50
12May04 6Bel⁷	Jessica's Angel	L	3 118	3	1	2ʰᵈ	4¹	6	6	Pezua J M	26.50

OFF AT 2:10 Start Good . Won driving. Track fast.
TIME :22², :46², :59², 1:13³ (:22.44, :46.40, :59.44, 1:13.78)

$2 Mutuel Prices:

3 – E. TICKET.	5.40	3.20	2.50
8 – MAIDEZ.		3.40	2.50
2 – MYSTICAL SEA.			3.10

$2 EXACTA 3–8 PAID $19.00 $2 TRIFECTA 3–8–2 PAID $51.00

Dk. b or br. f, (Mar), by Langfuhr – Special Date , by He's Bad . Trainer Aquilino Joseph. Bred by John Valentino (NY).

E. TICKET dropped far back early, raced wide, rallied outside and was along in the final strides. MAIDEZ quickly opened a long lead, set the pace, took a clear advantage into deep stretch and was caught at the wire. MYSTICAL SEA raced inside and finished well. MISTRESS HEMMING raced wide throughout and had no response when roused. LET'S GET PERSONAL had no response when roused. JESSICA'S ANGEL stumbled at the start and tired.

Owners– 1, J and Vee Stables; 2, Titone Joe; 3, Santangelo George L; 4, Happy Hill Farm; 5, Armstrong Harold D and Conley Judy; 6, De Stefano Peter

Trainers– 1, Aquilino Joseph; 2, Miceli Michael; 3, O'Brien Colum; 4, Pugh Peter D; 5, Friedman Mitchell; 6, O'Brien Leo

Scratched– Andriana (16Apr04 4Aqu⁵) , Factual Contender

It was an amazing performance from a visual standpoint, but the race was slow, and Biancone never purchased the filly. Maybe he never intended to do so in the first place. E. Ticket didn't become a star, but she was certainly special that day, and the early money should have tipped everyone off that she could run.

I discussed Sun King in the last chapter. After his eye-catching debut at Saratoga, he was entered in a tough maiden special weight at Belmont. Despite the quality of his opposition, Sun King opened at 6-5 and soon dropped to even money. Handicappers seeking "value" started to bet his competition, and Sun King went off at a juicy 2-1. Sun King showed advanced maturity, and a good deal of heart, to win a long stretch duel.

Watch out for first-time starters and lightly raced horses that open up well beneath their morning-line odds. It could be an indication that they are live.

BODY TYPE AND BODY LANGUAGE

It's always exciting to go down to the paddock and get a glimpse of a first-time starter. Who knows if the baby that you are eyeballing is the next great champion? In our mind's eye, we all have a snapshot of what the perfect horse looks like. I have yet to find mine on the track, but there are definitely things to look out for when watching babies prepare for their debuts. Looking at the horses is simply a logical part of the handicapping process. Would you buy a car without first getting a look at the merchandise? The same goes for the Thoroughbred. It is essential to get a feel for the horse on which you are investing your hard-earned money.

Sprinters
When looking for precocious sprinters in maiden races, bigger isn't necessarily better. I like the blocky, linebacker types. Look for a

powerful hind end, muscular thighs, and a shiny coat. Look for dapples on the rump.

Routers

While I look for a strong hind end in sprinters, I'm searching for a powerful chest, a long, strong neck, and long legs with routers. Here, I look for the big boys and girls. They will need the extra body mass to handle the longer distances. I love routers that are dappled out on the barrel of their bodies.

Turf

I look for many of the router's attributes, but I like a broad hoof, and a muscular shoulder. I have also found that several good turf horses not only have the powerful chest of a router, but also have the strong hind end of a sprinter. These traits are necessary in those slow-paced turf routes where the horses begin to sprint from three-eighths of a mile out.

Mud

I've never really liked big horses on muddy tracks. They tend to sink deeper in the mud, and have more trouble getting into a smooth rhythm. Downgrade horses that "high-step" when they are walking in the post parade over a muddy surface. They will gingerly place their hooves down on the mud, and quickly pick them up looking for a dry patch.

First-Time Starters

Look for some attitude. I love it when 2-year-olds announce to the world that they're ready for action with various snorts and battle cries. It's nice to see them prance around in a rhythm after the jockey gets a leg up. An arched neck is a good sign. Look for horses that are really mouthing the bit. You'll even see some foam coming out of their mouths as they attack the bit. Once the horses are on the track, look out for the ones that break off into a gallop with speed and intensity. If all else fails, look for the biggest, most physically impressive baby. They are often the ones that have matured quicker than the others.

Some tracks have enclosed saddling areas. Avoid horses that kick at the back of their stalls, and are generally hard to handle. When a trainer has to circle his runner a dozen times in order to get the saddle on, that's not very promising. Horses that are washed out on the neck on cool days, or have a large amount of kidney sweat between their legs, should be avoided. Keep away from paunchy runners with baby fat, or skin-and-bones types.

8

PROJECTING DRASTIC IMPROVEMENT WITH ANGLES

MAIDENS CAN IMPROVE greatly in almost no time at all. Let's consider some of the angles where handicappers can attempt to project improvement.

BACK BEYERS

We'll start with the fifth race at Monmouth on August 7, 2004. It's a statebred maiden special weight, and the form isn't very impressive. When I give seminars to beginning handicappers, I like to teach them this elementary way of utilizing the Beyer Speed Figures. I go back to an individual horse's best Beyer earned under circumstances that will be similar to today (one-turn sprint, same medication/equipment as his best Beyer, etc.).

5

Monmouth Park 6 Furlongs (1:07⁴) ⑤Md Sp Wt 46k Purse $46,000 (include $9,000 NJB – NJ Bred Enhancement) For Registered New Jersey Breds Maidens, Three Year Olds And Upward. Three Year Olds, 118 lbs. Older, 122 lbs.

---

1 Jackety Jack (58)
Own: Debra Sones
White, Blue Inverted Triangle, Blu
Gr/ro. g. 4 (May)
Sire: Two Punch (Mr. Prospector) $25,000
Dam: Winged (Triocala)
Br: Debra J Sones (NJ)
Tr: Sones Debra(12 2 1 1 .17) 2004:(12 2 .17)

ROCCO J (39 27 3 .05) 2004: (257 24 .09)
L 122

(4C.4)

	Life	4 M 0 1	$7,360	55	D.Fst	4 0 0 1	$7,360	55
	2004	4 M 0 1	$7,360	55	Wet(380)	0 0 0 0	$0	–
	2003	0 M 0 0	$0	–	Turf(156)	0 0 0 0	$0	–
	Mth	4 0 0 1	$7,360	55	Dst(368)	4 0 0 1	$7,360	55

25Jly04-11Mth fst 6f :22 :45¹ :57¹1.11 3↑⑤Md Sp Wt 46k — 0 8 2 3nk 67¼ 81⁵ 92⁹ Bravo J L122 fb 4.10 56– 14 DancinDusty118¾ Itsackewlk118⁹ IdeRejoice118¹ Broke thru,unseated jk 10
3Jly04-10Mth fst 6f :21³ :45 :58¹1.12¹ 3↑⑤Md Sp Wt 46k 55 11 1 3²¼ 3²¾ 33 Ortiz F L L122 fb 19.70 81– 15 BigNanasBoy113²¾ FourOWon118nk JacketyJack 124¾ 4-wide,gaining late 12
20Jun04- 2Mth fst 6f :22² :46⁴ :59¹1.13¹ 3↑⑤Md Sp Wt 46k 3⁴ 3 2 1½ 2¹ 3²¼ 4⁴⁸ Ortiz F L L122 f 2.70 69– 20 CalabriBell117³ ArielleCrown117¹¾ Bombzine117nk Steadied drifting turn 10
31May04-1Mth fst 6f :22 :46¹ .53¾¹ 24 21 367¾ 817 Ortiz F L 122 f 11.20 65– 09 Salt Flat Kid116²¼ A Toast to Life116¹ Life After116⁴ Vied early, tired 10

WORKS: Jly16 Mth 4f fst :49² ʙ 21/64 Jun29 Mth 5f fst :37³ ʙg 9/11 Jun12 Mth 5f fst 1:02¹ ʙ 10/32 May22 Mth 5f fst 1:01⁴ Hg 27/86 May15 Mth 5f fst :40 ʙ 19/20
TRAINER: MdnSpWt(25 .16 $2.62) MdnSpWt(11 .00 $0.00)

---

2 See Frankie 7
Own: Carlo Dethomasi
White, Red, White Cr In Green Circle, White
Ch. c. 3 (Apr)
Sire: Innkeeper (Secretariat) $1,000
Dam: Smart Flapper (Gallant Wings)
Br: Kenneth Levari (NJ)
Tr: Ruggiero Phil Jr(—) (—)

TRUJILLO E (105 10 14 16 .10) 2004: (312 30 .10)
L 119

	Life	1 M 0 0	$260	2	D.Fst	1 0 0 0	$260	2
	2004	1 M 0 0	$260	2	Wet(277)	0 0 0 0	$0	–
	2003	0 M 0 0	$0	–	Turf(285)	0 0 0 0	$0	–
	Mth	1 0 0 0	$260	2	Dst(259)	1 0 0 0	$260	2

Entered 6Aug04– 4 MTH
Previously trained by Perkins Ben W Jr
9Jun04- 4Mth fst 6f :22 :46 1.13² 3↑⑤Md 50000(50–45) 3 8 73¾ 74½ 56¼ 718 Bravo J L117 *1.20 55– 22 Hare's Love120⁴ Olivers Crossing120³¼ J. D. Belle117²¼ No speed, no rally 8
WORKS: Jly29 Mth 5f gd 1:01¹ Hg 2/12 Jly23 Mth 4f fst :54 ʙ 41/64 Jun2 Mth 4f fst :49³ ʙg 11/23 May27 Mth 4f fst :49⁴ ʙg 15/27 May21 Mth 4f fst :50 ʙ 33/65

---

3 Czar d'Or 3
Own: Dependable Stables
Black, Yellow Star Sash, Yellow Star On
Ch. g. 3 (Mar)
Sire: Tour d'Or (Medaille d'Or) $10,000
Dam: Talking Czarina (Dancing Czar)
Br: Robert L Edwards (NJ)
Tr: Hamer William E(10 0 0 0 .00) 2004:(77 1 .01)

GOMEZ O (67 5 5 7 .07) 2004: (165 8 .05)
L 115⁷

	Life	2 M 0 0	$920	42	D.Fst	2 0 0 0	$920	42
	2004	2 M 0 0	$920	42	Wet(375)	0 0 0 0	$0	–
	2003	0 M 0 0	$0	–	Turf(266)	0 0 0 0	$0	–
	Mth	2 0 0 0	$920	42	Dst(370)	2 0 0 0	$920	42

19Jun04-10Mth fst 6f :22³ :46¹ :59¹1.12³ 3↑⑤Md Sp Wt 46k — 2 9 — Wales T L122 b 30.70 – 18 A Toast to Life117¼ Colt Python122²¼ Runaway Train117² Stumbled start 9
30May04-12Mth fst 6f :21⁴ :44⁴ :57¹1.10⁴ 3↑⑤Md Sp Wt 46k 1 10 10¹⁰ 10¹⁰⅔ 5¹⁰ 51¹¼ Bracho R A 122 b 78.20 74– 12 Road Builder116⁵¾ Runaway Train117³ Dancin Dusty116²¼ Slow into stride 10

WORKS: Jly20 Pha 4f fst :50 ʙ 18/30 Jun15 Pha 3f fst 1:02³ ʙ 10/11 May25 Pha 4f fst 1:04 Hg 4/15 May18 Pha 4f fst :49¹ ʙg 12/29 May11 Pha 4f fst :51 ʙ 21/21
TRAINER: 31-60Days(16 .00 $0.00) Dirt(148 .05 $0.50) Sprint(96 .05 $0.60) MdnSpWt(27 .07 $1.15)

---

4 Quoit Rich 42
Own: Barry Kling
Royal Blue, Red Chevron, Red Cuffs On
Ch/ro. g. 3 (Apr)
Sire: Waquoit (Relaunch) $5,000
Dam: Dodge City Riches (Citidancer)
Br: Lilliput Farm (NJ)
Tr: Kling Barry(3 0 1 0 .00) 2004:(20 2 .10)

ORTIZ F L (175 18 15 17 .10) 2004: (283 25 .09)
119

+5 Blinkers ON

	Life	1 M 0 0	$460	32	D.Fst	1 0 0 0	$460	32
	2004	1 M 0 0	$460	32	Wet(374)	0 0 0 0	$0	–
	2003	0 M 0 0	$0	–	Turf(242)	0 0 0 0	$0	–
	Mth	1 0 0 0	$460	32	Dst(366)	1 0 0 0	$460	32

25Jly04- 4Mth fst 6f :22 :45³ :58¹1.12⁴ 3↑⑤Md Sp Wt 46k 10 3 57¼ 57 67¼ 79 Ortiz F L 118 11.90 71– 14 Four O Won118nk Colt Python117²¾ A Bag of Gold118¹ Mid track, outrun 10

WORKS: Jly31 Bow 4f fst :49² Hg 12/38 ●Jly21 Bow 3f fst :35² H 1/5 ●Jly2 Bow 3f fst :37 ʙg 6/10 Jly2 Bow 3f fst 1:01³ H 1/3 ●Jun23 Bow 3f gd :36⁴ Hg 1/5
TRAINER: 2ndStart(3 .00 $0.00) 1stBlink(2 .00 $0.00) Blink(30 .07 $0.07) Dirt(34 .12 $1.65) Sprint(26 .12 $1.64) MdnSpWt(5 .00 $0.00)

---

5 Runaway Train (59)
Own: Stacey and J A Frangella Jr
Black, Gold Collar And Jf, Gold Dots On
B. r. 4 (Apr)
Sire: Runaway Groom (Blushing Groom*Fr) $15,000
Dam: Marjoram (Muttering)
Br: Stacey Frangella & James Frangella Jr (NJ)
Tr: Perry William W(19 4 2 2 .21) 2004:(40 4 .10)

ELLIOTT S (305 45 43 42 .15) 2004: (821 164 .20)
L 122

	Life	12 M 2 2	$28,065	59	D.Fst	8 0 2 2	$26,915	59
	2004	5 M 2 2	$24,910	59	Wet(348)	3 0 0 0	$930	45
	2003	7 M 0 0	$3,155	57	Turf(236)	1 0 0 0	$220	57
	Mth	6 0 2 1	$23,700	59	Dst(308)	7 0 2 1	$24,955	59

Previously trained by Shaw Tim J
11Jly04- 5Mth fst 6f :22³ :46¹ :59¹1.12¼ 3↑⑤Md Sp Wt 46k 4 8 61¾ 32 22½ 23 Baze M C⁵ L117 b *1.60 76– 14 OliversCrossing122³ RunwyTrin117⁴ SpeclHff118⁴ Btwn 1/4,bid,2nd best 9
19Jun04-10Mth fst 6f :22³ :46¹ :59¹1.12³ 3↑⑤Md Sp Wt 46k 9 2 87¼ 66¼ 53¼ 33² Baze M C⁵ L117 fb 28.10 80– 12 AToasttoLife117¼ ColtPython122²¼ RunwyTrin117² Steadied between 1/8 9
30May04-12Mth fst 6f :21⁴ :44⁴ :57¹1.10⁴ 3↑⑤Md Sp Wt 46k 5 3 58 56¼ 35½ 37 25⅜ Baze M C⁵ L118 fb 11.70 74– 16 Cool Cafe123⁵¼ Lawrenson123¹¼ Runaway Train118nk Failed to menace 5
2May04- 5Pha fst 6f :22¹ :46 1.12³ 3↑ M d Sp Wt 20w 5 3 58 56¼ 44½ 38¾ Baze M C⁵ L118 fb 10.70 — 06 Western Reveng117⁶¼ UnclBruc122¼ SintdColony117¾ Brief speed, tired 7
18Jan04- 1Aqu gd 1¼ ⊡ :24 :493 1:15² 1:48⁴ 3↑ M d Sp Wt 42k 7 4³ 4² 76¾ 82⁵ 83⁶¼ Clemente A V L122 fb 113.50 34– 20 WesternReveng117⁶¼ UnclBruc122¼ SintdColony117¾ Failed to respond 8
28Dec03- 1Aqu fst 6f :23 :46¹ 1.12² 1.14¼ 3↑ M d Sp Wt 45k 7 5 88¾ 68¼ 66¾ 65¾ Clemente A V L121 fb 34.50 71– 15 Blue Skies Ahead121⁴ Falconer123⁴ Portlandale137 Failed to respond 8
30Nov03- 2Aqu fst 6f :22¹ :45⁴ :58¹1.12³ 3↑ M d Sp Wt 45k 1 8 88¾ 68½ 66¾ 62²¼ Pizarro J L121 fb 107.25 73– 21 BahamaJohn114¼¾ PrimoNova121nk BlueSkiesAhead121½ Wide trip, no rally 9
5Nov03- 6Med sly 170 :22² :45⁴ 1:11 1:43³ 3↑ M d Sp Wt 22k 3 2nd 2nd 43⅛ 61⁰ 62²¼ Pizarro J L108 f 39.30 62– 19 Reel Slam122¼ Bad Gambler120⁶ Perimeter115¹⅜ Steadied 1/4,gave way 9
Previously trained by Lozano Adalberto
80ct03- 4Med fm 1½ ⊕ :43³ 1:42 3↑ M d Sp Wt 22k 7 10⁴ 10⁵¼ 104⅔ 62¾ Pizarro J L116 f 86.20 69– 17 Hot Soup122¹⅓ Rare Bush119½ Integer119³ Step slow start 10
11Sep03-10Mth fst 6f :22³ :47 1.11¼1.42 3↑ M d Sp Wt 30k 4 81³ 81⁶ 81² 711 714 Baze M C⁷ L108 f 9.90e 79– 15 GovernorBennett118nk SpdingJim122¼¼ BdGmblr118²¾ Well back, no rally 8

WORKS: Jly31 Mth 4f gd :49¹ ʙ 16/65 Jun13 Mth 4f fst :38 ʙ 12/18 ●May23 Mth 3f fst :35² ʙ 1/2 May16 Mth 4f fst 1:01 ʙ 18 May15 Mth 4f fst :50 ʙ 47/85
TRAINER: 1stW/Tm(13 .08 $0.54) Dirt(86 .07 $1.02) Sprint(76 .08 $1.08) MdnSpWt(11 .27 $2.71)

---

6 A Bag of Gold (56)
Own: Colonial Farm
White, Gold Braces And F, Gold Cuffs On
B. g. 3 (Apr)
Sire: Abajanner (Devil's Bag) $3,000
Dam: Dixie Sunrise (Dixieland Band)
Br: Colonial Farms (NJ)
Tr: Thompson J Willard(90 12 12 .08) 2004:(134 12 .08)

LOPEZ C C (211 40 44 51 .19) 2004: (522 91 .16)
L 119

(4C.2)

	Life	2 M 0 2	$10,120	51	D.Fst	2 0 0 2	$10,120	51
	2004	2 M 0 2	$10,120	51	Wet(305)	0 0 0 0	$0	–
	2003	0 M 0 0	$0	–	Turf(161)	0 0 0 0	$0	–
	Mth	2 0 0 2	$10,120	51	Dst(265)	2 0 0 2	$10,120	51

25Jly04- 4Mth fst 6f :22 :45³ :58¹1.12⁴ 3↑⑤Md Sp Wt 46k 49 6 2 2² 21¼ 37 Lopez C C L118 7.70 77– 14 Four O Won118nk Colt Python117²¾ A Bag of Gold118¹ Briefly led,chased 10
11Jly04-10Mth fst 6f :22³ :45³ :57¹1.10¹ 3↑⑤Md Sp Wt 46k 51 110 95 37 35¾ Lopez C C L118 8.60e 76– 14 Why Oh Why118¹⅝ Oro de Oro122¾ ABagofGold118²¼ Dropped back turn 10

WORKS: Jly2 Mth 5f fst 1:01² ʙg 3/9 Jun25 Mth 4f fst :49¼ ʙg 9/42 May15 Mth 5f fst 1:02⁴ ʙg 24/41 May9 Mth 4f fst :49 H 10/76
TRAINER: Dirt(341 .07 $1.19) Sprint(256 .06 $0.96) MdnSpWt(109 .09 $0.96)

---

7 Twice Onabet (65)
Own: Anthony M Foglia
White, Red Collar And Blocks, Red
Dk. b or br. g. 4 (Apr)
Sire: Polish Pro (Mr. Prospector) $1,000
Dam: Wononabet (Bet Twice)
Br: Anthony Foglia (NJ)
Tr: Lima Rolando J(6 0 0 0 .00) 2004:(27 4 .15)

BAZE M C (200 22 21 27 .11) 2004: (359 43 .11)
L 117⁵

	Life	15 M 3 1	$26,570	65	D.Fst	15 0 3 1	$26,570	65
	2004	5 M 0 1	$1,840	40	Wet(327)	0 0 0 0	$0	–
	2003	7 M 3 0	$24,730	65	Turf(177)	0 0 0 0	$0	–
	Mth	5 0 1 0	$1,840	40	Dst(321)	14 0 3 1	$24,540	65

25Jly04-11Mth fst 6f :22 :45¹ :57¹1.11 3↑⑤Md Sp Wt 46k 39 7 9 79¾ 511 511¾ Rivera L Jr L122 fb 66.00 73– 14 Dancin Dusty118¾ Itsacakewalk118⁹ Ide Rejoice118¹ Outside, no rally 10
3Jly04-11Mth fst 6f :21³ :45 :58¹1.12¹ 3↑⑤Md Sp Wt 46k 33 8 6 1119 1116 1014 913¾ Rivera L Jr L122 fb 86.70 67– 15 Big Nana's Boy113²¾ Four O Won118nk Jackety Jack 122¾ Outrun 12
19Jun04-10Mth fst 6f :22³ :46¹ :59¹1.12³ 3↑⑤Md Sp Wt 46k 40 5 5 87¼ 88½ 810½ Rivera L Jr L122 fb 47.40 66– 18 A Toast to Life117¼ Colt Python122²¼ Runaway Train117² Faded quickly turn 9
30May04-12Mth fst 6f :21⁴ :44⁴ :57¹1.10⁴ 3↑⑤Md Sp Wt 46k ● 10 — 88 1014 91½ Rivera L Jr L122b 15.40 64– 12 Road Builder116⁵¾ Runaway Train117³ Dancin Dusty116²¼ Outrun 10
1Jan04- 8Pha fst 6f :22¹ :46² :58¼1:13³ 3↑ M d Sp Wt 21k 24 5 1 55¼ 51⁰ 61² 62²¼ Rivera L Jr L122 fb 23.60 64– 14 Full Cooler123²¾ Insanity Defense120² Hot Josh122¼ Outrun 6
20Dec03- 7Pha fst 6f :22¹ :47¹ 1:13 1:43³ 3↑ M d Sp Wt 19k — 0 10 32 10¹² 101⁷ 101⁹ Santana D⁵ L116 25.70 37– 14 AlltheNumbers121nk SlthDI121¼⁹ Rockonbmbm121nk Outside,through 1/2 10
30Nov03- 7Pha fst 6f :22¹ :47¹ 1:13 1:43 3↑ M d Sp Wt 20k 28 1 4 71½ 79¾ 99½ 814 Santagata N L120 b 6.50 61– 25 RunwyStorm120½ InsnityDefense121nk Bmboozlr121²¼ Shuffled into turn 10
7Nov03-10Med fst 6f :22¹ :45³ :57¼1:10³ 3↑ M d Sp Wt 27k 58 2 3 11 11 2nd 2¼ Santagata N L121 fb 4.40 83– 11 Hey Chub121nk Primo Nova121⁵ Twice Onabet121¼ Brk out,brushed start 9
170ct03-10Med fst 6f :23¹ :47³ :58¹1:12³ 3↑ M d Sp Wt 27k 50 3 4 3²¼ 31 31 41¾ Santagata N L121 fb *4.50 79– 13 He's My Idol120no Nicosia120³³ R Coastocoast121no Drifted out,level off 10
40ct03-10Med fst 6f :22³ :45³ :58¹1:11³ 3↑ M d Sp Wt 27k 65 2 6 1½ 1½ 2nd 2½ Santagata N L120 fb *1.90 86– 13 JaysWish120⅞ TwiceOnabet120² CallnInterview115no Game, only 1/16 ʙ 10

WORKS: ●Jly17 Pha 3f fst :34³ ʙ 1/34 Jun30 Pha 3f fst :38¹ ʙ 8/14 May22 Pha 5f fst 1:00⁴ ʙ 2/18 May15 Pha 5f fst 1:00³ ʙ 2/25 May8 Pha 4f fst :48 ʙ 2/55
TRAINER: Dirt(96 .06 $2.00) Sprint(64 .06 $2.37) MdnSpWt(18 .00 $0.00)

8 **Danzig's Jade** 51
Own: Robert M Bennett
Hunter Green, Pink Blocks, Green Cap
GARCIA ALAN (128 18 15 17 .14) 2004: (333 31 .09)
Ch. g. 3 (Apr)
Sire: Slavic (Danzig) $5,000
Dam: Budra (Jade Hunter)
Br: Robert Bennett (NJ)
Tr: Carlesimo Charles Jr(22 3 3 3 .14) 2004:(36 4 .11)
L 119
Life 3 M 0 0 $4,140 46 | D.Fst 3 0 0 0 $4,140 46
2004 3 M 0 0 $4,140 46 | Wet(300) 0 0 0 0 $0 -
2003 0 M 0 0 $0 - | Turf(230) 0 0 0 0 $0 -
Mth 3 0 0 0 $4,140 46 | Dst(273) 3 0 0 0 $4,140 46
25Jly04-4Mth fst 6f :22 :45³ :58¹ 1:12 3↑ⓈMd Sp Wt 46k 46 7 4 3³ 4² 4² 43½ Garcia Alan L118 b 12.10 76- 14 Four O Won118nk Colt Python117²¼ A Bag of Gold118¹ Steadied near turn 10
11Jly04-10Mth fst 6f :22² :45¹ :57³ 1:10¹ 3↑ⓈMd Sp Wt 46k 5 8 6⁸ 55½ 4⁷ 415¼ Garcia Alan L118 23.70 74- 14 Why Oh Why118¹¹¼ Oro de Oro122¹¾ ABagofGold118²¼ Pinched back early 10
9Jun04-5Mth fst 6f :22² :46¹ :58⁴ 1:12¹ 3↑ⓈMd Sp Wt 46k 7 6 4² 4² 64¾ 918¼ Bravo J L117 3.70 61- 22 CllnIntrviw122²¼ OnLstVictory117²¾ Awdwin122⁴¼ Chased turn,gave way 10
WORKS: ●Jly21 Mth 3f fst :36⁴ B 1/10 Jly7 Mth 4f fst :50⁴ B 39/48 ●Jun30 Mth 5f fst 1:01 Hg 1/12 Jun20 Mth 5f fst 1:02⁴ B 11/18 Jun5 Mth 4f fst :49 Bg 15/94 May31 Mth 6f fst 1:14⁴ H 4/11
TRAINER: Dirt(133 .09 $1.40) Sprint(83 .08 $1.54) MdnSpWt(15 .07 $0.46)

9 **Linden Lane**
Own: Irene Habernickel
Blue, White Diamond Framed Ih, White
KING E L JR (205 22 31 29 .11) 2004: (473 51 .11)
Gr/ro. c. 3 (Apr)
Sire: Runaway Groom (Blushing Groom*Fr) $15,000
Dam: Mi Mariposa (Two Punch)
Br: Irene Habernickel (NJ)
Tr: Hartman Mary(39 6 5 2 .15) 2004:(61 8 .13)
119
Life 0 M 0 0 $0 - | D.Fst 0 0 0 0 $0 -
2004 0 M 0 0 $0 - | Wet(400) 0 0 0 0 $0 -
2003 0 M 0 0 $0 - | Turf(243) 0 0 0 0 $0 -
Mth 0 0 0 0 $0 | Dst(358) 0 0 0 0 $0 -
WORKS: Jly30 Mth 5f fst 1:01⁴ H 11/56 Jly23 Mth 4f fst :49 Bg 3/44 Jly17 Mth 5f fst 1:01⁴ B 10/5 Jly10 Mth 4f fst :48³ B 6/58 Jly3 Mth 4f fst :51⁴ B 41/49 Jun19 Mth 3f fst :38 B 24/32 Mar23 GP 3f fst :36 B 1/2
TRAINER: 1stStart(13 .23 $1.78) Dirt(181 .13 $1.25) Sprint(127 .13 $0.96) MdnSpWt(20 .25 $2.21)

10 **Robert's Legacy** 30
Own: DArrigo Racing Stable
Hot Pink, Turquoise Cross, Pink And
PENNINGTON F (4 1 1 1 .25) 2004: (733 93 .13)
B. g. 4 (Mar)
Sire: Cryptoclearance (Fappiano) $15,000
Dam: Mama Nook (Belong to Me)
Br: Robert L Edwards (NJ)
Tr: Shavelson Pam(2 0 0 0 .00) 2004:(113 16 .14)
L 117⁵
Life 14 M 2 2 $13,962 66 | D.Fst 7 0 0 1 $2,465 30
2004 2 M 0 0 $702 52 | Wet(334) 3 0 1 0 $2,095 28
2003 4 M 1 0 $1,950 30 | Turf(235) 4 0 1 1 $9,402 66
Mth 3 0 0 1 $2,240 30 | Dst(303) 0 0 0 0 $0 -
Entered 7Aug04- 6 PHA
9Jly04-2Pen fm 5f Ⓣ:22² :45 :57¹ 3↑Md Sp Wt 14k 2 8 87½ 7¹¹ 78¾ 6⁴ Molina V H L122 f 7.90 83- 13 Star Optimist116½ Parrott116hd Secret Punch118²½ 3w,late gain 12
24Jun04-1Pen fm 5f Ⓣ:22¹ :45¹ :57² 3↑Md Sp Wt 13k 10 1 31½ 3⁵ 46½ 46½ Duarte J C Jr L122 f 6.00 79- 13 Lawrenson122½ Secret Punch118²½ Parrott115³½ 3w, fell back turn 11
Previously trained by Lynch Cathal
3Nov03-10Pha fst 1 1/16 :23¹ :46⁴ 1:13¹ 1:50¹ 3↑Md 8000(8-7) 1 65¾ 8¹³ 8¹⁰ 78¾ 6¹¹ Glasser T P L120 7.00 50- 30 Oceanic120³½ *Boo Yeah*122³½ Good for Me118no Showed little 11
28Sep03-4Pha sly 5½f :23 :47² 1:00² 1:07² Md 7500 3 3 67½ 66½ 55¼ 44¼ Glasser T P L122 3.20 72- 20 Cape Prince122¹¼ Voltemort115²¼ *Allthechips*117¾ Poor action, too late 7
20Sep03-10Pha fst 7f :23¹ :46⁴ 1:12¹ 1:25 3↑Md 13000(15-13) 3 8 95¾ 12¹⁷ 12²² 1238½ Rocco J L116 f 36.90 43- 16 ⒹCosmic Verse118⁴¼ Yaz Am Smart118¹¼ Jeffery118½ Outrun 12
Placed 11th through disqualification
31Aug03-9Pha wf 5½f :22⁴ :47¹ 1:00 1:07 Md 7500 27 8 7 53¾ 51¼ 2¹ 22¼ Glasser T P L122 f *2.60 76- 14 BeyondtheSe122²¼ RobrtsLgcy122¹ *HmlockBy*122¹¾ 5 wide move, 2nd best 8
9Dec02-1Pha fst 1 1/16 :23⁴ :48 1:14³ 1:51 Md 12500 12 1½ 1hd 32½ 87¾ 1022¼ Alvarado R Jr L118 f 21.40 33- 33 Sidler118¹¾ *Heat*118no Blue's Prospecter113¹¾ Vied to far turn,tired 12
12Nov02-2Med sly 1 :23⁴ :48¹ 1:14² 1:40² Md 12500(12.5-10.5) 4 2¹ 2½ 2hd 4⁶ 6¹⁸ Alvarado R Jr L118 *1.70e 52- 24 GrtitudeAttck118nk GreggiesStr118¹³¾ *SesidTony*118hd Bore out 1/4,faded 8
29Oct02-6Med fst 1 1/16 :23¹ :47⁴ 1:13 1:47⁴ ⓈMd Sp Wt 22k 8 52¾ 5² 65¼ 11¹⁶ 1133¾ Alvarado R Jr L118 3.90 36- 27 MssAttck118nk *MightyOk*111⁵½ BluesProspctr118½ Weakened 7wd far turn 12
10Oct02-4Med fm 1 Ⓣ:23³ :48⁴ 1:13 1:38 Md Sp Wt 29k 2 3¹ 3¹ 2hd 1hd 2² Alvarado R Jr L118 5.10 77- 19 CriticlBull115² RobertsLgcy118²¾ AidnsTurn118no Dueled,led,outfinished 9
WORKS: Jly27 Pha 4f fst :50² B 22/32 May14 Pha 4f fst :50 B 11/18
TRAINER: Turf/Dirt(10 .00 $0.00) Dirt(279 .13 $1.85) Sprint(199 .13 $1.62) MdnSpWt(17 .29 $4.48)

1. Jackety Jack: Earned a solid 55 Beyer Speed Figure at this level two starts back. Had an excuse last time out when he broke through the gate before the race. I usually give horses 10 starts before I give up on their learning curve. For babies with less than 10 starts, I add 10 Beyer points to their previous best. For 3-year-olds, I give a five-point Beyer credit. For 4-year-olds and older, I will only give three extra points. Because he is a 4-year-old, I was going to assume that Jackety Jack could run a 58 Beyer on his best day. **"A-day Beyer": 58**

2. See Frankie: Was terrible in the debut as the favorite despite starting for a top first-out barn. The pedigree doesn't excite. Add five points for being a lightly raced 3-year-old. **"A-day Beyer": 7**

3. Czar d'Or: Off slowly in both lifetime starts. Now has to deal with a layoff line. Earned a 42 Beyer in his debut, but that was before he was given Lasix. You'll notice that I scratched out the 42, as I only want to deal with past performances that will be similar to today's race. In his only race with Lasix, he failed to finish. Add three points to this 4-year-old with only two previous starts. **"A-day Beyer": 3**

4. **Quoit Rich:** Earned a 32 Beyer in debut, and now adds blinkers. I'll give him a five-point credit for being a lightly raced sophomore, and an extra five points for the equipment change. I would give five points extra if Lasix were added, blinkers were removed, or if the horse is announced as a first-time gelding. More-experienced handicappers with their own notes may add points if the horse is using mud caulks, bend shoes, etc. for the first time. **"A-day Beyer": 42**

5. **Runaway Train:** His best race was the 59 Beyer earned on June 19. He has already made 12 starts so I won't add any points to his total. **"A-day Beyer": 59**

6. **A Bag of Gold:** Scratched

7. **Twice Onabet:** Earned a 65 Beyer on the last past-performance line on the page. Has made 15 starts so can't bank on any further improvement. **"A-day Beyer": 65**

8. **Danzig's Jade:** Earned a career-best 46 Beyer when making his first start with blinkers. Another that gets five extra points for being a lightly raced 3-year-old. **"A-day Beyer": 51**

9. **Linden Lane:** First-time starter shows two quick works for capable debut barn, but the pedigree doesn't leap off the page, and he will be stuck on the far outside.

10. **Robert's Legacy:** Best races came on turf. Couldn't beat Penn National maidens on turf. After 14 starts, there doesn't seem to be much hope for improvement. **"A-day Beyer": 30**

I tell novice handicappers to find your top "A-day Beyer" and give yourself a 10-point margin for error. That would leave the top contenders as Jackety Jack, Runaway Train, and Twice Onabet.

Runaway Train was the 5-2 morning-line favorite. He had hit the board in his last four races, and was getting a favorable rider switch. The major knock on him was that he had already been to the post 12 times. Was he a professional maiden in waiting?

Jackety Jack was second choice at 7-2. He had good early speed, but I didn't like that he had broken through the gate prior to his recent race. He seemed like a fidgety sort, was losing the services of leading rider Joe Bravo, and would have to deal with the inside post position. Seemed like an underlay.

FIFTH RACE
Monmouth
AUGUST 7, 2004

6 FURLONGS. (1.07⁴) MAIDEN SPECIAL WEIGHT . Purse $46,000 (includes $9,000 NJB – NJ Bred Enhancement) FOR REGISTERED NEW JERSEY BREDS MAIDENS, THREE YEAR OLDS AND UPWARD. Three Year Olds, 119 lbs.; Older, 122 lbs.

Value of Race: $46,000 Winner $27,600; second $8,740; third $5,060; fourth $2,300; fifth $460; sixth $460; seventh $460; eighth $460; ninth $460. Mutuel Pool $191,877.00 Exacta Pool $176,808.00 Trifecta Pool $115,612.00

Last Raced	Horse	M/Eqt. A. Wt	PP	St	¼	½	Str	Fin	Jockey	Odds $1
11Jly04 5Mth2	Runaway Train	L b 4 122	5	7	4hd	23½	23	12	Elliott S	1.90
25Jly04 11Mth9	Jackety Jack	L bf 4 122	1	6	12	1½	1hd	2hd	Rocco J	3.50
25Jly04 11Mth5	Twice Onabet	L bf 4 117	6	8	82	75	43	37	Baze M C5	36.70
	Linden Lane	3 119	8	3	62	61	53	41½	King E L Jr	2.60
25Jly04 4Mth4	Danzig's Jade	L b 3 119	7	2	5hd	3hd	3hd	52¾	Garcia Alan	4.90
25Jly04 4Mth7	Quoit Rich	b 3 119	4	4	31	5½	61	6½	Ortiz F L	10.60
19Jun04 10Mth9	Czar d'Or	L b 4 115	3	9	9	9	83	79½	Gomez O7	51.00
9Jun04 2Mth7	See Frankie	L 3 119	2	5	21½	41	71	84	Trujillo E	27.10
9Jly04 2Pen6	Robert's Legacy	L f 4 122	1	1	74	82	9	9	Ferrer J C	33.00

OFF AT 2:53 Start Good . Won driving. Track fast.

TIME :22¹, :46¹, :58⁴, 1:11⁴ (:22.22, :46.21, :58.88, 1:11.95)

$2 Mutuel Prices:	5 – RUNAWAY TRAIN	5.80	3.00	2.60
	1 – JACKETY JACK		3.60	3.20
	7 – TWICE ONABET			6.40

$2 EXACTA 5–1 PAID $20.20 $2 TRIFECTA 5–1–7 PAID $193.20

B. r, (Apr), by Runaway Groom – Marjoram , by Muttering . Trainer Perry William W. Bred by Stacey Frangella & James Frangella Jr (NJ).

RUNAWAY TRAIN advanced inside into the turn, eased outside the pacesetter on the bend and finished steadily while edging clear late. JACKETY JACK saved ground while posting the early fractions and was no match late while holding the place. TWICE ONABET in close early, saved ground on the turn then closed well late along the inside. LINDEN LANE unseated the rider at the gate, was bumped at the start and lacked the needed stretch response. DANZIG'S JADE broke outward, raced well placed to the drive and tired. QUOIT RICH came out early, chased and raced five wide turning for home and tired. CZAR D'OR slow early, raced greenly down the backstretch and lacked a rally. SEE FRANKIE chased early and gave way in upper stretch. ROBERT'S LEGACY was through early.

Owners– 1, Frangella Jr Stacey and J A; 2, Sones Debra; 3, Foglia Anthony M; 4, Habernickel Irene; 5, Bennett Robert M; 6, Kling Barry; 7, Dependable Stables; 8, Dethomasi Carlo; 9, D'Arrigo Racing Stable

Trainers– 1, Perry William W; 2, Sones Debra; 3, Lima Rolando J; 4, Hartman Mary; 5, Carlesimo Charles Jr; 6, Kling Barry; 7, Hamer William E; 8, Ruggiero Phil Jr; 9, Shavelson Pam

Scratched– A Bag of Gold (25Jul04 4Mth3)

Twice Onabet earned the best "A-day Beyer." He was listed at 50-1 on the morning line, and rightly so. His recent races weren't pretty to look at, but he had passed tired horses in his last two races, and one could make an argument that he was rounding back into form, since he was making his fifth start of the form cycle. If you felt that the other "A-day Beyer" horses had holes in their form, and you were a very courageous handicapper, then you could play Twice Onabet at a big price. I decided to go for the home run, and play Twice Onabet to win and place, and use him in exacta boxes with Jackety Jack and Runaway Train.

As *Daily Racing Form* handicapper Jim Kachulis would say, "Aggravation for life." Jackety Jack made the lead as expected, but was soon met by Runaway Train heading into the turn. Twice Onabet had a smidgen of trouble at the start, raced inside for most of the way, and just missed second by a head. All at 36-1 odds. No win tickets cashed. No place tickets cashed. All I got was a measly $20.20 for the exacta box. Another appropriate Kachulisism would be "That's why you work."

Many followers of Beyer Speed Figures have trouble finding big prices because the world is in on the Beyer phenomenon. By unearthing a horse's best back Beyer, you may be able to uncover a nugget at a price once in a while.

SECOND-TIME STARTERS, FIRST-TIME LASIX

I had the good fortune to participate in the Daily Racing Form Horseplayers Expo 2004 in Las Vegas. Not only did I get to meet and greet some of the best handicappers in the world, but I was also able to fine-tune my selection-making process by utilizing some of their excellent advice. I've always been a big fan of Mark Cramer, and I got a big kick out of moderating his "Form Cycle Analysis" forum with Joe Cardello. Mark mentioned several profitable angles worth watching, and one concerned second-time-starting maidens that were receiving Lasix for the first time. He claimed that this was an extremely potent angle, and it seemed to make perfect sense. What if a live first-time starter bleeds? The resulting poor performance can be excused, and the horse can still be considered live for his next start with Lasix. Only with higher odds.

All Trumps
Own: Lazy F Ranch

Dk. b or b. c. 2 (Apr) FTSAUG03 $260,000			
Sire: Grand Slam (Gone West) $75,000			
Dam: Kris's Intention (Kris S.)			
Br: Kidder, Griggs, J & J Corp (Ky)			
Tr: Penna A J Jr(0 0 0 0 .00) 2004:(45 7 .16)			

	Life	2 1 0 0	$28,350	76	D.Fst	2 1 0 0	$28,350	76
	2004	2 1 0 0	$28,350	76	Wet(416)	0 0 0 0	$0	–
	2003	0 M 0 0	$0	–	Turf(335)	0 0 0 0	$0	–
	Sar	2 1 0 0	$28,350	76	Dst(305)	1 0 0 0	$1,350	45

4Sep04–4Sar fst 7f	:22 :45² 1:11² 1:24⁴	Md Sp Wt 45k	76 9 4 4⁴ 3⁵ 2¹ 1² Velasquez C	L119	3.05	80– 19 All Trumps119² Silent Bid119² Our FriendTimmy119no	Resolutely outside 10
7Aug04–2Sar fst 6f	:22⁴ :46¹ :59 1:12⁴	Md Sp Wt 45k	45 4 6 63½ 6⁸ 56½ 56½ Velasquez C	118	*2.30	72– 13 Funk118⁵½ Lion Cat118½ One Fein Dad118no	Bumped stretch 8

WORKS: Sep14 Bel 4f fst :51 B 20/23 Sep1 Sar 4f fst :48 B 8/69 Aug25 Sar 4f fst :48³ B 15/41 Aug18 Sar 4f fst :48 B 9/105 ●Aug4 Sar 3f fst :35 B 1/11 Jly30 Sar 4f fst :49⁴ B 43/151

All Trumps was bet down to 2-1 odds in the Funk race at Saratoga. A son of top debut sire Grand Slam, All Trumps cost $260,000 as a yearling, and showed bullet works for his first race. Trainer Angel Penna Jr. isn't known for his success with first-time starters, however, and it was surprising that All Trumps took so much money considering that Funk was going out for the formidable team of Todd Pletcher and John Velazquez. The long comment for All Trumps' debut was "bumped start, greenly turn, between rivals stretch, bumped." It sounded like a strenuous trip for such an inexperienced runner, and he bled to boot. Adding Lasix for the first time on September 4, All Trumps went off at 3-1 odds, and he did not disappoint.

The theory works with second-time starters that use blinkers for the first time. Take Accurate, for example.

Accurate
Own: Pugilsi Stables

Dk. b or b. c. 2 (Apr) OBSAPR04 $85,000			
Sire: Precise End (End Sweep) $6,000			
Dam: Love Destiny (Silver Deputy)			
Br: Sez Who Thoroughbreds (NY)			
Tr: Klesaris Steve(0 0 0 0 .00) 2004:(389 78 .20)			

	Life	2 1 0 0	$24,718	70	D.Fst	2 1 0 0	$24,718	70
	2004	2 1 0 0	$24,718	70	Wet(343°)	0 0 0 0	$0	–
	2003	0 M 0 0	$0	–	Turf(254°)	0 0 0 0	$0	–
	Sar	2 1 0 0	$24,718	70	Dst(360)	2 1 0 0	$24,718	70

5Sep04–2Sar fst 6f	:22² :46⁴ :59⁴ 1:12³	Ⓢ Md Sp Wt 41k	70 3 4 31½ 3² 1½ 13½ Velasquez C	L119 b	18.30	79– 14 Accurte119³½ NughtyNewYorker119⁶ Thundrprinc119²	3 wide move, clear 12
11Aug04–1Sar fst 6f	:22³ :46² :59¹ 1:12³	Ⓢ Md Sp Wt 41k	50 5 12 72¾ 76½ 68¼ 76¼ Velasquez C	L118	51.75	73– 17 UpLkThndr118no UrbnConqst118¹ MrMlprop118½	Ducked out start, wide 12

WORKS: Sep2 Sar 3f fst :37⁴ B 8/11 Aug27 Sar 4f fst :49⁴ B 21/26 Aug6 Sar 4f fst :49⁴ B 20/61 Jly31 Sar 4f fst :50 B 73/90 Jly22 Bel tr.t 4f fst :49¹ B 5/9

He went off at a huge price for his debut, and he showed some immaturity. The long comment states that he "ducked out at the start, four-wide trip, tired stretch." One would think that the new blinkers would cure his start woes, and help him to focus better on the task at hand. They did. He showed better speed in his second start, and went on to easily win at 18-1 odds.

Whenever a runner adds blinkers or Lasix for the second lifetime start, pay attention. The trainer is showing intent, and if the horse flashed any little bit of ability in the debut, the equipment change may spur on the improvement needed to find the winner's circle.

TRIP HANDICAPPING

We've discussed the advantages of speed in maiden races. But what happens when a maiden gets caught up in a hot speed duel and is found wanting in the stretch? Do we classify the horse as a quitter? I've always tried to give the benefit of the doubt to lightly raced runners with speed. Let's look at J P Jewel.

I loved J P Jewel when she made her debut for Nick Zito on August 5, 2004, at Saratoga. She showed some sharp workouts, and I was very pleased that she took some early tote action. She shot to the front along the inside, but was soon joined by three other pace rivals. She went 21³/₅ for the first quarter, and still had a nostril in front when the field turned for home. Understandably, she faltered in the final furlong, and jockey Edgar Prado wrapped up on her in the late stages. Taking a peek at the race chart, you would see that the first three finishers were racing in ninth, fourth, and 10th at the first call. Closers simply benefited from the scorching pace.

When J P Jewel showed up for her second start on September 3, many handicappers were apprehensive about betting her. She was stretching out a quarter of a mile to seven furlongs, and people were questioning whether she would have the stamina to hold on. All I knew was she had good speed, and was trained by a man that historically did better with second-time starters than with firsters. It also helped that I was very familiar with the race favorite. Lemon Lady, a Pletcher-Velazquez production by Lemon Drop Kid, caught my eye in her debut. I thought she would run well, but was disappointed when she raced greenly in the stretch, and couldn't keep up with the competition.

J P Jewel earned a 50 Beyer in her debut. Lemon Lady received a 64. Was Lemon Lady really 14 Beyer points better? Visually, I didn't think so. Plus, J P Jewel figured to be on the lead. Trip handicappers knew that J P Jewel was fast and that Lemon Lady was green. Pace handicappers marked down J P Jewel's debut fractions, and were impressed. She seemed worth a play, and I threw her in with a few others in multi-race wagers.

FOURTH RACE
Saratoga
SEPTEMBER 3, 2004

7 FURLONGS. (1.20²) MAIDEN SPECIAL WEIGHT . Purse $45,000 (UP TO $8,550 NYSBFOA) FOR MAIDENS, FILLIES TWO YEARS OLD. Weight, 119 lbs.

Value of Race: $45,000 Winner $27,000; second $9,000; third $4,500; fourth $2,250; fifth $1,350; sixth $180; seventh $180; eighth $180; ninth $180; tenth $180. Mutuel Pool $504,578.00 Exacta Pool $498,158.00 Quinella Pool $52,632.00 Trifecta Pool $335,848.00

Last Raced	Horse	M/Eqt. A. Wt	PP	St	¼	½	Str	Fin	Jockey	Odds $1
5Aug04 4Sar6	J P Jewel	L	2 119	8	3	1hd	1½	18	16½	Castellano J J	2.80
9Aug04 4Sar6	Winning Season	L	2 119	10	1	21½	21½	21½	22¾	Day P	12.70
9Aug04 4Sar4	Theschemeofthings	L	2 119	3	5	32½	3½	32½	3¾	Migliore R	9.60
	Burant Orange		2 119	9	4	93	92½	5hd	43½	Sellers S J	21.80
18Aug04 2Sar5	Lemon Lady	L	2 119	5	6	4hd	42½	41½	51½	Velazquez J R	2.30
9Aug04 4Sar5	Marchonin	L	2 119	4	7	71	61½	61½	61¾	Albarado R J	43.25
1Aug04 4Sar5	Key Causeway	L	2 119	7	2	62½	73½	72	72	Fragoso P	7.20
	Stock Tip	b	2 119	1	9	81½	8hd	82	83¾	Prado E S	6.90
	Hooky	L	2 119	6	10	10	10	93½	911½	Dominguez R A	8.80
	Taramundi–UAE	L	2 119	2	8	5½	54½	10	10	Velasquez C	50.75

OFF AT 2:38 Start Good . Won driving. Track fast.
TIME :22³, :45², 1:10³, 1:24¹ (:22.66, :45.51, 1:10.76, 1:24.31)

$2 Mutuel Prices:

8 – J P JEWEL	7.60	5.20	4.00
10 – WINNING SEASON		10.20	6.40
3 – THESCHEMEOFTHINGS			5.10

$2 EXACTA 8–10 PAID $102.50 $2 QUINELLA 8–10 PAID $69.00
$2 TRIFECTA 8–10–3 PAID $545.00

Dk. b or br. f, (May), by Dixie Union – Easy 'n Gold , by Slew o' Gold . Trainer Zito Nicholas P. Bred by Kilroy Thoroughbred Partnership (Ky).

J P JEWEL bumped at the start, rushed up along the inside to gain the early advantage, set the pace under pressure to the turn, shook loose in upper stretch and drew off while being kept to the task. WINNING SEASON pressed the pace outside the winner to the top of the stretch but couldn't stay with that one through the lane. THESCHEMEOFTHINGS checked in tight at the start, raced just off the pace for a half, lodged a mild bid while three wide leaving the turn then lacked a strong closing response. BURANT ORANGE ducked out after the start, raced well back to the turn then failed to threaten with a mild late rally. LEMON LADY raced up close while four wide for five furlongs and faded in the stretch. MARCHONIN ducked in at the start, raced in the middle of the pack to the turn and lacked a strong closing bid. KEY CAUSEWAY bumped at the start, failed to mount a serious rally while three wide. STOCK TIP broke awkwardly then race greenly in the early stages and failed to threaten thereafter. HOOKY was outrun after breaking slowly. TARAMUNDI (UAE) failed to menace while saving ground.

Owners– 1, Ol Memorial Stable; 2, Overbrook Farm; 3, Never Tell Farm; 4, Rutherford Mike G; 5, MerryDale Farm; 6, Goodman John B; 7, Evans Edward P; 8, Flying Zee Stable; 9, Egan Jaye and Thomas J; 10, Darley Stable

Trainers– 1, Zito Nicholas P; 2, Lukas D Wayne; 3, Ward John T Jr; 4, Mott William I; 5, Pletcher Todd A; 6, Matz Michael R; 7, Hennig Mark; 8, Biancone Patrick L; 9, Bond Harold James; 10, Albertrani Thomas

FIRST-TIME MAIDEN CLAIMERS

This angle is commonly referred to as the most powerful class drop in racing. That statement can be considered true, as horses dropping from maiden special weights are obviously facing weaker competition when they meet maiden claimers. The reason I didn't rank this angle higher on the list is that so many handicappers have caught on to it. While the class-drop angle consistently produces winners, the prices have decreased over the years. Still, it is a very effective tool to have in your handicapping arsenal. Especially when the horse dropping in class has good early speed.

Sis City raced twice at Churchill Downs for Steve Asmussen. She showed speed both times, but faded badly when the real running began. Asmussen dropped her in for $50,000 at Saratoga, and that seemed like a reasonable spot for the homebred daughter of a stallion that stands for only five grand. Many folks believe that when trainers drop horses in for a tag, they are ready to give up on the runner. I don't buy that. I feel that every horse has a winning class level. If a horse with a moderate pedigree drops into a maiden claimer, don't be afraid. The connections are trying to find the right spot in order to get the money. People are in this business to win races and make money. Running fourth and fifth in maiden specials isn't going to pay the feed man.

Dropping a horse in class is a risk worth taking when the runner was bought (or, in this case, bred) for less than the claiming price. When a son of Seattle Slew that sold for $500,000 at Keeneland drops in for $50,000, then you have to worry. In Sis City's case, she was properly placed, and just held on to win by a nose. Unfortunately for Asmussen and company, she was claimed by Richard Dutrow Jr., and won her next start by 16 lengths in a Monmouth stakes event.

Northern Concorde is another example of a drop-down worth playing.

Northern Concorde
Own: Robsham Mrs. E P

Dk. b or b. c. 2 (Feb) OBSAPR04 $65,000
Sire: Concorde's Tune (Concorde Bound) $2,000
Dam: Pocket Beauty (Storm Bird)
Br: E. Paul Robsham (Fla)
Tr: Hough Stanley M(0 0 0 0 .00) 2004:(201 40 .20)

Life	4	1	1	0	$31,040	65	D.Fst	2	1	1	0	$28,400	63
2004	4	1	1	0	$31,040	65	Wet(347)	2	0	0	0	$2,640	65
2003	0	M	0	0	$0	-	Turf(343)	0	0	0	0	$0	-
Sar	2	1	0	0	$21,150	65	Dst(370)	4	1	1	0	$31,040	65

12Aug04-3Sar	fst	5f	:22	:454		:591	Md 75000	63	2	4	1½	11½	11½	11¾	Castellano J J	L118 f	2.80	91-09	NorthernConcorde1181¾ DecemberFir1182¼ *StndRdy*1181½	Set pace, clear	6
28Jly04-5Sar	my	5½f	:22	:453	:581	1:05	Md Sp Wt 45k	65	3	4	36½	34	33	56¾	Castellano J J	L118 f	9.40	84-15	Royal Moment118¾ Malheur1182¾ Flagstaff1181½	Chased inside, no bid	9
5Jly04-4Bel	fst	5½f	:222	:452	:581	1:05	Md Sp Wt 43k	62	1	1	1½	1hd	2hd	23¼	Castellano J J	L118 f	*1.50	85-15	Vicrg1183¼ NorthrnConcord1181¼ MrHrtbrkr1185¾	Vied inside, weakened	7
18Jun04-4Bel	gd	5f	:221	:46		:59	Md Sp Wt 43k	45	2	6	77¾	78½	612	57½	Castellano J J	118 f	4.60	81-10	*Schiloh*110hd Tip City1184½ *Storm Creek Rising*1182¾	Greenly	8

WORKS: Sep11 Bel tr.t 5f fst 1:012 B *2/21* Sep1 Sar 4f fst :483 B *19/69* Aug24 Sar 4f fst :481 B *10/45* Jly22 Bel 5f fst 1:032 B *22/24* Jly15 Bel tr.t 4f gd :48 B *3/8* Jun28 Bel 5f fst 1:00 Hg *3/16*

He failed to meet his reserve at auction and was bought back for $65,000 by his breeder in April 2004, and shortly thereafter made his debut in a maiden special weight. He showed improved speed in his second start with the addition of Lasix, and was entered in the opening-day maiden special weight of the 2004 Saratoga meet. He couldn't keep up with those horses early and tired in the stretch. Although he had lost ground from the stretch call to the finish in his last two starts, his good speed combined with the drop in class made him an instant contender when he was entered for $75,000. Instead of facing some of the most promising maidens around, he was tackling several proven losers. Northern Concorde didn't have fancy breeding, and figured to need a class adjustment in order to win. He did, and 5-2 odds were very juicy.

Why bet a horse like Countless Gold in a maiden claimer?

Countless Gold
Own: J. Jeps Stable

B. c. 3 (Feb) FTSAUG02 $175,000
Sire: Formal Gold (Black Tie Affair*Ire) $7,500
Dam: Countless Affairs (Storm Cat)
Br: Gainesway Thoroughbreds Ltd. (Ky)
Tr: Synnefias Dimitrios K(0 0 0 0 .00) 2004:(166 21 .13)

Life	6	M	0	0	$3,805	64	D.Fst	4	0	0	0	$1,550	44
2004	6	M	0	0	$3,805	64	Wet(378)	2	0	0	0	$2,255	64
2003	0	M	0	0	$0	-	Turf(294)	0	0	0	0	$0	-
Aqu	1	0	0	0	$205	40	Dst(372)	1	0	0	0	$205	40

20Aug04-5Mth	fst	1 1/16	:25	:503	1:153	1:462	3↑ Md 32000(32-28)	30	5	53	54½	55	515	521¾	Baze M C5	L113	11.10	51-27	SphonsGlory1222 Cmpnd1184¼ Snglbrrlshtgn1182¾	Away bit slowly,no bid	5
12Aug04-6Mth	fst	6f	:212	:442	:57	1:11	3↑ Md Sp Wt 37k	44	3	11	1010	911	911	911¾	Ortiz F L	L119 f	123.10	73-14	Cambaco1192¾ Little Dovefeather119nk *Sargasso*1192¾	Outrun	12
20Mar04-1Aqu	my	7f	:22	:451	1:113	1:262	3↑ Md Sp Wt 41k	40	7	8	914	918	918	78¾	Beitia A O	L115 f	10.00e	64-27	D Two My Son's1101 Augusttown Maxi124¾ Jack's Jet124¾	Had no rally	10
Placed 6th through disqualification																					
28Feb04-6Aqu	fst	1⅛	⊡ :50	1:15	1:394	1:52	Md Sp Wt 42k	9	8	64	72½	88¼	832	843	Pimentel J	L121	18.80	39-16	Cuba1215¾ Old Gold121nk Gibbons Terrace116hd	Wide throughout, tired	8
4Feb04-1Aqu	my	6f	⊡ :23	:452	:572	1:094	Md Sp Wt 41k	64	1	8	88½	714	518	412½	Beitia A O	L121	23.80	77-14	Abbondanza1215¾ *Pisgah*1212¼ Torun1214½	Came wide, no rally	8
22Jan04-4Aqu	fst	6f	⊡ :231	:464	:593	1:123	Md c-(20-18)	44	6	8	1212	1114	89¾	54¾	Lopez C C	L121 f	10.40	71-17	*Clever Greek*1211½ A. P. Lax109¾ Master Painter1211¾	Belatedly outside	12
Claimed from Centennial Farms for $20,000, Rice Linda Trainer 2003: (352 51 53 52 0.14)																					

WORKS: Aug4 Mth 4f fst :50 B *12/18* Jly16 Mth 5f fst 1:012 Hg *6/32* Jly3 Mth 4f fst :494 B *21/49*

He sold for $175,000 as a yearling, and wasn't even given a chance to debut in a maiden special weight. If he had at least raced once against nonclaimers, then perhaps I would have given him a chance on the class drop. But on January 22, 2004, at Aqueduct, Linda Rice tossed Countless Gold in for $20,000. Powerful owners like Centennial Farms do not fool around. This was a definite throwaway horse. They were fortunate that someone took the bait.

FIRST-TIME FAST TRACK

I am a very forgiving handicapper. If a horse has a pedigree I like, or if he has some speed, or if he showed me anything in a trip, then I'm willing to follow him to the ends of the earth. Many times, such horses lead me down blind alleys. Then, a Lure of Gold comes along.

Lure of Gold
Own: Grant Mary and Joseph and Kelly, Thom

Gr/ro. f. 3 (Mar)
Sire: Formal Gold (Black Tie Affair*Ire) $7,500
Dam: Concolour (Our Native)
Br: Thomas J. Kelly & Joseph M. Grant (Ky)
Tr: Kelly Patrick J(0 0 0 0 .00) 2004:(167 11 .07)

Life	10	1	0	0	$30,833	74	D.Fst	2	1	0	0	$25,505	61
2004	5	0	0	0	$1,553	74	Wet(346)	3	0	0	0	$3,580	58
2003	5	1	0	0	$29,280	64	Turf(273)	5	0	0	0	$1,748	74
Aqu ⊡	2	1	0	0	$25,505	61	Dst(356)	2	1	0	0	$25,505	61

5Sep04-5Sar	fm	1	Ⓣ :242 :483 1:122 1:361	ⒻAlw 48000N2L	74	6	74½	51½	82	86½	84½	Albarado R J	L117 b	20.70e	86-06	RightThisWy119no Muguet117hd TuesdyPryr1191½	Between foes, no rally	10
22Aug04-8Sar	sf	1	Ⓣ :243 :49 1:15 1:392	3↑ ⒻAlw 48000N1X	52	9	44	42½	64¾	810	814	Espinoza J L	L115 b	11.20e	60-26	GoRobin1171½ WinlocsGloryDys1151 MedowBll120¾	Chased outside, tired	10
25Apr04-6Aqu	fm	1	Ⓣ :24 :491 1:134 1:38	ⒻAlw 44000N2L	38	2	74¾	61½	1010	1015	919	Garcia Alan5	L112 b	34.25	68-13	FortunteDmsel1174¾ TnTrsurs119½ MissPrkPlc1121	Drift out second turn	10
18Mar04-5Aqu	my	1	:232 :463 1:111 1:382	ⒻAlw 44000N1X	58	2	55	54½	68½	68½	67¾	Fragoso P5	L112 b	15.00	65-25	GrandPrayer117¾ *FortunateDamsel*1123½ SpecilTctics119½	Inside trip, tired	6
11Feb04-8Aqu	fst	1 1/16	⊡ :233 :49 1:15 1:471	ⒻⓇNijana60k	51	1	74½	61¾	51½	811	815½	Bridgmohan S X	L115 b	26.00	59-28	ExclusivelyWild1154 TemptingNot117nk TittingrRos1151½	4 wide, bumped	9
28Dec03-3Aqu	fst	170	⊡ :244 :494 1:151 1:454	ⒻMd Sp Wt 42k	61	1	1hd	11	1hd	11	12¼	Thornton T5	L114 b	8.50	65-29	LureofGold1142¼ AftertheTone1142 RingaringRosie114¾	Set pace, driving	6
7Nov03-3Aqu	my	1⅛	:48 1:14 1:41 1:543	ⒻMd Sp Wt 46k	31	3	612	49½	68½	616	621¾	Castellano J J	L119 b	4.20e	41-30	Smash Hit119no Unshuttered11911¼ *Tig*119no	Steadied first turn	6
10Oct03-4Bel	fm	1⅛	Ⓣ :494 1:144 1:40 1:514	ⒻMd Sp Wt 46k	59	8	95½	95½	94¼	75¾	57¾	Fragoso P5	L114	16.10	63-29	LucifersStone1193½ IndyChrmer119nk *HoneyRydr*1193½	Steadied first turn	10
28Sep03-5Bel	sly	7f	:223 :461 1:12 1:254	ⒻMd Sp Wt 45k	52	5	1	53	57½	413	413	Guidry M	L119	5.70	58-23	Rare Gift1195½ Grand Prayer114nk Mystified1197¼	3 wide trip, no rally	6
11Sep03-4Bel	fm	1	Ⓣ :231 :463 1:103 1:352	ⒻMd Sp Wt 46k	64	8	1115½	1111	98¾	98	84¾	Guidry M	118	37.75e	78-09	PleseTkeMOut1182 RoylTromp1181¼ HonyRydr118no	5 wide turn, no rally	12

WORKS: Aug30 Sar 4f fst :482 B *23/63* Aug16 Sar tr.t Ⓣ 4f fm :482 B *9/23* Aug9 Sar tr.t Ⓣ 4f hd :483 B *12/24* Aug4 Sar tr.t Ⓣ 4f fm :494 B(d) *16/24* Jly30 Sar 3f fst :38 B *19/25* Jun18 Bel 3f my :362 B(d) *1/2*

Lure of Gold is a half-sister to Evening Attire, one of the most consistent handicap horses of recent years. My fellow *Daily Racing Form* handicapper Paul Malecki and I positively loved her chances on December 28, 2003, at Aqueduct. Why were we so confident? She had never cracked the trifecta up to that time, and her past-performance lines were filled with uninspiring comments such as "no rally." We liked her because we could forgive her for all of her past indiscretions. The race in question was a two-turn maiden special weight over a fast Aqueduct inner strip. Lure of Gold had made her debut on the turf. Throw the race out. She then sprinted in the slop (bet down to 5-1, no less). Throw the race out. Another turf try followed. Another toss-out. Then a two-turn try in the mud (again taking money). We drew another line through that race.

If you dismissed all of the races, as Paul and I did, you were left with what was essentially a first-time starter that happened to be a half-sister to Evening Attire. She had an inside post, which is essential in two-turn races over the inner track. She was facing ordinary horses. At best, she was a great value play. At worst, she had a chance. At 8-1, we were willing to take that gamble.

FIRST TIME ROUTING

It's in the Mail
Own: The Maltese Cross

Ch. g. 3 (Apr) EASOCT02 $8,500
Sire: Deposit Ticket (Northern Baby) $3,000
Dam: Video Sister (Horatius)
Br: Mr. & Mrs. Charles McGinnes (Md)
Tr: Robinson Catherine H(0 0 0 0 .00) 2004:(84 11 .13)

Life	4 1 0 0	$3,135 59	D.Fst	3 1 0 0	$7,075 59
2004	4 1 0 0	$3,135 59	Wet(329)	1 0 0 0	$1,260 41
2003	0 M 0 0	$0 –	Turf(280)	0 0 0 0	$0 –
Lrl	0 0 0 0	$0 –	Dst(323)	2 1 0 0	$7,575 59

11Sep04–5Pim fst 1⅛ :23 :46¹ 1:10⁴ 1:43³ 3↑ Clm 25000(25–20)x2l 59 7 5¹¹ 6¹¹ 4¹⁰ 4¹¹ 4¹⁴ Hamilton S D L120 f 18.70 75– 21 Fast Exercise120¹⁰½ Legend's Silver120²¼ Aspen Moon116¹ No factor 9
19Aug04–1Pim fst 1⅛ :24¹ :48⁴ 1:13⁴ 1:46⁴ 3↑ Md 14000(16–14) 57 4 3¹ 32 32¼ 1¹ 13¼ Hamilton S D L115 f 8.40 73– 22 ItsintheMil115³¼ BKsOnthePrk115² SilOnKent120¹½ Stalked pace, driving 8
Previously trained by Merryman Ann W
21Jly04–1Del fst 6f :22¹ :46¹ :59 1:11⁴ 3↑ Md 40000(40–35) 23 3 2 75¼ 75¾ 6¹² 6¹⁸¾ Castillo O O 117 9.00 63– 20 Doctor Rock117³¼ Drew's Delight122ⁿ⁰ Saga Boy115¹ Outrun 7
25Jun04–2Del wf 6f :21⁴ :44 :56² 1:09¹ 3↑ Md 40000(40–35) 41 5 7 7¹⁰ 7¹⁵ 7¹⁶ 4¹⁸¼ Castillo O O 116 8.00 76– 12 Mr Playboy116¹⁶¾ Sly Doc120¹ Dangerous Ridge116¹¼ Passed tiring rivals 7
WORKS: Aug14 Pim 4f fst :50⁴ B 18/24 Jly11 Pim 4f fst :49¹ B 2/5 Jun22 Pim 3f fst :37 Bg 2/4

It's in the Mail had shown nothing in two previous sprint starts at Delaware, but he was stretching out for the first time on August 19, 2004, in the first race at Pimlico. Could it be that all he ever wanted was a route race? Certainly, a forgiving handicapper could dismiss the sprint tries, and the first-time routing angle is even more powerful when it goes hand in hand with the two-sprints-to-a-route move.

It's not like It's in the Mail was completely dead on the board in his two races at the tougher Delaware circuit. He went off at less than 10-1 both times. He figured to have sufficient bottom to go the extra distance with those two sprints on his page, and he had a plethora of other angles going for him as well. He was dropping from a $40,000 maiden claimer to a $14,000 seller. That's a completely reasonable drop in class for a $9,500 auction purchase. He was adding Lasix for the first time and was making his first start for a new barn. Chasing hot quarter-miles in those sprint races sharpened his speed for the stretch-out, and he remained prominent throughout the running before drawing off to win by open lengths.

When one maiden angle is on display, a handicapper should definitely take notice. When two or more are obvious, then the horse should be respected as a top contender. Also, when a horse is trained by one of our listed horsemen, or is sired by one of our hot stallions, it's definitely worth considering that horse the first time he tries something new. It's very possible that it took some time and experimentation before he found his niche on the racetrack.

THE PROFESSIONAL MAIDEN

Being a forgiving handicapper, I want to believe that every horse has a winning class level. Most of them do. Then there are the professional maidens. The follow-the-leader types. The Bucksome Girls of this world.

Bucksome Girl
Own: Rublee Marianne

B. f. 4 (Mar)
Sire: Thats Our Buck (Buckaroo) $1,000
Dam: Pepsgorgeousgirl (Hello Gorgeous)
Br: Marianne Rublee (Fla)
Tr: Rountree Cathy(3 0 2 0 .00) 2004:(43 8 .19)

Life	15	M	2	2	$8,844	60	D.Fst	9	0	2	2	$7,578 60
2004	6	M	1	0	$2,627	60	Wet(264)	2	0	0	0	$770 42
2003	9	M	1	2	$6,217	48	Turf(183)	4	0	0	0	$496 53
Crc	5	0	1	1	$4,390	48	Dst(288)	0	0	0	0	$0 -

11May04-4Crc	fst	6½f	:223 :462 1:132 1:202	3↑ⒻMd 22500(25-22.5)	34	3	8	86¾	85½	65¾	69¾	Boulanger G	L119	9.00	67-18	Sailor's Gold1172¼ Miss Maronie1171 *Starlana*1101	Off slowly	8
17Apr04-7Tam	fm	*1 1/16 Ⓣ	:243 :504 1:17 1:474	4↑ⒻMd Sp Wt 16k	35	10	96¾	913	108¼	812	714¼	Garcia J J	L120	15.70	57-25	Oh So Wonderful1205¼ Latin Storm1202 *Gigiski*1202¼	No threat	10
13Mar04-6Tam	fm	*1 1/16 Ⓣ	:234 :502 1:161 1:49	4↑ⒻMd Sp Wt 13k	53	2	94¾	106¾	108¼	105½	73¼	Garcia J J	L120	21.00	62-27	KingsFancy120hd HearMeClerly120½ SpecilTpestry1201	Failed to menace	10
28Feb04-11Tam	fst	1⅛	:474 1:143 1:413 1:551	4↑ⒻMd Sp Wt 13k	60	9	1013	1114	105¾	64½	54¼	Arango L E	L120	11.70	84-13	Chaos1202¼ Cateress120¾ Miss Ruby Jo1201¼	Passed tiring rivals	11
5Feb04-6Tam	fst	7f	:232 :471 1:131 1:264	4↑ⒻMd 25000(25-20)	48	3	8	87¾	86	72¼	22¾	DHGarcia J J	L120	4.70	76-13	RnsApprl1202¾ DHBcksGrl120 DHSplshnPrncss1201¼	Split horses, gaining	8
20Jan04-10Tam	wf	7f	:233 :473 1:14 1:284	4↑ⒻMd Sp Wt 13k	42	9	6	74¾	79	69¼	42½	Arango L E	L120	8.10	66-21	*La Joconde*120nk Glamorama120nk Silver Ruckus1202	Closed gap too late	9
23Dec03-2Crc	fst	1	:243 :491 1:151 1:43	3↑ⒻMd 25000(25-22.5)	46	8	88¾	811	78½	66	66¾	Velasquez C	L119	3.50	59-29	Pixel1193½ Miss Vice Regent1191 Princess K K119¾	Outrun	8
1Dec03-10Crc	fst	7f	:23 :471 1:132 1:273	3↑ⒻMd 25000(25-22.5)	48	1	8	87	78	54½	22¼	Arango L E	L119	9.40	74-14	*PointSunshine*1192¼ BucksomGirl119½ HonorblGl1142¼	Slow st, closed well	8
21Nov03-1Crc	fst	6½f	:23 :47 1:123 1:192	3↑ⒻMd 25000(25-22.5)	39	3	7	66	67	57	39¼	Arango L E	L119	11.00	73-18	NoRsrvtions1145 MissVcRgnt1194¼ BucksomGrl1191¾	Broke in air, 3 wide	7
Previously trained by Bernhart Walter																		
26Oct03-11Crc	fst	7f	:224 :47 1:141 1:283	3↑ⒻMd 25000(25-22.5)	34	6	4	78½	78½	64½	56½	Toribio A Jr	L119b	11.00	64-15	Texas Prez1193¾ Cymbidium1191½ Skip's Best Girl119½	Outrun	7

On paper, Bucksome Girl didn't look like she was on the road to being a lifetime loser. She had made the trifecta in four of her first 12 starts, and her Beyer Speed Figures weren't bad at all for a maiden at Tampa Bay Downs. The astute handicapper, however, knew that Bucksome Girl didn't have much heart. She often broke slowly, a sign that a horse doesn't want to win. She showed no early interest in her races. Another poor sign. She would take off after horses when she was well behind, but on the rare instances that she got into contention, she would start to hang noticeably. Her stride would shorten, and she would go into a circle gallop (up-and-down motion, even finish) for the remainder of the race. She wasn't a leader, but merely content to follow.

Her connections tried everything. They gave her blinkers, they took the blinkers off. They tried Lasix. They tried turf. They tried sprinting on the dirt, and then tried to go long. Maiden special weights. Maiden claimers. It didn't matter.

For those handicappers that don't have the time to do extensive trip analysis, here are some code words in the short comment lines that will alert you to the possibility of an older professional maiden. Remember that I'm willing to forgive the babies and the lightly raced runners. When an older maiden shows these comments on his page, raise the red flags.

Lunged start	Greenly	Pulled up
Drifted start	Bled	Balked
Ducked out start	Sore	Dwelt
Hung	Vanned off	Unruly
Drifted out	Walked off	Swerved
Drifted in	Broke out	Impeded Rival
Lugged out	Broke in	Bumped rival
Lugged in	Fractious	Veered in
Broke through gate	Left lead	Bore out
Rank	Threw head	Bolted
Pulled	Washy	

I think you get the picture. Professional maidens are pretty easy to spot. They are horses that have basically tried everything, and still haven't made an impact. Sometimes these horses take money because their Beyer Speed Figures compare well with the rest of the field. Still, that does not make them good betting propositions.

FASTER DIVISIONS OF SPLIT RACES:
How to Spot Key and Negative Key Races

FAST HORSES WIN fast races, and fast horses place in fast races. With that in mind, let's jump into a discussion of split divisions of maiden events, and how to profit in the long term from them. The Keeneland spring meet is a wonderland place for fans of maiden races. The young juveniles are being unveiled, late-blooming 3-year-olds are hoping to leap into classic contention, and older maidens usually find themselves in excellent betting heats. I feel that one can find key races by zoning in on the faster divisions of split maiden heats on a given day.

Opening day at Keeneland 2004 showcased a pair of maiden special weights at $8\frac{1}{2}$ furlongs for 3-year-olds. The first division went in 1:45.60. The other was completed in 1:47.05. From the looks of things, the first division was definitely filled with better horses. A key angle in handicapping maiden races is to look for the top three to five finishers in the faster division of split races. Logically, if those horses ran in the slower division, they either would have won the race, or finished much closer to the leader. These horses usually run very well the next time they tackle maiden competition.

I'm usually not fond of maiden winners when they tackle open company for the first time, but Ecclesiastic, the winner of the first division, was able to handle the jump up in class. He won a N1X allowance at Belmont in his next start at 2-1 odds. Mr. Mabee, the runner-up in the first division, returned to win a maiden race at Churchill Downs in his next start, but was unfortunately pounded to 2-5 favoritism. I decided to follow the split divisions for the rest of the Keeneland meet, and see if I could find some upcoming key races.

Sunday, April 4
Race 3 - Seven Furlongs, Maiden Special Weight, 3-Year-Olds. Final Time - 1:24.73
Race 5 - Seven Furlongs, Maiden Special Weight, 3-Year-Olds. Final Time - 1:25.13
Winners coming out of the faster division:
Mahzouz (finished second): Won next two starts at Belmont (Maiden Special at 1-1, N1X at 7-1).
J Town (finished third): Won next two starts (Maiden Special at Keeneland, N1X at Churchill, both at 6-5 odds).

Wednesday, April 14
Race 4 - Six Furlongs, Maiden Special Weight, 3-Year-Old Fillies. Final Time - 1:11.58
Race 6 - Six Furlongs, Maiden Special Weight, 3-Year-Old Fillies. Final Time - 1:12.64
Winner from the faster division:
Navajo Breeze (finished third): Won Maiden Special at Mountaineer at 1-2 odds.

Thursday, April 22
Race 6 - Seven Furlongs, Maiden Special Weight, 3-Year-Old Fillies. Final Time - 1:24.26

Race 4 - Seven Furlongs, Maiden Special Weight, 3-Year-Old Fillies. Final Time - 1:25.58

Winners from the faster division:

Eye of the Sphynx (winner): Won Fury Stakes at Woodbine at 3-2 odds, then won next two stakes races.

Present Danger (finished third): Won Maiden Special at Monmouth at 5-2 odds.

Friday, April 23

Race 7 - About Seven Furlongs, Maiden Special Weight, 3-Year-Olds. Final Time - 1:26.72

Race 5 - About Seven Furlongs, Maiden Special Weight, 3-Year-Olds. Final Time - 1:28.67

Winners from the faster division:

J Town (winner): Won N1X at Churchill Downs at 6-5 odds.

Storm Legacy (second): Won Maiden Special at Belmont at 2-1 odds.

Three of the four faster divisions came back as key races. I was definitely intrigued, but I needed more data. So I decided to break out a copy of the 2004 *Saratoga Players' Guide,* and checked out the results of the previous year's Spa meet.

Saturday, July 26

Race 3 - 6½ Furlongs, Maiden Special Weight, 2-Year-Olds. Final Time - 1:16.88

Race 5 - 6½ Furlongs, Maiden Special Weight, 2-Year-Olds. Final Time - 1:17.22

Winners from the faster division:

Undisclosed (fourth): Won $75,000 Maiden Claimer at 7-2 odds.

Donaldson Flats (seventh): Won $50,000 Maiden Claimer at 9-1 odds.

Commendation (eighth): Won Maiden Special on turf at 14-1 odds.

Sunday, August 3

Race 2 - Seven Furlongs, Maiden Special Weight, NY-bred, 3-Year-Olds and Up. Final Time - 1:24.45

Race 4 - Seven Furlongs, Maiden Special Weight, NY-bred, 3-Year-Olds and Up. Final Time - 1:24.63

Winner from the faster division:

My Salute to You (eighth): Won Maiden Special at Finger Lakes at 3-2 odds.

Monday, August 4

Race 1 - Six Furlongs, Maiden Special Weight, NY-bred, 3-Year-Olds and Up, Fillies and Mares. Final Time: 1:12.27

Race 4 - Six Furlongs, Maiden Special Weight, NY-bred, 3-Year-Olds and Up, Fillies and Mares. Final Time: 1:12.68

Winners from the faster division:
None.

Wednesday, August 6

Race 4 - 5^1/$_2$ Furlongs, Maiden Special Weight, NY-bred, 2-Year-Olds. Final Time - 1:05.74

Race 1 - 5^1/$_2$ Furlongs, Maiden Special Weight, NY-bred, 2-Year-Olds. Final Time - 1:06.62

Winners from the faster division:
None.

Thursday, August 7

Race 4 - 5^1/$_2$ Furlongs, Maiden Special Weight, NY-breds, 2-Year-Old Fillies. Final Time - 1:04.18

Race 2 - 5^1/$_2$ Furlongs, Maiden Special Weight, NY-breds, 2-Year-Old Fillies. Final Time - 1:04.48

Winners from the faster division:
None.

Monday, August 11

Race 1 - Nine Furlongs, Maiden Special Weight, NY-breds, 3-Year-Olds and Up, Fillies and Mares. Off the turf. Final Time - 1:55.27

Race 9 - Nine Furlongs, Maiden Special Weight, NY-breds, 3-Year-Olds and Up, Fillies and Mares. Off the turf. Final Time - 1:55.35

Winners from the faster division:

None.

Saturday, August 16

Race 2 - Six Furlongs, Maiden Special Weight, 2-Year-Olds. Final Time - 1:10.89

Race 5 - Six Furlongs, Maiden Special Weight, 2-Year-Olds. Final Time - 1:12.25

Winners from the faster division:

Purge (winner): Won N1X at Gulfstream at 3-5 odds.

Wildly (third): Won Maiden Special at Belmont at 3-5 odds.

Under Caution (fourth): Won Maiden Special at Arlington at 1-1 odds.

Charismatic Rob (sixth): Won Maiden Special at Saratoga at 15-1 odds.

Cool Conductor (seventh): Won turf Maiden Special at Belmont at 9-2 odds.

Thursday, August 28

Race 6 - 8½ Furlongs (Turf), Maiden Special Weight, 2-Year-Olds. Final Time - 1:44.22

Race 3 - 8½ Furlongs (Turf), Maiden Special Weight, 2-Year-Olds. Final Time - 1:44.99

Winner from the faster division:

Potomac Chase (fourth): Won dirt Maiden Special at Laurel at 2-1 odds.

Sunday August 31

Race 5 - 8½ Furlongs (Turf), Maiden Special Weight, 2-Year-Old Fillies. Final Time - 1:43.78

Race 2 - 8½ Furlongs (Turf), Maiden Special Weight, 2-Year-Old Fillies. Final Time - 1:43.79

Winners from the faster division:

None

Monday, September 1

Race 3 - 6½ Furlongs, Maiden Special Weight, 2-Year-Olds. Final Time - 1:18.03

Race 7 - 6½ Furlongs, Maiden Special Weight, 2-Year-Olds. Final Time - 1:19.08

Winners from the faster division:

Eurosilver (winner): Won Grade 2 Breeders' Futurity at Keeneland at 11-1 odds.

Grand Score (third): Won Maiden Special at Keeneland at 1-1 odds.

Three out of 10 key races isn't that bad. The divisions on August 11 and August 31 were very close in time. If you want to throw those two days out, then you're left with a 3-for-8 mark. What is also interesting about some of the faster divisions at the Spa in 2003 is that some of the horses that failed to win their next starts went on to become nice horses. Value Plus, Capeside Lady, and Lucifer's Stone earned black type, and several other horses in the faster divisions won their second start after the quick heat.

If we can look to the faster divisions of split maiden races as possible key events, can we try and find negative key races out of the slower ones? Let's discuss Scipion, the much-hyped half-brother to juvenile champion Vindication. Sent off as a red-hot 4-5 for his debut at Saratoga on August 14, 2004, Scipion soon dropped back to last, and looked absolutely beaten when the field turned for home. Once he leveled off, however, Scipion put in one of the most visually impressive stretch runs that I've ever seen from a juvenile. He flew down the center of the track, passed every horse in the field, and won going away. You could hear the "oohs" and "aahs" at the Spa when Scipion crossed the wire. A future champion was crowned. Or so it seemed.

Scipion's final time for the seven-furlong test was 1:24.72. When United won the second division of that day's maiden specials in 1:23.93, I began to wonder how good Scipion really looked. Visually, he was great. He showed all the tools of a future stakes winner. But would he be worth the expected short price in his next start? And what about the other runners coming out of that race?

Scipion went off at even money in the Cradle Stakes at River Downs in his next start. He pressed the slow pace in his first two-turn test, but couldn't finish with the others, and tired to third. The runner-up in Scipion's debut, Royal Sultan, returned to run fifth at 7-2 odds at Belmont. Sixth-place finisher Devine Cozzene shipped to Turfway Park, and finished up the track at 3-1 odds. Seventh-place runner Our Friend Timmy returned to run third at 8-1 odds. Stephen Got Lucky, last on August 14, came back to try turf. He finished off the board at 12-1.

Handicapping baby races is tricky, because you have to find a common ground between speed figures and visual impressions. Scipion showed dogged determination and heart in his debut, and he should be a nice horse down the road. But he was a terrible bet in the Cradle after coming out of the slower division.

10

THE MYTH ABOUT MAIDEN CLAIMING FIRSTERS

MOST HANDICAPPERS DISCOUNT debut runners in maiden claiming events. I've always stood firm in the belief that every horse has a winning level. In 2001, I did a study on first-time starters in maiden claiming events and found some very surprising statistics. From January 1 to March 26 of that year, 95 of the 521 maiden claiming races that included at least one first-time starter were won by horses making their career debuts, a 19 percent win rate.

Why do handicappers dislike backing beginners in maiden selling races? Conventional wisdom states that by putting a firster in a claiming heat, the connections of the horse are admitting failure. If the horse had potential, surely he would be running in a maiden special weight, safe from being taken by another barn. For many horseplayers, a firster entered in a maiden claimer has a "For Sale— As Is" sign on his back. Take my horse, please!

But numbers do not lie. First-time starters are winning maiden claiming races in bunches, and paying big prices to boot. Perhaps trainers are getting more realistic about their runners' ability. Getting to the winner's circle is the bottom line, and horses that are a bit behind in their schooling (though not untalented) may better fit a maiden claiming race. A trainer may think he can find an easy spot in a maiden claimer, thus boosting his horse's confidence for the eventual move up the class ladder.

With the explosion of purses at small tracks with slot machines and card rooms, trainers can "get the money" with a solid horse in a maiden claimer. This game is about winning. The high-percentage trainers know the ability levels of their horses, find the right spots in the condition book, and take aim. You should obviously be more confident when playing first-time starters in maiden special weights. Still, you shouldn't discount maiden claiming firsters.

Once a trainer wins or runs a winning race with a debut maiden claimer, he bears watching later on. Not many handicappers took notice when Steve Asmussen connected with 11-1 firster Saintly Charm in a $15,000 maiden claimer going $1\frac{1}{16}$ miles at Oaklawn on February 23, 2001. But followers of trainer patterns saw a prime wagering opportunity a month later when Asmussen entered My Extolled Honor in a $1\frac{1}{16}$-mile maiden claimer at Fair Grounds.

Asmussen had proven that he was capable of saddling a maiden claiming firster to win a route race. So why was his horse, My Extolled Honor, dismissed at 24-1 at Fair Grounds? After My Extolled Honor swept from the back of the pack to score a decisive $9\frac{1}{2}$-length victory, astute trainer handicappers were not shaking their heads in disbelief. They were at the windows, cashing.

There are three key factors to picking first-time-starter maiden claimers:

1. Trainer statistics. Note *Daily Racing Form* trainer statistics for First Start and Maiden Claiming. Once a trainer has proven himself with a debuting maiden claimer, watch for other maiden claiming firsters from the same barn.

2. **Common work tabs.** Many trainers work two or more unraced horses in tandem. Check the daily work tabs for "company" works.

3. **Pattern handicapping.** Make notes on trainers' successful moves involving jockeys, owners, equipment, and workout patterns (long, short, fast, slow, gate, etc.). Winning patterns will surface for certain barns, sometimes at huge payoffs.

Becoming a successful handicapper of maiden races requires a very open mind. Don't be afraid to think outside the box; don't be afraid of debut runners in maiden claiming races.

11

SLEEPER DEBUT SIRES
FOR OLDER MAIDENS

SOME SIRES PRODUCE 2-year-old winners in bunches. I listed a bunch of them earlier in the book. Other sires, however, have stouter pedigrees. Their progeny may not get to the races until their 3-year-old year or later. Here are some sires to watch with older first-time starters.

CARSON CITY

Pedigree: Mr. Prospector—Blushing Promise, by
    Blushing Groom
Race Record and Earnings: 15 starts, 6 wins, 2 seconds,
    0 thirds, $306,240
2004 Stud Fee: $35,000
2004 Stud Farm: Overbrook Farm (KY)

Most handicappers consider Carson City to be merely a precocious sire of swift juvenile runners. While he is excellent with 2-year-old debut runners (he scored a "B" earlier in the text), the public often bets his juvenile runners down to favoritism.

He does get a good deal of older debut winners, however, and those runners are not bet so heavily. Watch for Carson City's older firsters early in the 3-year-old season. These are probably runners that had some small setbacks as juveniles that cost them their 2-year-old campaigns. Making their debuts as 3-year-olds, they are now healthy and ready to go, and still have the precocious genes of their sire. He crosses very well with mares from the Northern Dancer line as well as mares by Valid Appeal. A son of the great Mr. Prospector, Carson City was a swift sprinter with a compact build. His progeny are often a bit on the small side, but don't be afraid if they aren't as physically imposing as their rivals. Most of them are very quick.

Older Debut Sire Ranking: A

IN EXCESS

Pedigree: Siberian Express—Kantado, by Saulingo (GB)
Race Record and Earnings: 25 starts, 11 wins, 2 seconds,
    3 thirds, $1,740,861
2004 Stud Fee: Private
2004 Stud Farm: Vessels Stallion Farm (CA)

I loved In Excess as a racehorse. After breaking his maiden in Europe, In Excess was imported to the United States, and quickly became a multiple Grade 3 winner on grass. He excelled at age 4 on the dirt, however, winning the "sire-making" Grade 1 Metropolitan Handicap, the Grade 1 Suburban (10 furlongs in 1:58$^{1}/_{5}$), the Grade 1 Woodward, and the Grade 1 Whitney. His excellent tactical speed served him well between eight and 10 furlongs, but his progeny usually do well first-out in sprint races at age 3. He was a tough and hearty runner, and crosses well with both Mr. Prospector- and Northern Dancer-line mares. In Excess is one of California's best sires, and his older debut runners should be respected in statebred maiden special weights. They usually have excellent early speed.

Older Debut Sire Ranking: A

GILDED TIME

Pedigree: Timeless Moment—Gilded Lilly, by What a Pleasure
Race Record and Earnings: 6 starts, 4 wins, 0 seconds, 1 third, $975,980
2004 Stud Fee: $17,500
2004 Stud Farm: Vinery (KY)

Who knows how good Gilded Time would have been if he hadn't gotten injured. He won the first four starts of his career, including the Breeders' Cup Juvenile, and earned a 107 Beyer Speed Figure as a 2-year-old. He then missed almost a year of racing, and trainer Darrell Vienna picked a difficult spot for his return: the Breeders' Cup Sprint. Facing the quickest horses in the world, Gilded Time pressed fractions of 21.14 and 43.94 before understandably tiring to a third-place finish. After a disappointing run in the Malibu Stakes, Gilded Time was retired, and has been a dependable source of older debut winners. He could successfully stretch his speed to a mile and a sixteenth, and his best runners are capable of going that long. Gilded Time is a nice outcross for most Thoroughbred bloodlines, and he was a very sturdily built runner. His firsters often have the same blocky appearance, and they can be quick from the gate. Respect them in debut races for older runners.

Older Debut Sire Ranking: A

SEEKING THE GOLD

Pedigree: Mr. Prospector—Con Game, by Buckpasser
Race Record and Earnings: 15 starts, 8 wins, 6 seconds, 0 thirds, $2,307,000
2004 Stud Fee: $150,000
2004 Stud Farm: Claiborne Farm (KY)

Seeking the Gold won his only start at 2 by 12 lengths, and was a multiple Grade 1 winner at 3, although he was perhaps best known for his heartbreaking near-misses in big races. He finished behind Alysheba in the Breeders' Cup Classic, missed by a dirty nose to Forty Niner in both the Travers and Haskell, and placed behind Private Terms in both the Wood Memorial and Gotham. He has sired over 35 graded stakes winners, is perhaps the best son of Mr. Prospector at stud, and usually is bred to classy mares. Not surprisingly, he crosses very well with the Northern Dancer line, but his progeny may need a bit of time to get to the races. He often is mated with stout mares, and the resulting foals are sometimes best with added maturity and distance. He consistently gets good results from his older debut runners, and his progeny are usually trained by top horsemen. An absolute no-brainer for fans of pedigree. *Older Debut Sire Ranking: A*

TWO PUNCH
Pedigree: Mr. Prospector—Heavenly Cause, by Grey Dawn II
Race Record and Earnings: 8 starts, 4 wins, 0 seconds,
   1 third, $89,795
2004 Stud Fee: 25,000
Stud Farm: Northview Stallion Station (MD)

Two Punch is the result of the mating between legendary sire Mr. Prospector and multiple Grade 1 winner (Acorn, Fantasy, Kentucky Oaks, Selima, Frizette) Heavenly Cause. A stakes-winning sprinter, Two Punch is perennially among the leading sires in the Mid-Atlantic region, and he usually sends out between 30 and 50 winners a year. He crosses well with the Northern Dancer and Turn-to lines, and is certainly capable with Bold Ruler-line mares also. He is the sire of champion sprinter and successful sire Smoke Glacken, and his get usually can stretch their speed to a mile. Two Punch sires

hard-hitting racehorses, and should continue to be among the top stallions on the East Coast. His older debut runners are usually live.
Older Debut Sire Ranking: A

A.P. INDY

Pedigree: Seattle Slew—Weekend Surprise, by Secretariat
Race Record and Earnings: 11 starts, 8 wins, 0 seconds, 1 third, $2,979,815
2004 Stud Fee: $300,000
2004 Stud Farm: Lane's End Farm (KY)

A precocious pedigree is almost always a prerequisite for a juvenile debut winner. For older runners, look more toward classy bloodlines. The late Unbridled showed surprisingly successful results with his older firsters. Despite being bred for extra distance, the Unbridleds regularly won at first asking as 3-year-olds and older. I believe that it was his class that pushed his progeny to the winner's circle, and the same may apply for top stallion A.P. Indy. The son of Seattle Slew and multiple graded winner Weekend Surprise cost $2.9 million as a yearling, and has beautiful conformation. A.P. Indy won his second start at 2, and won seven races in a row at one point, including the Grade 1 Hollywood Futurity, the Grade 1 Santa Anita Derby, and the Grade 1 Belmont Stakes. He finished his successful career with a 114 Beyer performance and a win in the Breeders' Cup Classic. A.P. Indy had a wonderful stride. He had a low running action, and was always reaching out for more ground. Many of his successful runners have inherited that trait. A.P. Indy's older debut runners can win sprinting or at longer distances, and they can be depended on to bring lots of class to the table. One of the best sires in the world, A.P. Indy should continue to send out high-quality racehorses.
Older Debut Sire Ranking: A

MR. GREELEY

Pedigree: Gone West—Long Legend, by Reviewer
Race Record and Earnings: 16 starts, 5 wins, 6 seconds,
0 thirds, $474,452
2004 Stud Fee: $50,000
2004 Stud Farm: Spendthrift Farm (KY)

I've already mentioned how much I respect the Gone West strain of the Mr. Prospector line, and Mr. Greeley is yet another success story by Gone West. It took Mr. Greeley a couple of starts to win a maiden race, and he didn't win his first stakes race until early in his 3-year-old season. He ran off an impressive series of races between January and April of his sophomore year, but didn't reach the winner's circle after that. He earned a 111 Beyer when second in the Jerome Handicap at a mile, and he ended his career with a runner-up performance in the Breeders' Cup Sprint. Mr. Greeley is very powerfully built, and his progeny can stretch their speed around two turns. Watch out for his older maidens when they debut early in their 3-year-old seasons. A solid sire, Mr. Greeley should send out several older debut winners each year.
Older Debut Sire Ranking: A

STORM CAT

Pedigree: Storm Bird—Terlingua, by Secretariat
Race Record and Earnings: 8 starts, 4 wins, 3 seconds,
0 thirds, $570,610
2004 Stud Fee: $500,000
2004 Stud Farm: Overbrook Farm (KY)

Storm Cat received a deserving mention in the juvenile debut sire section, and it would be sloppy not to include him in this list. He is simply one of the five best sires in the world, and his class shines through in almost every occasion. He has sired over 25 Grade 1 winners, and over 100 stakes winners. You can pretty much cross him with any sire line, and his progeny are dangerous on any surface at any age. Some of the Storm Cats can be pretty temperamental, and will need maturing before they do their best. Perhaps that is why he does as well with older firsters as he does with juveniles. He is bred to the best mares in the world, and the class of his runners makes them dangerous when they debut as older runners. An obvious pedigree threat in any maiden special weight race.

Older Debut Sire Ranking: A

COZZENE

Pedigree: Caro—Ride the Trails, by Prince John
Race Record and Earnings: 24 starts, 10 wins, 5 seconds, 5 thirds, $978,152
2004 Stud Fee: $60,000
2004 Stud Farm: Gainesway Farm (KY)

Many handicappers think of Cozzene as merely a sire of excellent turf runners. And while the Breeders' Cup Mile winner sends out grass winners in bunches, he also gives his progeny enough speed and class to win first time out on dirt as older runners. By Caro, Cozzene doesn't have a precocious pedigree, and his runners usually need plenty of time to grow into their bodies. His son Alphabet Soup won the Breeders' Cup Classic, so we know that he can sire good dirt runners. His older firsters usually go off at good odds thanks to Cozzene's reputation as a grass sire. Don't fail to take advantage of his classy pedigree in older maiden races.

Older Debut Sire Ranking: B

DIXIELAND BAND

Pedigree: Northern Dancer—Mississippi Mud, by Delta Judge
Race Record and Earnings: 24 starts, 8 wins, 3 seconds, 4 thirds, $570,610
2004 Stud Fee: $50,000
2004 Stud Farm: Lane's End Farm (KY)

Year after year, Dixieland Band sends out multiple older debut winners, and is one of the most underrated sires in the country. He has sired almost 100 stakes winners, and is a great cross for Mr. Prospector-, Damascus-, and Ribot-line mares. His runners seem to love the turf almost as much as they appreciate the main track, and there doesn't seem to be a distance limit for them. Dixieland Band won a stakes race as a juvenile around two turns, won the Grade 2 Pennsylvania Derby at 3, and the Grade 2 Massachusetts Handicap at 4. He isn't a flashy sire, but he gets the job done time after time, especially with his older debut runners.

Older Debut Sire Ranking: B

FOREST WILDCAT

Pedigree: Storm Cat—Victoria Beauty, by Bold Native
Race Record and Earnings: 20 starts, 9 wins, 2 seconds,
   1 third, $478,462
2004 Stud Fee: $40,000
2004 Stud Farm: Brookdale Farm (KY)

I may have underestimated this exciting young stallion by giving him a C+ for his juvenile debut rating. As a speedy, graded-stakes-winning son of Storm Cat, he certainly has the class and pedigree to succeed first-out, and he has sent out plenty of older debut winners. Forest Wildcat won five of his last seven races with Beyers ranging between 107 and 117. He may be most successful when crossed with other speedy sire lines, but looms an intriguing debut possibility in races with older maidens.

Older Debut Sire Ranking: B

CAPOTE

Pedigree: Seattle Slew—Too Bald, by Bald Eagle
Race Record and Earnings: 10 starts, 3 wins, 0 seconds,
   1 third, $714,470

2004 Stud Fee: $30,000
2004 Stud Farm: Three Chimneys Farm (KY)

Capote was brilliant at 2, winning all three of his races, including the Breeders' Cup Juvenile. He failed to crack the exacta at 3, but has asserted himself as one of the great Seattle Slew's leading sons at stud, and he is very strong with debut runners. Capote not only has class on the top of his pedigree but on the bottom as well. His dam won 13 of 24 starts, and was named Broodmare of the Year in 1986. Capote is a half-brother to multiple Grade 1 winner Exceller, Grade 3 winner Vaguely Hidden, and stakes winners and precocious sires American Standard and Baldski. He makes a nice outcross for Mr. Prospector- and Northern Dancer-line mares, and is a big, nicely conformed individual. He should be on everyone's debut sire list for older runners.
Older Debut Sire Ranking: B

SILVER DEPUTY

Pedigree: Deputy Minister—Silver Valley, by Mr. Prospector
Race Record and Earnings: 2 starts, 2 wins, 0 seconds,
  0 thirds, $41,820
2004 Stud Fee: $40,000
2004 Stud Farm: Brookdale Farm (KY)

Silver Deputy was perfect on the track, and he has become very successful at stud. A $200,000 yearling purchase, Silver Deputy won his debut in gate-to-wire fashion by over six lengths, and then won the Swynford Stakes as a front-runner. He has sired over 50 stakes winners, and his two-time Eclipse Award-winning daughter, Silverbulletday, earned almost $3 million. His late sire is a top broodmare sire, and I think that Silver Deputy will follow in Deputy Minister's footsteps in that category. Silver Deputy offers good value at a $40,000 stud fee, and should continue to sire classy runners. He'll continue to impress with his older debut runners.
Older Debut Sire Ranking: B

THEATRICAL
Pedigree: Nureyev—Tree of Knowledge, by Sassafras
Race Record and Earnings: 22 starts, 10 wins, 4 seconds,
   2 thirds, $2,940,036
2004 Stud Fee: $75,000
2004 Stud Farm: Hill 'n' Dale Farms (KY)

Classy Theatrical won six Grade 1 events including the Breeders'
Cup Turf. He won his debut at 2 in Ireland, but didn't fully come
to hand until his 5-year-old year. His progeny also seem to do better as they age, but don't be fooled by Theatrical's stellar grass
record and pedigree. While he usually is among the leaders in siring turf runners, Theatrical is certainly capable of getting a good
dirt horse, especially when he is crossed with mares from the Mr.
Prospector line. For a big horse, Theatrical has nice conformation,
and his progeny usually appreciate longer distances. His produce
can be hard to handle, and often need maturing before they are
mentally ready for the rigors of racing. Still, he provides plenty of
class to his offspring, and he has done very well with older debut
runners both on dirt and turf. Don't simply think of Theatrical as
a turf sire. He can surprise with his dirt performers at good prices.
Older Debut Sire Ranking: B

A. P JET
Pedigree: Fappiano—Taminette, by In Reality
Race Record and Earnings: 36 starts, 4 wins, 5 seconds,
   5 thirds, $1,622,369
2004 Stud Fee: $5,000
2004 Stud Farm: Sugar Maple Farm (NY)

Being a good New Yorker, I had to throw in a sire based in the
Empire State. A. P Jet has found a nice home in New York after racing exclusively in Japan. A group winner by Fappiano, A. P Jet has

done surprisingly well with his older first-time starters. He has had success crossing with Northern Dancer-line mares, and his progeny have shown good bursts of speed at sprint distances. A. P Jet has an excellent pedigree. He is a full brother to millionaire Tappiano out of a full sister to the good sires Tentam and Known Fact. He is also a half to Secrettame, the dam of Gone West. He hasn't shown great results at the sales, but all that means is that his runners may offer value when they debut at ages 3 and up.

Older Debut Sire Ranking: B

GONE WEST

Pedigree: Mr. Prospector—Secrettame, by Secretariat
Race Record and Earnings: 17 starts, 6 wins, 4 seconds,
   2 thirds, $682,251
2004 Stud Fee: $125,000
2004 Stud Farm: Mill Ridge Farm (KY)

If you've gotten this far in the text, then you know what sort of affinity I have for Gone West. But he's not just a great sire of sires. The old boy is still siring good winners, including top sprinter Speightstown. His produce sell very well at auction, and perform at high levels on both dirt and turf. He has sired over 70 stakes winners and is a great match for Northern Dancer- and Bold Ruler-line mares. His expensive stud fee underscores his quality. He gets stone-cold runners. Beware of his older debut runners in maiden races.

Older Debut Sire Ranking: B

HOLY BULL

Pedigree: Great Above—Sharon Brown, by Al Hattab
Race Record and Earnings: 16 starts, 13 wins, 0 seconds,
   0 thirds, $2,481,760
2004 Stud Fee: $15,000
2004 Stud Farm: Darley at Jonabell (KY)

In a game where "great" is thrown around way too liberally, I can say without hesitation that Holy Bull was a great horse. The big gray had a modest pedigree, but he didn't know it. In his debut run at Monmouth as a juvenile, he blitzed his hapless foes with a 101 Beyer Speed Figure. He was a perfect 4 for 4 as a 2-year-old, including a victory over top juvenile Dehere in the Grade 1 Futurity. After convincing wins in the Florida Derby and Blue Grass Stakes, the popular Holy Bull went off as the favorite in the Kentucky Derby. He broke slowly over a sloppy Churchill Downs strip, and never made a serious impact. Holy Bull returned 23 days later to whip older horses with a 122 Beyer in the Metropolitan Handicap. He would then win the Dwyer and Haskell without much fuss before prevailing in one of the best Travers races ever run. Defying a Wayne Lukas-trained rabbit through quick fractions, Holy Bull dug down deep, and held off subsequent Breeders' Cup Classic winner Concern in the stretch. He ended his 3-year-old season with a dominant performance in the Woodward at Belmont, and earned Horse of the Year honors. Many analysts, myself included, doubted that Holy Bull could match his track performance in the breeding shed. While he hasn't been a sensation at stud, he has given us Breeders' Cup Juvenile winner Macho Uno, and Grade 1 winner Confessional. He has sired some rather large runners, and they need some time to develop. That may be why he is proficient at siring older debut winners. He usually provides value for pedigree handicappers. *Older Debut Sire Ranking: B*

OLDER DEBUT SIRE RANKING: B

(Percentages and ROI's from 1/1/00 through 9/25/04)

West Acre: 33% winners, $8.09 ROI
Tactical Cat: 29% winners, $6.61 ROI
Barkerville: 23% winners, $6.29 ROI
Red River Gorge: 22% winners, $5.54 ROI
Harriman: 23% winners, $5.40 ROI
Dazzling Falls: 21% winners, $5.13 ROI
Indian Charlie: 30% winners, $2.36 ROI
Raise a Rascal: 26% winners, $3.95 ROI
Eltish: 25% winners, $4.49 ROI
Native Factor: 24% winners, $2.89 ROI
Relaunch a Tune: 24% winners, $4.50 ROI
Flying Chevron: 24% winners, $4.94 ROI
Double Honor: 23% winners, $2.05 ROI

OLDER DEBUT SIRE RANKING: B-/C+

Cahill Road
Unbridled's Song
Meadowlake
Gold Case
Moscow Ballet
Royal Academy
Salt Lake
Smart Strike
Thunder Gulch
Grand Slam
Not For Love
Tale of the Cat
With Approval

12

RECORD-KEEPING
Go With What You Know

IT TAKES A lot of work to be a successful handicapper of
maiden races. It's not easy keeping track of everything. Which sires
are hot with their debut runners? Which trainer is making an impact
first-out? What are the patterns that the successful debut trainers
employ? It is extremely important to keep detailed records on both
trainers and sires. Here's how I do it. My best friend is *DRF Simulcast Weekly*. Each week, I peruse the charts published there, and
immediately input every debut winner into my computer database
(I used to keep a marble notebook, but finally succumbed to tech-
nology). You can tell in the chart if a horse won his debut by scanning the "Last Raced" section, located on the far left of the chart.
If there is nothing listed under "Last Raced," then the horse was a
first-time starter. I have two separate databases, one for trainers and
one for sires.

SIRE	AGE	DISTANCE	TRACK	TRAINER	CLASS
Ago	2yo	5.5f	HOO	Kohnhorst	MSW
Alamocitos	2yo	2f	PRM	Pogue	MSW
Alamocitos	2yo	6f	FP	Pogue	MSW
Alfaari	2yo	6.5f	HST	Murray	MCL

In one easy listing you get the sire and age of the debut winner, the distance and track where the debut win took place, the trainer of the winner, and the class level of the race in question.

With trainers, I use several other categories. In this order, I list trainer, track, date, distance, class, sire, odds, medication/equipment, jockey, age, owner. By keeping and updating a list like this, you can easily answer whether or not a trainer likes to win first time out in maiden claiming races. Or if he uses blinkers on his successful first-time starters. You will see potent jockey-trainer combinations at work, or if the owner-trainer combination likes to win early. Do the stable's firsters take money? You'll know with a list like this. It is essential to keep these kinds of records.

DRF Simulcast Weekly is excellent in covering the larger circuits. Really industrious handicappers will check the free daily charts on *www.drf.com* for every track, and mark down the debut winners that the weekly misses.

An information advantage is crucial in handicapping maiden races. By keeping track of the latest sire and trainer trends, you will be ahead of the game.

GO WITH WHAT YOU KNOW

Trainers tend to win first-out in bunches. With your new handicapper's database at your disposal, you can spot trends before the rest of the public. Trainer Phillip Sims shocked the fans at Turfway Park when he sent out Miss O. on February 25, 2001. The 3-year-old daughter of Olympio was making her debut in a $30,000 maiden claimer with rider Axel DaSilva aboard. She won at 19-1 and paid $41.80.

Sims was at it again a week later. On March 4, 2001, he entered 3-year-old filly Elsie for a $15,000 tag with DaSilva named to ride. Without even studying the work tab (Miss O. and Elsie had both worked on the same days with Miss O. getting the better of her mate), stat-keeping maiden handicappers knew that Sims could pop at a price with a 3-year-old filly in a maiden claimer. Stat-keeping handicappers would know that DaSilva was the barn's go-to rider with debut runners. They could go to the window and bet with confidence. They would also cash on Elsie and collect a $66.40 mutuel.

William White made our list of juvenile debut trainers to watch. On August 14, 2004, at Calder, White teamed up with rider Abdiel Toribio for D'court's Speed's first-out victory in a juvenile maiden special weight. The very next day, White and Toribio returned with Hide and Chic, a first-time starter in a maiden special weight for juvenile fillies. Handicappers up-to-date with their statistics knew the hot trainer-jockey combination. Not surprisingly, Hide and Chic won by five, and could have been the single to start off an $895.60 pick three.

The trainer stats in *Daily Racing Form* are magnificent handicapping tools. But they only go back a year and a half. What if a capable debut trainer was in a prolonged cold streak? Only the handicappers with their own records or with access to *Daily Racing Form*'s Formulator 4 long-term trainer database could have found this gem at Delta Downs on January 17, 2004. The field shaped up like this.

1. **Larry and Pete:** Finished fourth and eighth in two starts at 2 with a top Beyer of 26. Now was making his first start since November 2003, and did not show a recent workout.

2. **Wouldja:** First-time starter by Gift of Gib. Homebred showed a bullet work for this, and the trainer was hitting at a 36 percent clip.

3. **E O's Flash:** Ran third in his debut with a 64 Beyer Speed Figure. Now was getting Lasix for the first time, but had not worked out in the last 26 days.

4. **Goldtariat:** Firster by Gold Token out of a Secretariat mare. New York-bred with slow works.

5. **News Alert:** Firster by Langfuhr. Showed a bullet work for a 15 percent barn. Sold for beneath the stud fee.

6. **Schisler:** Firster by Leestown. Several gaps in the published work tab.

7. **B's Buddy:** Firster by Excavate. Showed sharp gate work. Leading rider named, but trainer 0 for 24 on *Daily Racing Form* "First Start" stats.

8. **Dona Dance:** Firster by Emancipator. Showed a quick work and made debut with Lasix.

9. **Coin Patch:** Firster by Game Coin. Several gaps in the tab. Low-percentage rider named.

10. **B. J.'s Secret:** Earned 0 Beyer Speed Figure at Suffolk Downs. Claimed from that race, and adds blinkers, but is now stuck in a tough outside post position.

E O's Flash looked like a deserving favorite. His debut Beyer was above par for this level, but I didn't like the fact that he failed to show a recent (14 days or less) workout. He seemed like an underlay. Wouldja was playable based on his trainer's winning percentage at the meet, and the fact that he had a bullet workout. Dona Dance could also be considered based on the steady stream of workouts.

But what about B's Buddy? I seemed to remember that trainer Donald Cormier had sent out past debut winners. What was up with the 0-for-24 in the paper? Going back through my database, I found that Cormier had five debut winners in 2001. One of them came with this rider aboard. Clearly, Cormier knew how to get a runner to win at first asking. Plus, I figured that I was one of the few handicappers privy to that information. I had to use B's Buddy now that I had double-checked with my stats, and I boxed him with E O's Flash, Wouldja, and Dona Dance. B's Buddy dueled with E O's Flash early, put him away on the turn, and beat back Wouldja's stretch challenge to win by a neck. B's Buddy paid $21 to win for Cormier. The exacta with Wouldja returned $254.20, and the trifecta with favored E O's Flash in the third slot paid $1,182.80.

Keeping trainer and sire stats can be an arduous task, but it certainly can be profitable in difficult maiden races.

13

WORKOUT PATTERNS AND FORM CYCLES

*T*RAINERS LOOKING TO prepare successful first-time runners can't rely on pedigree alone. They have to get the runner fit enough to handle the rigors of a demanding new distance. Most of these horses have not worked six or seven furlongs, and if they debut at one of those trips, it will probably be the first time they have attempted going that far. I have always been a big fan of firsters that show at least one five-furlong workout in preparation for their debuts. I believe that the five furlong work gives the runner the perfect combination of speed and stamina. The time of the workout is unimportant. If the runner can go five furlongs in the morning, I am much more confident in his chances to win first-out at six or seven. Here's a look at the workout patterns of the debut winners at the 2004 Saratoga meet.

July 28, 2004

Royal Moment: juvenile by Two Punch - trained by Steven Asmussen - $5\frac{1}{2}$ furlongs - maiden special weight - seven uninterrupted workouts prior to debut - two at five furlongs - paid $7.40.

July 29, 2004

Play With Fire: juvenile filly by Boundary - trained by Mark Hennig - $5\frac{1}{2}$ furlongs - maiden special weight - seven uninterrupted workouts prior to debut - one at five furlongs - paid $99.

July 30, 2004

Big Apple Daddy: juvenile by Precise End - trained by James Picou - $5\frac{1}{2}$ furlongs - New York-bred maiden special weight - seven uninterrupted workouts prior to debut - none at five furlongs - paid $4.30.

Caribbean Cruiser: juvenile by Silver Ghost - trained by Donna Bireta - $5\frac{1}{2}$ furlongs - New York-bred maiden special weight - nine uninterrupted workouts prior to debut - three at five furlongs - paid $6.30.

July 31, 2004

Proud Accolade: juvenile by Yes It's True - trained by Todd Pletcher - $6\frac{1}{2}$ furlongs - maiden special weight - eight uninterrupted workouts - four at five furlongs - paid $5.80.

August 1, 2004

Sense of Style: juvenile filly by Thunder Gulch - trained by Patrick Biancone - $6\frac{1}{2}$ furlongs - maiden special weight - eight uninterrupted workouts - one at five furlongs - paid $5.30.

August 2, 2004

Megascape: juvenile filly by Cape Canaveral - trained by Steven Asmussen - $5\frac{1}{2}$ furlongs - New York-bred maiden special weight - four uninterrupted workouts - two at five furlongs - paid $3.90.

Kiki B: juvenile filly by Williamstown - trained by John Hertler - 5½ furlongs - New York-bred maiden special weight - five uninterrupted workouts - none at five furlongs - paid $6.70.

August 4, 2004

Upscaled: juvenile by Sir Cat - trained by Todd Pletcher - five furlongs - maiden special weight - six uninterrupted workouts - two at five furlongs - paid $13.60.

August 5, 2004

Ready's Gal: juvenile filly by More Than Ready - trained by Todd Pletcher - five furlongs - maiden special weight - 11 uninterrupted workouts - three at five furlongs - paid $5.50.

August 6, 2004

English Channel: juvenile by Smart Strike - trained by Todd Pletcher - 8½ furlongs on turf - maiden special weight - five uninterrupted workouts - two at five furlongs - paid $8.20.

August 7, 2004

Funk: juvenile by Unbridled's Song - trained by Todd Pletcher - six furlongs - maiden special weight - 13 uninterrupted workouts - two at five furlongs - paid $9.50.

August 8, 2004

Say Hey Willie: 3-year-old filly by Artax - trained by Jennifer Pedersen - six furlongs - New York-bred maiden special weight - four uninterrupted workouts, two at five furlongs - paid $25.80.

August 9, 2004

Commentator: 3-year-old by Distorted Humor - trained by Nicholas Zito - seven furlongs - New York-bred maiden special weight - five uninterrupted workouts - two at five furlongs - paid $11.60.

Should Be Royalty: juvenile filly by Pine Bluff - trained by Patrick Biancone - six furlongs - maiden special weight - two uninterrupted workouts - none at five furlongs - paid $3.80.

August 11, 2004
Up Like Thunder: juvenile by War Chant - trained by Nicholas Zito - six furlongs - New York-bred maiden special weight - six uninterrupted workouts - none at five furlongs - paid $5.60.

Solid Platinum: 3-year-old filly by Mr. Greeley - trained by Dallas Stewart - six furlongs - maiden special weight - 10 uninterrupted workouts - two at five furlongs - two at six furlongs - paid $11.20.

August 13, 2004
Blue Sunday: juvenile by A. P Jet - trained by Thomas Albertrani - 5$\frac{1}{2}$ furlongs - New York-bred maiden special weight - three uninterrupted workouts - one at five furlongs - paid $6.80.

August 14, 2004
Scipion: juvenile by A.P. Indy - trained by Patrick Biancone - seven furlongs - maiden special weight - one uninterrupted workout - one at five furlongs - paid $3.70.

August 16, 2004
Wallstreet Scandal: juvenile by Mt. Livermore - trained by Richard Violette Jr. - 5$\frac{1}{2}$ furlongs - maiden special weight - three uninterrupted workouts - none at five furlongs - paid $17.80.

Kwondo: juvenile by Grindstone - trained by Todd Pletcher - 5$\frac{1}{2}$ furlongs - maiden special weight - six uninterrupted workouts - two at five furlongs - paid $4.80.

Rowdy: 3-year-old filly by Malibu Moon - trained by Thomas Voss - eight furlongs (turf) - maiden special weight - three uninterrupted workouts - one at five furlongs - paid $22.40.

August 18, 2004

Alfonsina: juvenile filly by Grand Slam - trained by Nicholas Zito - 5$^1/_2$ furlongs - maiden special weight - four uninterrupted workouts - three at five furlongs - paid $10.

Lady H: juvenile filly by Silver Deputy - trained by Todd Pletcher - 5$^1/_2$ furlongs - maiden special weight - 13 uninterrupted workouts - four at five furlongs - paid $4.70.

August 20, 2004

Yankee Trick: juvenile filly by Yankee Victor - trained by George Weaver - five furlongs - New York-bred maiden special weight - 10 uninterrupted workouts - three at five furlongs - paid $6.30.

August 22, 2004

Galloping Grocer: juvenile by A.P Jet - trained by Dominick Schettino - five furlongs - New York-bred maiden special weight - two uninterrupted workouts - two at five furlongs - paid $3.60.

August 23, 2004

Carminooch: juvenile by Tomorrows Cat - trained by Todd Pletcher - 5$^1/_2$ furlongs - New York-bred maiden special weight - seven uninterrupted workouts - two at five furlongs - paid $3.90.

August 25, 2004

Closing Argument: juvenile by Successful Appeal - trained by Kiaran McLaughlin - five furlongs - maiden special weight - eight uninterrupted workouts - one at five furlongs - paid $13.20.

August 27, 2004

Fixed Amount: juvenile filly by Precise End - trained by Ramon Hernandez - 5$^1/_2$ furlongs - New York-bred maiden special weight - three uninterrupted workouts - none at five furlongs - paid $19.40.

August 29, 2004

My Typhoon: juvenile filly by Giant's Causeway - trained by William Mott - 8$^1/_2$ furlongs on turf - maiden special weight - two uninterrupted workouts - one at six furlongs - paid $4.40.

September 1, 2004

Peter's Puddles: 3-year-old by Thunder Puddles - trained by Harold James Bond - nine furlongs on turf - New York-bred maiden special weight - three uninterrupted workouts - one at five furlongs - paid $12.40.

September 6, 2004

Social Virtue: juvenile filly by Elusive Quality - trained by Richard Dutrow Jr. - six furlongs - New York-bred maiden special weight - one uninterrupted workout - none at five furlongs - paid $6.

French Dressing: 3-year-old by French Deputy - trained by Christophe Clement - 8$^1/_2$ furlongs on turf - maiden special weight - seven uninterrupted workouts - none at five furlongs - paid $38.60.

So what have we learned from all this? We learned that Pletcher is phenomenal. We learned that Boundary continues to send out huge-priced juvenile debut winners. We also found out that 25 of the 33 debut winners at Saratoga 2004 (75 percent) had at least one five-furlong or longer workout before their first race. Of the eight debut winners that didn't have a five-furlong work, four of them (50 percent) made their debuts at the abbreviated sprint distance of 5$^1/_2$ furlongs. Perhaps we can make an exception for the "at least one five-furlong work rule" at distances less than six furlongs. We do see that a five-furlong workout is definitely beneficial for a first-time starter.

This rule can be applied to maidens that have already raced. If a runner is returning from a layoff of 31 days or more, I need to see at least one five-furlong workout before I have confidence at the windows. The horse must also show at least one workout within two weeks of the race, at any distance.

Here is where record-keeping comes in. What if a trainer's M.O. is *not* to work a horse five furlongs or more before the debut? Trainers such as Bill Mott, Shug McGaughey, Richard Dutrow Jr., Christophe Clement, David Donk, and Ramon Hernandez often fail to work their horses at that distance. It is very helpful to jot down the trainers that don't give their charges long workouts. That way, you can feel better when you see one of their runners without the five-furlong drill.

FORM CYCLES

For older maidens, it is very important to realize when a runner is rounding into form. Some of these horses have been away from the races due to some kind of physical ailment. We've discussed how important it is to give runners a chance to shine the first time they are trying something. Whether it's Lasix, blinkers, distance, turf, etc., a runner can show a tremendous amount of improvement the first time he does something new. But what if said runner has been away from the races for a while, and is trying something new? Should we give him the benefit of the doubt if he runs poorly off the layoff, and give him another chance the second, or even third, time back? I think we should. Here are some ways to look at form cycles of maiden runners.

Second Off the Layoff
I hate tips. I despise receiving them from "someone in the know," and I hate giving them out. When I'm at any kind of a social

function, I usually don't tell people what I do for a living. If I do tell them that I'm a handicapper, the usual response is, "So, got any hot tips for me?" It's rather annoying. My new response is that I tell people that I work on Wall Street (true, since our offices are on Broadway and Wall in New York City). Unfortunately, people then ask me for stock tips.

Anyway, I was sitting in a bar one evening during the 2004 Saratoga meet, and an acquaintance of mine gave me a tip on a horse that would be running in the next few days. This guy was an excellent handicapper, and I respected his opinion, but I just don't like hearing about "hot" horses. He told me about a maiden named Wateree. The 3-year-old filly had been campaigning in Kentucky, Illinois, and Arlington without reaching the winner's circle, but would be making her first start against New York-breds. According to the toutster, the horse could run.

Wateree made her first start in New York on August 16, 2004, in a seven-furlong statebred maiden special weight. (It turned out that she had the top Beyer figure in the field and was pounded down to 3-2 on the tote board; so much for hot tips.) Wateree didn't show much early speed, got caught behind a moderate pace, rallied five-wide into the stretch, and closed for the runner-up spot. All in all, a good effort for a horse that hadn't run in 42 days.

Perhaps the layoff had Wateree a bit short; if so, then surely she could improve in her second start against statebreds. She did. Wheeling back on 17 days' rest for the excellent yet underrated Lisa Lewis, Wateree made a four-wide move to the front, and drew off to win by over five lengths. She surprisingly offered some value as well, going off at 2.35-1.

The lesson I learned was that I can forgive a layoff horse that fails when she tries something for the first time. Perhaps she needs a race or two to get back to her best form. Be patient. Give horses a few starts off the layoff before categorizing them as professional maidens.

Two Sprints to a Route

Shadow Play cost $400,000 as a yearling, and as a daughter of Breeders' Cup Turf winner Theatrical, was expected to make an impact on the grass. She started six times on the turf without winning, but earned a creditable 79 Beyer Speed Figure on one of those occasions. After she failed to make good at even money at Tampa Bay Downs, trainer Barclay Tagg gave her some time off, and then returned her in a dirt sprint. Had the Kentucky Derby-winning trainer given up? Shadow Play had no dirt pedigree to speak of, and she certainly wasn't bred to sprint. Why was Tagg doing this?

Shadow Play went off at 8-5 in her main-track debut and finished off the board. The next obvious step was to go back to turf, right? Not in Tagg's mind. He actually dropped Shadow Play back a furlong to six panels and tried the dirt again, this time at Gulfstream. Not surprisingly, Shadow Play finished off the board again. Tagg then shipped north to Aqueduct, and returned Shadow Play to turf in a nine-furlong maiden special weight. He was utilizing one of the most powerful form-cycle angles in racing—a maiden going two sprints to a route in the third start of the form cycle with a surface switch. I watched as Shadow Play dueled throughout from the inside, and barely held on to win at $23.60. Tagg was "legging up" Shadow Play with the dirt sprints, and then unleashed her on her preferred surface when she was ready to rock and roll. The two-sprints-to-a-route angle is one that bears watching, especially when it coincides with an equipment, medication, or surface switch, and also when it occurs in the third start off a layoff of at least 31 days.

14

TURF MAIDENS:
Leading Turf-Debut Sires
and Trainers

SOME STALLIONS GET their best results from their turf runners. Here are 10 from my database that should be respected when
their first-time starters make their debuts on the grass.

GONE WEST
Pedigree: Mr. Prospector—Secrettame, by Secretariat
Race Record and Earnings: 17 starts, 6 wins, 4 seconds,
    2 thirds, $682,251
2004 Stud Fee: $125,000
2004 Stud Farm: Mill Ridge Farm (KY)

I'm sorry. I just love Gone West and it's not like he doesn't deserve
the publicity. From 2001 through 2003, he sired 14 North
American-bred debut winners on turf throughout the globe. Among
his top runners are English 2000 Guineas winner Zafonic, German
champion Royal Abjar, Breeders' Cup Turf winner Johar, Breeders'

Cup Mile winner Da Hoss, and millionaire Lassigny. He's as close to a complete sire as there is.

Turf-Debut Sire Ranking: A

DIESIS

Pedigree: Sharpen Up—Doubly Sure, by Reliance II

Race Record and Earnings: 6 starts, 3 wins, 1 second, 0 thirds, $152,700

2004 Stud Fee: $30,000

2004 Stud Farm: Mill Ridge Farm (KY)

Mill Ridge Farm stands two of the top turf sires in the world. Diesis was champion juvenile in England after winning the Group 1 Middle Park Stakes at six furlongs and Group 1 Dewhurst Stakes at seven furlongs. He has broken into the top 15 of sires on the English-Irish list on six occasions, and crosses well with just about any mare. He sired 12 turf-debut winners from 2001 through 2003, and some of his best runners are European champions Halling, Docksider, Diminuendo, Elmaamul, Magistretti, Knifebox, Three Valleys, and Look Daggers. His progeny excel on grass, and he brings plenty of class to the table so respect his runners when they make their career debuts on turf.

Turf-Debut Sire Ranking: A

STORM CAT

Pedigree: Storm Bird—Terlingua, by Secretariat

Race Record and Earnings: 8 starts, 4 wins, 3 seconds, 0 thirds, $570,610

2004 Stud Fee: $500,000

2004 Stud Farm: Overbrook Farm (KY)

Storm Cat dominates on just about every level. Whether it's with juveniles, older maidens, or turf runners, his class shines through almost every time. He had 12 North American-bred turf-debut

winners throughout the world from 2001 through 2003, and some of his best runners include European champions Giant's Causeway, Black Minnaloushe, Mistle Cat, Catrail, Denebola, and Munaaji. By now, you know that he is one of the best stallions in the world.
Turf-Debut Sire Ranking: A

THEATRICAL
Pedigree: Nureyev—Tree of Knowledge, by Sassafras
Race Record and Earnings: 22 starts, 10 wins, 4 seconds, 2 thirds, $2,940,036
2004 Stud Fee: $75,000
2004 Stud Farm: Hill 'n' Dale Farms (KY)

The Nureyev branch of the Northern Dancer sire line does beautifully with grass runners, and Theatrical was a champion in Ireland as well as an Eclipse Award-winning turf male. He's had 12 North American-bred turf-debut winners from 2001 through 2003, and he is usually among the leading grass stallions. He has done very well when crossed with Bold Ruler- and Mr. Prospector-line mares, and has sired Japanese champion Hishi Amazon, and European champions Zagreb and Theoretically. Another sire with lots of class, Theatrical's firsters should get at least a second look when they make their debuts on turf.
Turf-Debut Sire Ranking: A

WOODMAN
Pedigree: Mr. Prospector—Playmate, by Buckpasser
Race Record and Earnings: 5 starts, 3 wins, 0 seconds, 1 third, $32,011
2004 Stud Fee: $25,000
2004 Stud Farm: Ashford Stud (KY)

Ireland's champion 2-year-old of 1985, Woodman has been one of the most durable and dependable stallions in the world. He gets plenty of class from his sire, Mr. Prospector, and his good conformation probably comes from broodmare sire Buckpasser. His progeny do very well going long, and his turf runners usually provide good value at the windows. Among Woodman's best runners are Japanese champion Hishi Akebono and European champions Hawk Wing, Hector Protector, Dr Johnson, Way of Light, and Mujtahid. Woodman can be counted on to sire plenty of debut winners on the turf.

Turf-Debut Sire Ranking: A

COZZENE

Pedigree: Caro—Ride the Trails, by Prince John
Race Record and Earnings: 24 starts, 10 wins, 5 seconds,
5 thirds, $978,152
2004 Stud Fee: $60,000
2004 Stud Farm: Gainesway Farm (KY)

Eclipse Award-winning turf runner Cozzene topped the sire's earning list in 1996 when his Alphabet Soup upset the great Cigar to win the Breeders' Cup Classic. He is best known for siring hard-hitting turf runners that do their best between eight and 12 furlongs. Some of his best turf runners include Japanese champion Admire Cozzene, Arlington Million winner Star of Cozzene, Breeders' Cup Turf winner Tikkanen, Cozzene's Prince, Maxzene, and Gaviola. Cozzene sent out 10 turf-debut winners from 2001 through 2003, and he should continue to sire good grass runners.

Turf-Debut Sire Ranking: A

DYNAFORMER

Pedigree: Roberto—Andover Way, by His Majesty
Race Record and Earnings: 30 starts, 7 wins, 5 seconds,
2 thirds, $671,207
2004 Stud Fee: $75,000
2004 Stud Farm: Three Chimneys Farm (KY)

Dynaformer is from the turf-loving Roberto branch of the Turn-to line, and he has quietly been a five-time top-15 sire by earnings in the United States. Dynaformer is a big horse, standing 17 hands, and he gives his progeny plenty of bone, class, and the ability to go long distances on the grass. Some of his top runners are grass stakes winners Ocean Silk, Riskaverse, Vergennes, and Film Maker. He crosses well with all different types of sire lines, and remains one of the most underrated sires in the world. He is a very dangerous turf-debut sire. *Turf-Debut Sire Ranking: A*

KINGMAMBO

Pedigree: Mr. Prospector—Miesque, by Nureyev
Race Record and Earnings: 13 starts, 5 wins, 4 seconds, 2 thirds, $733,139
2004 Stud Fee: $225,000
2004 Stud Farm: Lane's End Farm (KY)

Kingmambo was bred to be a top turf runner and sire. By Mr. Prospector out of two-time Breeders' Cup Mile winner and Hall of Fame inductee Miesque, Kingmambo won his second start at 2, but enjoyed his best successes the following season. A brilliant miler, he won the French 2000 Guineas, the Group 1 Prix du Moulin de Longchamp, and the Group 1 St. James's Palace Stakes at 3. He is bred to exquisite mares at Will Farish's Lane's End Farm, and his progeny are able to stretch their speed to 12 furlongs. He has sired champion older male Lemon Drop Kid, but his best runners have raced on turf. Japan Cup winner El Condor Pasa, French champion Okawango, British 1000 Guineas winner Russian Rhythm, and multiple Grade 1 winner Voodoo Dancer are among his best offspring. Kingmambo had nine North American-bred turf-debut winners between 2001 and 2003, and he crosses exceptionally well with Northern Dancer-line mares. He transmits speed and class to his young runners, and they should be able to win first-out between eight and 10 furlongs on the grass.
Turf-Debut Sire Ranking: A

ROYAL ACADEMY

Pedigree: Nijinsky II—Crimson Saint, by Crimson Satan
Race Record and Earnings: 7 starts, 4 wins, 2 seconds,
    0 thirds, $759,967
2004 Stud Fee: $20,000
2004 Stud Farm: Ashford Stud (KY)

Royal Academy cost $3.5 million as a yearling because of his beautiful pedigree and flawless conformation. A half-brother to multiple Grade 2 winners Pancho Villa and Terlingua (the dam of the mighty Storm Cat), Royal Academy earned championship honors at 3 in England and Ireland after winning the Breeders' Cup Mile at Belmont Park. Other stallion sons of Nijinsky II include Caerleon, Green Dancer, and Ile De Bourbon, so Royal Academy is definitely from a turf-loving line. He has been among the top 15 sires by earnings on the English-Irish stallion list on five occasions, and had nine North American-bred turf-debut winners between 2001 and 2003. His offspring usually provide good value when they are unveiled on the turf.
Turf-Debut Sire Ranking: A

SEEKING THE GOLD

Pedigree: Mr. Prospector—Con Game, by Buckpasser
Race Record and Earnings: 15 starts, 8 wins, 6 seconds,
    0 thirds, $2,307,000
2004 Stud Fee: $150,000
2004 Stud Farm: Claiborne Farm (KY)

Seeking the Gold has sired such main-track stars as Flanders, Heavenly Prize, Dream Supreme, Cash Run, and Cape Town, but he is classy and versatile enough to have given us the brilliant Dubai Millennium, French champion Seeking the Pearl, and Japanese Group 1 winner Meiner Love. I have already mentioned his success rate with older first-out runners on dirt, but he has had seven North

American-bred turf-debut winners between 2001 and 2003. He is always dangerous.

Turf-Debut Sire Ranking: A

TURF-DEBUT SIRE RANKING: B

Distant View
Red Ransom
A. P. Indy
Quest for Fame
Spinning World
Grand Slam
Pulpit

LEADING TURF-DEBUT TRAINERS

Some horsemen won't use a prep race to get their horses ready to win on the turf. These excellent turf trainers are very capable at the demanding task of getting their inexperienced runners to win first-out on the grass. Here are some trainers to keep an eye on.

CHRISTOPHE CLEMENT

Clement has always been one of my favorite trainers, and he is fantastic with turf runners. He sent out eight debut winners on grass from 2001 through 2003, and he goes against the grain of my long-workout theory. Clement rarely works his horses longer than four furlongs, but he usually has them fit and ready to go first-out. He only used Lasix on two of his eight debut winners in the study, and three of them were ridden by Edgar Prado. Watch out for his turf firsters in New York, Florida, and Virginia.

Turf-Debut Trainer Ranking: A

MICHAEL DICKINSON

The "Mad Genius" is best known for his work with layoff runners, so it isn't surprising that he does very well with first-time starters. A fresh horse is a live horse when it comes to Dickinson. He used Lasix on all eight of his turf-debut winners in my study, and he has had good success with rider Mario Pino. Dickinson's runners usually have excellent pedigrees, and they are trained to perfection on his revolutionary Tapeta Farm. His high winning percentage tells the story. Dickinson is a winner, and his turf firsters must be respected at Delaware, Fair Grounds, Laurel, Aqueduct, Belmont, Pimlico, and Colonial.

Turf-Debut Trainer Ranking: A

HAROLD JAMES BOND

Agent 007 is lethal when he sends out a debut runner on grass. He sent out seven first-out turf winners in the study, and is exceptionally deadly when Edgar Prado is his jockey of choice. Bond usually sends out his turf winners in Florida in the winter, and in New York the rest of the year. He is not averse to putting blinkers on his winning firsters. Bond's debut winners usually get plenty of action on the tote so it isn't hard to spot a live one from his barn.

Turf-Debut Trainer Ranking: A

TODD PLETCHER

Pletcher's firsters are so nice that he gets mentioned twice. His stable is full of runners with immaculate pedigrees, and he popped with seven horses that were making their debut in grass races from 2001 through 2003. Pletcher's successful debut runners usually show at least one five-furlong workout before their first start. He does his best work when he administers Lasix, and gives a leg up to John Velazquez.

Turf-Debut Trainer Ranking: A

ROBERT FRANKEL

Frankel usually receives top-class runners from the famed international breeder-owner Juddmonte Farms, and many of their horses are bred for success on the grass. Frankel sent out five debut winners on grass in the study, and has done very well with jockeys Alex Solis and Patrick Valenzuela. Frankel usually gives his winning firsters Lasix and Butazolidin, and they should be closely watched in Southern California.

Turf-Debut Trainer Ranking: A

WILLIAM MOTT

Mott is one of the finest horsemen around, and he has a world-class reputation for being a top turf trainer. Like Chris Clement, Mott often fails to give his horses long workouts, but they are certainly capable of popping at a price when they debut on the grass. Mott had five turf-debut winners in the study, and none of them used Lasix. He had success with Jerry Bailey, Cornelio Velasquez, and Javier Castellano, and should be watched when his firsters show up in New York and Florida.

Turf-Debut Trainer Ranking: A

TURF-DEBUT TRAINER RANKING: B

Mark Casse
Neil Drysdale
John Kimmel
Hugh Robertson
Dale Capuano
Daniel Smithwick Jr.
James Toner
Jonathan Sheppard

DISREGARD THAT DULL DIRT FORM

Turf and dirt are two completely different ball games. Some horses run equally well on both surfaces, but most have a distinct preference for one or the other. We've seen various pedigrees, and how certain sire lines prefer turf instead of dirt. The Nijinsky II branch of the Northern Dancer line adores grass, but I would question its potency on the main track. When observing maidens going dirt-to-turf for the first time, I completely ignore their dirt form. I don't care if the runner has earned high Beyer Speed Figures, or has been a complete flop on the main track. It simply doesn't matter to me what the runner has done in the past. Look for some of the angles mentioned in previous chapters with horses that are switching surfaces for the first time. Also, scan for some of the turf sires that have been discussed. Take War Trace, for example. A son of Storm Cat out of multiple Grade 1-winning turfer Memories of Silver, War Trace made his first two starts in dirt sprints. He ran poorly both times, but students of turf pedigree were merely biding their time, and waiting for him to try the turf. He did so in his third lifetime outing at Gulfstream. Making the important two-sprints-to-a-route move in the third start of the form cycle coupled with a surface switch, War Trace had the dangerous combination of a beautiful turf pedigree, and a powerful angle. He rolled home from eighth at the stretch call with a breathtaking late kick to win at 3-1 odds.

Trip handicappers weren't too concerned about the relatively uninspiring 77 Beyer Speed Figure that War Trace earned that day. They saw a lightly raced, regally bred turf runner with plenty of upside potential. He would go on to win the Choice Stakes at Monmouth later that year with a 97 Beyer.

15

ONCE AROUND THE BLOCK:
Experienced Turf Runners and European Imports

*I*N THE PREVIOUS chapter, I gave you a list of turf sires that you need to know when handicapping first-time starters in turf races. However, the majority of maiden races on grass, especially for juveniles, are won by experienced runners. Why? Most turf races are run around two turns, and young horses often lack the professionalism and stamina to handle both bends. Often the turf-course turns are tight, and these babies are frequently caught in traffic as they speed into the first corner. Horses with racing experience have probably already faced these conditions and are much better equipped to handle two-turn racing.

Most turf horses are bred to improve with distance and maturity. Although talented, they can be slow learners, and aren't prepared to be rated for the majority of the running while often in and among many other horses. It is a strenuous task for a firster to succeed in a turf race. Many turf races are won by "angle" horses, and several of the angles mentioned earlier involve a prep race. Whether going from a sprint to a route, or making his second or third start of the form cycle, a horse with experience is likely fitter to handle the demanding turf-route distance.

The result of a turf race for maiden juvenile fillies at Saratoga on August 27, 2004, should punctuate the point. The favorite of race 4 that day, and rightfully so, was the Todd Pletcher trainee Madison Dollie. Not only was she one of four runners in the 10-horse field with previous racing experience, but she was the only one that showed a turf line on her past-performance page. Several first-time starters looked intriguing. Misinformer, a daughter of top turf sire Dynaformer, took lots of money and went off at 7-2 despite breaking from the far outside post. Alcina, by Kingmambo, was very hot on the tote, and was released at 5-2 odds. The other firsters were relatively cold in the wagering, but most of them had excellent pedigrees. Here are the long comments for the firsters in the race.

Misinformer (finished second): broke slowly, steadied while being carried very wide on the first turn, raced in the middle of the pack for six furlongs, rallied along the inside on the turn, angled five-wide at the top of the stretch, then finished fastest but could not get up.

Aunt Dot Dot (finished third): settled in good position for five furlongs, swung four-wide while gaining on the turn, made a run outside the winner to threaten nearing the furlong marker, then held well for a share.

Slewbee Dubee (finished fifth): sprinted clear in the early stages, set the pace along the rail to the turn, then tired from her early efforts.

My Bert (finished sixth): was bumped and pinched back at the start, worked her way forward while circling five-wide on the turn, then lacked a strong closing response.

Alcina (finished seventh): bumped at the start, steadied in traffic between horses on the first turn, and failed to threaten thereafter.

Triple Schnied (finished tenth): bore out causing crowding on the first turn and was pulled up along the backstretch.

You'll notice that every firster had some kind of an excuse, and you could argue that it was the lack of racing experience and/or maturity that cost each and every one of them. Misinformer missed the break, a common occurrence for a young horse, and was forced very wide going into the tight first turn. Aunt Dot Dot had to swing four-wide on the turn, and the loss of ground coupled with her lack of racing experience may have had her a little short when she tried to rally late. Slewbee Dubee was unratable in the early stages. She set quick fractions of 22.71, 46.45, and 1:12.18 while opening up by seven lengths. My Bert and Alcina had traffic problems that they were probably very unfamiliar with. Triple Schnied couldn't handle the first turn, bore out, and was eased. Meanwhile, Madison Dollie, the only horse with previous turf experience, ended up overcoming her troubled trip, and gutted out the victory. Her long comment read: "reluctant to load into the starting gate, ducked out at the start, moved up from outside on the first turn, raced just behind the pacesetter while in hand along the backstretch, closed the gap between horses to take the lead on the turn, opened a clear advantage in midstretch then was fully extended to hold Misinformer in the closing stages."

Madison Dollie was surely still green. But, her prior races had her better prepared to overcome her immature tendencies than the firsters that lacked experience. Keep track of par times at your local track, and stick with them when it comes to handicapping maiden turf races. While you will occasionally find a nice-priced firster by one of the sires mentioned in the last chapter, your best bet may be to stick with the experienced maidens.

EUROPEAN MAIDEN IMPORTS

American handicappers have Beyer Speed Figures in *Daily Racing Form,* while European handicappers looking to get their hands on the crown jewels look to Timeform ratings, published exclusively by DRF in the United States. But what are Timeform numbers, exactly? How should we use them when comparing European runners with their American counterparts? Timeform has an excellent website at *www.timeform.com,* where the most comprehensive explanation of the ratings is available.

Basically, the Timeform ratings measure the distance of the race, the time of the race, the weight carried by each horse, his age, and the margins separating the runners. In the case of inexperienced horses, Timeform handicappers go more with the speed of the race, and the comparison of that race with those of years past. With more experienced runners, the handicapper not only deals with the time, weight, margins, etc., but also the form of the runners, as well as his personal opinions. The Beyer numbers are listed in a 0-to-120 ranking based on speed. The Timeform numbers establish, in terms of weight, how a horse's performance compares to that of others in the race. Horses rarely run a 120 Beyer in the United States, although the occasional Grade 1 superstar can achieve that figure, or even higher. Good horses run 120 Timeforms regularly in Europe. Remember that Beyers measure speed. Timeforms measure speed as well, but also are tilted heavily toward class, weight, and other factors. Therefore, a 120 Timeform rating shouldn't be confused with a 120 Beyer Speed Figure.

Since the Beyer Speed Figures are, at the very least, the starting point for most handicappers, it is important to attempt to convert the Timeforms to an estimated Beyer Speed Figure, and vice versa in the case of the Dubai World Cup card. This is obviously an inexact science, since we are not converting speed to speed, but speed to class, form, and weight. Many excellent handicappers have found that a subtraction of 12 to 14 pounds off the Timeform rating gives the American handicapper a proper Beyer Speed Figure estimation of the import's ability level.

I've found that theory to be acceptable in handicapping races with established form. But does it work when European nonwinners run in American maiden races? I would use that formula as a guide, but I feel that there are many other factors at work here. Two major angles in handicapping European maidens and juveniles are the "first-time Lasix" and "first-time blinkers on/off" moves. We've seen many cases where European horses with poor form add Lasix, and then reach their potential. This is probably due to the fact that there is a strict no-medication policy in Europe.

Stage Shy cost $725,000 as a yearling. As a full sister to Oaklawn Handicap winner Geri, she was expected to be a nice runner, and was immediately exported to Europe by the late Robert Sangster. She made her juvenile debut at Newmarket, in a sevenfurlong maiden on the turf, and was sent off as the 4-1 betting favorite. She made the running for a half-mile before plummeting to the back of the back, and finished last of 15. Trainer John Gosden found that his filly had sore shins after the race, and rested her for almost nine months. Stage Shy made her return in a maiden at Sandown going 10 furlongs, and although she was reluctant to enter the stalls at first, she recovered to sit a nice tracking trip en route to victory.

There was talk of running Stage Shy in the Ribbonsdale Stakes, but Gosden wheeled her back in 23 days to contest the Group 2 Pretty Polly Stakes at The Curragh. The class hike was simply too tough for the recent maiden winner, and she finished seventh of eight after attending the pace. Her next start was in the listed Chalice Stakes at Newbury, and she went off the lukewarm favorite off the class drop. The *Racing Post* has a wonderful website where American handicappers can access extensive trip notes and commentaries on just about every horse that has run in England

and Ireland. After going to www.racingpost.co.uk, I was able to find out what happened to this sister to Geri. The commentary after the race, in which Stage Shy finished last of seven, stated ". . . having dropped in class, was a bitter disappointment, and seems to have only limited ability." Her long comment said that she "chased leaders, ridden 3f out, soon no response, no chance when lost action over 1f out."

Sangster believed in Stage Shy, and he sent her to Neil Drysdale's barn in Southern California. Her latest Timeform figure was a 33, however. Her best Timeform rating was a 90. When converting to Beyers, she would be given a 76-78 speed figure. Let's say we gave her 10 extra points for the addition of Lasix and Butazolidin. Now she would get an 86-88. It was also possible that we could give her an additional three Beyer points, as she was a lightly raced 4-year-old that certainly could improve. That would give her an 89-91 Beyer, a reasonable number for a $40,000 optional claimer with a N1X condition. Stage Shy couldn't have been more visually impressive in winning that day with a 91 Beyer, and is now 3 for 4 in the United States. By being flexible with the Timeform numbers, and allowing for improvement from a lightly raced runner adding Lasix for the first time, Stage Shy became a contender despite her poor recent form.

Use the Timeform-to-Beyer conversion rate as a starting point, and then go to more common-sense issues. Did the horse show speed in Europe, and can he improve by rating in the faster-paced races in the States? Is there an equipment or medication change to consider? On the flip side, does the horse show the "warning" comment lines that I mentioned earlier? Was the horse rank? Does he drift out?

Also, consider who was training the horse overseas. If the runner was handled by a trainer that generally does well with lightly raced runners, such as those listed opposite, give the horse some extra credit. It's possible that a medication change in America will help the horse find his true potential.

Andrew Balding

G. B. Balding

Ian Balding

T. D. Barron

Pascal Bary

J. M. Beguigne

Gianluca Bietolini

Annalisa Borroni

Clive Brittain

J. G. Burns

Gerard Butler

Neville Callaghan

Henry Cecil

Mick Channon

Roger Charlton

Nicolas Clement

Paul Cole

J. G. Coogan

J. P. J. Dubois

Ed Dunlop

John Dunlop

Andre Fabre

James Fanshawe

R. Gibson

John Gosden

Bruno Grizzetti

William Haggas

John Hammond

Richard Hannon

Peter Harris

Christiane Head-Maarek

Barry Hills

Michael Jarvis

Mark Johnston

Carlos Laffon-Parias

Eric Libaud

Come Ligerot

David Loder

Brian Meehan

Jeremy Noseda

Aidan O'Brien

Jamie Osborne

Henri-Alex Pantall

J. W. Payne

Amanda Perrett

Kevin Prendergast

L. Riccardi

Jean-Claude Rouget

Peter Schiergen

D. Sepulchre

David Smaga

Sir Michael Stoute

Marcus Tregoning

David Wachman

You'll also want to follow the American trainers that do the best with imports. Bobby Frankel, Christophe Clement, and Bill Mott are obvious names. Thankfully, *Daily Racing Form* provides up-to-date statistics on each trainer with first-time imports. The higher the winning percentage and ROI, the more confidence you should have in backing these runners.

Daily Racing Form's foreign editor, Alan Shuback, wrote an excellent chapter on European racing in *Bet with the Best*. He shows us the class of each European racecourse, and which of them provide the best runners. You have probably heard of Longchamp, Epsom, and The Curragh, but how do you rate a maiden from Ayr, La Teste, or Listowel? Shuback's chapter is a must-read regarding foreign racing and how it relates to predicting a European runner's success in North America. He also distinguishes between the different condition levels. For maiden purposes, I don't like to see a horse that was racing in allowances or handicaps. They are weaker events than listed races, or in my opinion, even maiden races. I prefer horses coming out of straight maidens. If they have tried a listed stakes, that is a pretty good sign for me. I don't want to see them in handicaps against a bunch of inconsistent runners.

While many excellent horses have come to our shores from South America, I am hesitant to play them in maiden races unless the proven local commodities have failed to reach par for the class level. The same goes for horses from Mexico, Panama, and Puerto Rico. I usually like to see a race out of these runners before I play them in maiden events.

16

"NICKING" PATTERNS AND BROODMARE SIRES TO WATCH

IBRIEFLY TALKED about pedigree crosses in the sire profiles. Northern Dancer sires usually cross well with dams from the Mr. Prospector line and vice versa. "Nicks" are specific crosses. For example, A. P. Indy excels when bred to broodmares by Mr. Prospector (10 stakes winners from less than 60 foals), Deputy Minister (four stakes winners from less than 10 foals), Nureyev (two stakes winners from less than 25 foals), Cox's Ridge (two stakes winners from less than 10 foals), and Danzig. You could certainly give any A. P. Indy runner extra credit when he is bred to any mare by these broodmare sires. Here are some solid "nicks" that handicappers of maiden races should recognize.

SIRE	BROODMARE SIRE
Boundary	Alydar, Forty Niner
Mutakddim	Southern Halo
Storm Cat	Alydar
Valid Expectations	Carr de Naskra, Relaunch, Peterhof
Carson City	Valid Appeal
In Excess	Crafty Prospector, Crystal Water
Gilded Time	Afleet, Gulch, Mr. Prospector, Vice Regent, Wild Again
Seeking the Gold	Nijinsky II, Pleasant Colony, Seattle Slew
Mr. Greeley	Copelan, Desert Wine, Greinton, Relaunch, Silver Deputy
Dixieland Band	Damascus, Fappiano, Graustark, His Majesty, Mr. Prospector, Pleasant Colony
Forest Wildcat	Affirmed, Key to the Mint, Lord Avie, Pentelicus
Silver Deputy	Bold Ruckus, Fappiano
Theatrical	Alydar, Blushing Groom, Mr. Prospector, Riverman, Seattle Slew, Tyrant
Holy Bull	Slewpy
Woodman	Danzig, Nijinsky II, Riverman
Dynaformer	Dr. Blum
Kingmambo	Alleged, Danzig, Dixieland Band, His Majesty, Seattle Slew
Royal Academy	Bletchingly, Chief Singer
Elusive Quality	Dayjur
Is It True	Clever Trick, Haulpak, Carry a Smile
Two Punch	Magesterial, Smarten
Capote	Conquistador Cielo, Deputy Minister, Fappiano, Lyphard, Miswaki, Mr. Prospector, Rubiano, Vice Regent
Gone West	Cox's Ridge, El Gran Senor, Majestic Light, Seattle Slew, The Minstrel
Diesis	Deputy Minister, Nonoalco, Roberto

BROODMARE SIRES TO WATCH

I've talked about how the mare brings class to the pedigree, so it would seem logical that handicappers look for classy broodmare sires when handicapping maiden races. Buckpasser was one of the world's great broodmare sires. Why? Well, for one thing, he had almost flawless conformation. Also, he was a Hall of Fame runner and was bred to the classiest of mares. Even if his filly foals didn't show talent on the racetrack, they still had the genes of Buckpasser and their classy dams, and were apt to pass those traits on to the next generation. Here are some broodmare sires that should give a pedigree plenty of class and speed.

AFFIRMED
Pedigree: Exclusive Native—Won't Tell You, by Crafty Admiral
Race Record and Earnings: 29 starts, 22 wins, 5 seconds,
   1 third, $2,393,818

Triple Crown winner and Thoroughbred legend Affirmed was known as much for his iron will and courage as he was for his racetrack speed. Affirmed never seemed to get the best of his arch-nemesis, Alydar, in the breeding shed, but he sired hard-knocking racehorses that seemed to show an extra affinity for the turf. With over 20 crops to race, Affirmed sired more than 75 stakes winners including champion turf mare Flawlessly, Canadian champions Quiet Resolve and Peteski, and $2.3 million earner Affirmed Success. He has outdone himself as a broodmare sire, with multiple champions to his credit, including Breeders' Cup Classic and Dubai World Cup winner Pleasantly Perfect, and English Oaks and Irish Derby heroine Balanchine. You have to respect all of Affirmed's accomplishments, both on the track, and as a stallion. He should continue to have great success as a broodmare sire.

DANZIG

Pedigree: Northern Dancer—Pas de Nom, by
 Admiral's Voyage
Race Record and Earnings: 3 starts, 3 wins, 0 seconds,
 0 thirds, $32,400

The unbeaten Danzig has been one of the top sires in the world
over the past 20 years, and he has also made a big impression on
the breeding industry with his broodmares. A five-time North
American champion stallion by earnings, Danzig has sired over 150
stakes winners, and he is the broodmare sire of over 100 stakes winners. His versatility as a sire was what set Danzig apart from the rest.
Not only did he have success with top distaffers such as Dance
Smartly and Versailles Treaty, but he also sired top turf runners such
as Lure and War Chant, and major main-track players like Pine
Bluff and Langfuhr. He has proven to be a great sire of sires, and
he is the broodmare sire of Kentucky Derby winner Fusaichi Pegasus, top sprinter Caller One, Japanese champion Grass Wonder, and
many, many other classy performers. When you see Danzig on the
bottom half of a maiden's pedigree, you can be assured of speed
and class.

DEHERE

Pedigree: Deputy Minister—Sister Dot, by Secretariat
Race Record and Earnings: 9 starts, 6 wins, 2 seconds,
 0 thirds, $723,712
2004 Stud Fee: 49,500 AUS$
2004 Stud Farm: Arrowfield Stud (AUS)

Two-year-old champion Dehere almost immediately became one of
the top debut sires in the world not long after his retirement from
racing. He now plies his trade in Australia, but he did sire multiple
Grade 1 winner Take Charge Lady while he was here, and he has
the speedy genes to be a young, up-and-coming broodmare sire.

Take special note of Dehere broodmares when they are bred to other speed sire lines. His broodmares should throw quick, precocious runners that can break their maidens in their first or second start.

DIXIELAND BAND

Pedigree: Northern Dancer—Mississippi Mud, by Delta Judge
Race Record and Earnings: 24 starts, 8 wins, 3 seconds,
    4 thirds, $570,610
2004 Stud Fee: $50,000
2004 Stud Farm: Lane's End Farm (KY)

I've already mentioned Dixieland Band's excellent sire record. But, he is also a broodmare sire that you need to know. He has sired the dams of Kentucky Derby winner Monarchos, Grade 1-winning distaffers Exotic Wood and Dream Supreme, and millionaire Southern Image, among others, and his mares usually foal quality runners on both turf and dirt going long and short. As with a fellow son of Northern Dancer, Danzig, Dixieland Band provides plenty of versatility in a pedigree. He should continue to rank among the top broodmare sires for many years to come.

GONE WEST

Pedigree: Mr. Prospector—Secrettame, by Secretariat
Race Record and Earnings: 17 starts, 6 wins, 4 seconds,
    2 thirds, $682,251
2004 Stud Fee: $125,000
2004 Stud Farm: Mill Ridge Farm (KY)

As a top sire of sires, one would think that Gone West would have similar success as a broodmare sire. While he hasn't achieved that level of success, I'm willing to give Gone West the benefit of the doubt. He is still siring top-flight runners, and although he is the broodmare sire of solid stakes winners such as Saudi Poetry and Misty Sixes, I feel that the best is yet to come for Gone West mares.

When you see his name on the bottom of a maiden's pedigree, think grass and class.

KRIS S.

Pedigree: Roberto—Sharp Queen, by Princequillo
Race Record and Earnings: 5 starts, 3 wins, 1 second,
    0 thirds, $53,350

"Mr. Breeders' Cup" tasted victory on racing's championship day with Action This Day (Juvenile), Hollywood Wildcat (Distaff), Prized (Turf), and Soaring Softly (Filly and Mare Turf). Kris S. passed away in 2002, but is still going strong with top runners such as Kicken Kris. He has sired the dams of over 40 stakes winners and is a sure bet to be a perennial top-20 broodmare sire. His broodmares should be accorded extra consideration when their foals debut as older runners on the grass.

MEADOWLAKE

Pedigree: Hold Your Peace—Suspicious Native, by
    Raise a Native
Race Record and Earnings: 3 starts, 3 wins, 0 seconds,
    0 thirds, $308,580
2004 Stud Fee: $20,000
2004 Stud Farm: Darby Dan Farm (KY)

Meadowlake stands a majestic 17 hands, has excellent conformation, and was perfect during his short juvenile campaign. He has been a top debut sire for most of his career, with his best runner being juvenile filly champion Meadow Star. He also gives plenty of bone and muscle mass to many of his foals, and he has already sired the dams of several stakes winners. I think the precocity that he showed on the track will be transmitted through his broodmares to their foals. He adds lots of speed to a pedigree, and should be the broodmare sire of many debut winners.

NUREYEV

Pedigree: Northern Dancer—Special, by Forli
Race Record and Earnings: 3 starts, 2 wins, 0 seconds,
0 thirds, $42,522

The great Nureyev twice led the French sire standings, and sired over 130 stakes winners. One of Northern Dancer's best sons at stud, Nureyev gave both speed and class to his progeny, and now we see those traits through his broodmares and their foals. Nureyev broodmares figure to throw early-developing, classy runners that may prosper on the turf. In 2004 alone, Nureyev broodmares have accounted for over $5 million in earnings. He should continue to dance atop the broodmare sire list for several more years.

SEATTLE SLEW

Pedigree: Bold Reasoning—My Charmer, by Poker
Race Record and Earnings: 17 starts, 14 wins, 2 seconds,
0 thirds, $1,208,726

Seattle Slew had it all. He was the people's champion, a Hall of Famer, a leading sire, and a champion broodmare sire. The late Triple Crown winner sired over 100 stakes winners in his career, and was leading broodmare sire on three different occasions. He will go down as the broodmare sire of Cigar, Lemon Drop Kid, Escena, Golden Attraction, and many other top runners. Seattle Slew broodmares will give their babies all the class in the world. Pay special attention to maidens with the great Seattle Slew in their pedigrees.

SEEKING THE GOLD

Pedigree: Mr. Prospector—Con Game, by Buckpasser
Race Record and Earnings: 15 starts, 8 wins, 6 seconds,
0 thirds, $2,307,000
2004 Stud Fee: $150,000
2004 Stud Farm: Claiborne Farm (KY)

Seeking the Gold won't turn 20 until January 1, 2005, but he has already sired the dams of over 25 stakes winners, including champion Surfside, $1.8 million earner Lu Ravi, Grade 2 winner Pure Prize, and the speedy Pomeroy. He is bred to the very best pedigrees so he should continue to have great success as a broodmare sire. With Danzig pensioned, Seeking the Gold takes over as the "big horse" at legendary Claiborne Farm.

SILVER HAWK
Pedigree: Roberto—Gris Vitesse, by Amerigo
Race Record and Earnings: 8 starts, 3 wins, 4 seconds, 0 thirds, $163,885

Here's an underrated broodmare sire. Silver Hawk sired a couple of champions in his successful career at stud, and his mares have produced over 30 stakes winners. He's best known as a turf sire, and his name is one you need to know when tracking broodmare sires in maiden races. Silver Hawk should provide plenty of value, as well, as handicappers flock to better-known stallions.

STORM CAT
Pedigree: Storm Bird—Terlingua, by Secretariat
Race Record and Earnings: 8 starts, 4 wins, 3 seconds, 0 thirds, $570,610
2004 Stud Fee: $500,000
2004 Stud Farm: Overbrook Farm (KY)

He's the best sire in the world, and it wouldn't be surprising if one day, Storm Cat becomes the leading broodmare sire. When you have to pay $500,000 a pop for a shot at a Storm Cat foal, you know that he's receiving the cream of the broodmare crop. He is already the broodmare sire of 40 stakes winners, including Breeders' Cup Sprint winner Speightstown, Sky Mesa, Santa Catarina, and Buddha. Upgrade any maiden firster with Storm Cat listed as broodmare sire.

TWINING

Pedigree: Forty Niner—Courtly Dee, by Never Bend.
Race Record and Earnings: 6 starts, 5 wins, 1 second,
0 thirds, $238,140
2004 Stud Fee: Private
2004 Stud Farm: Shadai Stallion Station (JPN)

Here's a young broodmare sire in the mold of Dehere. Twining brings performance and pedigree to the table, and he was a top debut sire in the United States before being exported to Japan. Twining didn't make his first start until he was 3, but he rolled off five consecutive victories including wins in the Grade 2 Withers and Grade 2 Peter Pan Stakes. His only defeat came in his final start as he ran second to the great Holy Bull in the Grade 2 Dwyer. His career Beyers ranged between 91 and 107. Twining comes from one of the premier female families in the stud book. He is a half-brother to eight black-type earners, including Grade 1 winners Ali Oop, Ketoh, and Althea. He has sired some quick horses, such as Two Item Limit and Pie N Burger, and will bring lots of speed to the bottom of any maiden's pedigree.

UNBRIDLED

Pedigree: Fappiano—Gana Facil, by Killaloe
Race Record and Earnings: 24 starts, 8 wins, 6 seconds,
6 thirds, $4,489,475

Kentucky Derby and Breeders' Cup Classic winner Unbridled was expected to be an excellent sire of stout runners over long distances. But he was a surprisingly good debut sire, and his Anees and Unbridled's Song both won the Breeders' Cup Juvenile. Unfortunately, Unbridled passed away while still a relatively young sire, but his class and underrated precocity should still be felt through his broodmares. Beware Unbridled as a broodmare sire with older first-time starters. With his class, speed, and pedigree, he should quickly climb the broodmare-sire rankings.

17

HANDICAPPING THE BREEDERS' CUP BABY RACES

CHAMPIONSHIPS ARE USUALLY decided on Breeders' Cup Day. But, more importantly to the horseplayer, the Breeders' Cup offers full fields of competitive horses as well as many attractive wagering opportunities. One would think that handicapping the Juvenile and Juvenile Fillies would fall under one category. But those two races are as different as night and day.

According to the 2004 *American Racing Manual,* the Beyer par time for the Juvenile Fillies is a 95.93. From 2001 through 2003, the mean Beyer for the Juvenile Fillies was a 102.67. The baby girls ran faster than their male counterparts in each of those years. The trend continued in 2004 when Sweet Catomine earned a 102 Beyer for her Juvenile Fillies win while the European invader Wilko received a 98 for his Juvenile upset. The quality of the Juvenile has gone down as many trainers have opted to skip the race to begin early preparations for the Kentucky Derby. That has made the Juvenile a mess to handicap. The Juvenile Fillies, on the other hand, is one of the most formful races on the Breeders' Cup card.

It seems that almost every year, a filly comes along that is simply more physically and emotionally dominant than her peers. Whether it was Twilight Ridge (paid $3.20) at Aqueduct in 1985, Open Mind ($3.40) at Churchill in 1988, Meadow Star ($2.40) at Belmont in 1990, Eliza ($4.40) at Gulfstream in 1992, Flanders ($2.80) at Churchill in 1994, Storm Song ($5.20) at Woodbine in 1996, Silverbulletday ($3.60) at Churchill in 1998, Storm Flag Flying ($3.60) at Arlington in 2002, Halfbridled ($6.60) at Santa Anita in 2003, or Sweet Catomine ($6.60) at Lone Star in 2004, the Breeders' Cup Juvenile Fillies has usually featured a standout or two.

Fillies mature more quickly than the colts when it comes to reaching the races, but once they've made a start or two, it is the colts that improve faster from race to race. I believe that's why we've seen so many short-priced stickouts in the Juvenile Fillies. These gals are so far ahead in terms of precocity, physique, and ability that the late-developing runners fail to catch up until their 3-year-old seasons. Don't be afraid to play that short-priced runner that looks like a cinch on paper. Those horses usually run to their past-performance pages.

Look for a physically dominant runner in the race replays, and in the paddock and post parade. Halfbridled and Sweet Catomine, for example, were the equivalents of full-grown women facing mere girls from a physical standpoint. They had no problem with the distance of the Juvenile Fillies, and proved much the best in their respective races.

I don't think it is wise to try and pinpoint any single prep race for the Juvenile Fillies. Recent winners had their final preps in the Oak Leaf at Santa Anita, the Frizette at Belmont, the Del Mar Debutante at Del Mar, the Arlington-Washington Lassie at Arlington, and the Alcibiades at Keeneland. A Breeders' Cup Juvenile Fillies winner can come from anywhere. It might also be fruitless to try and find a Beyer pattern in predicting Juvenile Fillies success.

Halfbridled and Storm Flag Flying both earned 98 Beyer Speed Figures in their final preps, but Tempera, Caressing, and Cash Run (2001, 2000, and 1999 winners, respectively) showed Beyers ranging between 71 and 90 in their final races before the Breeders' Cup.

The key may be to look for horses that have shown early speed in their last prep races before the Cup. Of the last 11 Breeders' Cup Juvenile Fillies winners, seven of them were either on the lead, or within a length of the front-runner at the pace call. Pace makes the race, especially in the Breeders' Cup Juvenile Fillies.

The Juvenile, however, is a very tricky race to handicap. If you had Anees, Action This Day, or Wilko at boxcar odds, then congratulations. They certainly were tough to like on paper. Perhaps horseplayers should step outside the box, and handicap the Juvenile in a completely different way from their day-to-day exercises. Four of the last five winners won their final prep races, and three of them (European imports Johannesburg and Wilko were the exceptions) improved their Beyers by at least five points from their final prep to the Juvenile. Seven of the last 11 winners won their most recent prep races, so it certainly seems prudent to play sharp runners in the Breeders' Cup.

Let's look at how the betting favorites have fared in the last six runnings of the Juvenile. Forest Camp went off as the 5-2 favorite in 1999 after earning a 103 Beyer Speed Figure in the Norfolk at Santa Anita, a race in which he had tired to finish second at odds of 3-10 in his first start around two turns. He definitely had stamina issues. A P Valentine was the 2-1 chalk in 2000 after winning the Champagne with a 98 Beyer. He had not raced around two turns prior to the Juvenile, and finished last of 14. Officer was sent off at 75 cents to the dollar in 2001 after taking the Champagne with a 102 Beyer. By Bertrando, he was bred more for speed than stamina, and he faltered after pressing the pace in the Juvenile. Whywhywhy was favored in 2002 after winning the one-turn Futurity with a 102 Beyer. His pedigree was also geared toward sprinting, and he had yet to try two turns. He also tired in the stretch. The

2003 favorite was Cuvee. The son of speed influence Carson City had just won the Futurity with a 102 Beyer, and was another that had not gone two turns. He finished last of 12. Roman Ruler was bet to favoritism in 2004 despite being very green in his previous two races. Although he won the Grade 2 Norfolk in his final prep before the Juvenile, trainer Bob Baffert was apparently dissatisfied and made an equipment change (blinkers off) in the Breeders' Cup.

What have we learned? Four of the last seven winners of the Juvenile had at least one two-turn race under their belts before the big race. Two others, Johannesberg and Wilko, were tested over stamina-building courses in Europe. It is professionalism, not speed, that wins the Juvenile. The true stamina runners are being saved for the Derby while the Juvenile betting favorites often have sprint pedigrees and big Beyers.

In 2002, Vindication ran the most visually impressive race of any 2-year-old in the Kentucky Cup Juvenile in his final prep for the Breeders' Cup. He only earned an 87 Beyer that day, but it was the way he won that caught the eye. Action This Day only beat a maiden field at Santa Anita in 2003, but he chugged his way between horses after being far back in the early stages of the race. He only received a 79 Beyer for his maiden score, but you could tell by the gallant way in which he won that he could improve. Two-year-colts can improve 10 to 20 points a race. Don't be swayed too much by gaudy Beyer Speed Figures earned in sprints or one-turn routes. It is imperative to watch the replays of each horse with the ultimate goal of finding a runner that has overcome trouble, acts like he wants to go long, and/or has a fluid stride. If all else fails, you can't beat two-turn experience.

CONCLUSION: TYING IT ALL TOGETHER

Whew! Who knew that handicapping maidens involved so many names, numbers, and angles? Studying workouts, pedigrees, and trainer stats is fascinating to me despite the loads of work involved. Hopefully, whether you are a handicapper of 30 years or three days, you will find some of the pointers in this book helpful at the track. There is so much information out there that it is increasingly difficult to stay ahead of the game. Try to beat the crowd by keeping up-to-date records, and by using common sense instead of numbers alone. Keep an open mind, and be forgiving of horses that ran poorly in only their first or second starts. Respect speed and pedigree. Most importantly, have fun. This is the finest game out there. Cherish it.

ABOUT THE AUTHOR

DAN ILLMAN HAS been involved in the Thoroughbred-racing industry for the past seven years. After working as a racing writer, analyst, and handicapper for Sports Eye Inc., Illman joined *Daily Racing Form* in 1998, and was promoted to handicapper two years later.

He has written "A Closer Look" for many high-profile races and has also contributed handicapping articles, "Handicapper's Diary" columns, horse profiles, and feature-race advances to *Daily Racing Form* and *DRF Simulcast Weekly*. Illman supplied DRF's "Sweep" graded handicap for the 2001–2003 Gulfstream meetings, and formerly made the DRF morning line for the NYRA circuit.

Illman has appeared on numerous radio programs, and has given handicapping seminars at Rockingham Park, Colonial

Downs, and for New York City and Nassau Off Track Betting. He is currently the co-host of the "DRF News Desk" with Noel Michaels, and has appeared on TVG's "Blinkers Off," as well as on HRTV and "Horsin' Around TV." He specializes in juvenile, maiden, and turf races, and enjoys finding overlays by utilizing trip- and pedigree-handicapping techniques. Illman's "Spa Babies" column was featured daily on the DRF website for the 2004 Saratoga meet, and he wrote "The Skinny" for Kentucky Derby contenders on drf.com.

Illman graduated with a B.A. in Liberal Arts from Nova Southeastern University in 1997, and currently lives in Woodmere, New York.